First World War
and Army of Occupation
War Diary
France, Belgium and Germany

40 DIVISION
Headquarters, Branches and Services
Royal Army Medical Corps
Assistant Director Medical Services
2 June 1916 - 31 March 1919

WO95/2597/1

The Naval & Military Press Ltd
www.nmarchive.com
Published in association with The National Archives

Published by

The Naval & Military Press Ltd

Unit 10 Ridgewood Industrial Park,

Uckfield, East Sussex,

TN22 5QE England

Tel: +44 (0) 1825 749494

www.naval-military-press.com

www.nmarchive.com

This diary has been reprinted in facsimile from the original. Any imperfections are inevitably reproduced and the quality may fall short of modern type and cartographic standards.

© Crown Copyright
Images reproduced by permission of The National Archives, London, England, 2015.

Contents

Document type	Place/Title	Date From	Date To
Heading	WO95/2597/1		
Heading	Asst Dir. Medical Services Jun 1916-1919 Mar		
Heading	A.D. US 40th Division		
War Diary	Blackdown Camp	02/06/1916	02/06/1916
War Diary	Southampton	02/06/1916	02/06/1916
War Diary	Havre	03/06/1916	04/06/1916
War Diary	Lillers	05/06/1916	05/06/1916
War Diary	Norrent Fontes	05/06/1916	17/06/1916
War Diary	Bruay	19/06/1916	30/06/1916
Heading	Medical Service War Diary Of A.D.M.S. 40th Division for month of July 1916 Volume II		
War Diary	Bruay	01/07/1916	04/07/1916
War Diary	Noeux Les Mines	05/07/1916	17/07/1916
War Diary	Braquemont (Noeux Les Mines)	19/07/1916	31/07/1916
Miscellaneous	A.D.M.S. 40th Division		
War Diary	Braquemont (36. B. L25b.2.5)	01/08/1916	10/08/1916
War Diary	Braquemont	11/08/1916	31/08/1916
Heading	A.D.M.S. 40th Div.		
War Diary	Braquemont. (36. B. L. 25.b.2.5)	01/09/1916	30/09/1916
Heading	A.D.M.S. 40th Division		
War Diary	Braquemont 36. B. 1.25.b.2.5	01/10/1916	30/10/1916
War Diary	Roellecourt Sheet 36. B. 1.40,000 T.20. C. 2.8	30/10/1916	31/10/1916
Heading	A.D.M.S. 40th Division		
War Diary	Roellecourt Sheet 36 B. 1.40,000 T.20. C. 2.8	01/11/1916	02/11/1916
War Diary	Frohen-Le-Grand	03/11/1916	04/11/1916
War Diary	Bernaville (Sheet 1,100,000	05/11/1916	05/11/1916
War Diary	Lens Sheet	07/11/1916	14/11/1916
War Diary	Frohen-Le-Grand	15/11/1916	18/11/1916
War Diary	Bouquemaison	19/11/1916	21/11/1916
War Diary	Doullens	22/11/1916	22/11/1916
War Diary	Canaples	23/11/1916	23/11/1916
War Diary	Ailly-Le-Haut Clocher	24/11/1916	30/11/1916
Heading	A.D.M.S. 40th Division		
War Diary	Ailly-Le-Haut-Clocher (map Abbeville 1,100,000)	01/12/1916	14/12/1916
War Diary	Chipilly (Amiens Sheet 1,100,000)	15/12/1916	27/12/1916
War Diary	Map. Albert 1,40,000 T.16.d.4.9	28/12/1916	31/12/1916
Heading	A.D.M.S. 40th Division		
War Diary	Map Albert Amiens Sheet 1,100,000) L, 16.d,1.9	01/01/1917	27/01/1917
War Diary	Corbie	28/01/1917	31/01/1917
Heading	A.D.M.S. 40th Division		
War Diary	Corbie Amiens Sheet 1,100,000	01/02/1917	12/02/1917
War Diary	L.16d 1.9	12/02/1917	13/02/1917
War Diary	L.16d 1.9 Amiens Sheet 1,40,000	14/02/1917	28/02/1917
Heading	Medical Services War Diaries Of A.D.M.S. 40th Division.		
War Diary	L 16d 1.9 Amiens Sheet 1,40,000	01/03/1917	08/03/1917
War Diary	Suzanne G.8.d.	09/03/1917	18/03/1917
War Diary	Amiens Sheet 1,40,000	19/03/1917	27/03/1917
War Diary	Craniere B16.d.38	28/03/1917	31/03/1917
Heading	A.D.M.S. 40th Division		

Type	Description	Start	End
War Diary	Craniere B16.d.3.8	01/04/1917	12/04/1917
War Diary	Manancourt V 13 c4.4	13/01/1917	30/04/1917
Heading	A.D.M.S. 40th Division		
War Diary	Manancourt V 13.c.4.4 Map France Sheet 57c	02/05/1917	31/05/1917
Operation(al) Order(s)	40th Division R.A.M.C. Operation Order No. 25 Appx A	03/05/1917	03/05/1917
Operation(al) Order(s)	40th Division. R.A.M.C. Operation Order No. 26 Appx B	11/05/1917	11/05/1917
Operation(al) Order(s)	40th Division. R.A.M.C. Operation Order No. 26 Appx C	19/05/1917	19/05/1917
Miscellaneous	To Accompany 40th Division R.A.M.C. Operation Order No. 27	19/05/1917	19/05/1917
Miscellaneous	40th Division R.A.M.C. Operation Order No. 28 App D	21/05/1917	21/05/1917
Miscellaneous	Medical Arrangement 40th. Division Appx F	28/05/1917	28/05/1917
Miscellaneous	Amendments To Medical Arrangements 40th Division.	30/05/1917	30/05/1917
Miscellaneous	A.D.M.S. 40th Div		
War Diary	Manancourt	01/06/1917	30/06/1917
Operation(al) Order(s)	40th Division R.A.M.C. Operation Order No. 29	30/06/1917	30/06/1917
Heading	A.D.M.S. 40th Division		
War Diary	Manancourt	01/07/1917	11/07/1917
War Diary	Sorel-Le-Grand V.18.d.5.7	12/07/1917	31/07/1917
Operation(al) Order(s)	40th Division. R.A.M.C. Operation Order No. 30	08/07/1917	08/07/1917
Miscellaneous	Medical Arrangements 40th Division	03/07/1917	03/07/1917
Miscellaneous	Medical Arrangements 40th Division	19/07/1917	19/07/1917
Miscellaneous	Amendment To Medical Arrangements 40th Division	29/07/1917	29/07/1917
Heading	Medical Service War Diaries Of A.D.M.S. 40th Division Field A Ambulance		
War Diary	Sorel-Le-Grand	01/08/1917	31/08/1917
Miscellaneous	Appendix Medical Arrangements		
Operation(al) Order(s)	40th Division R.A.M.C. Operation Order No. 32	21/08/1917	21/08/1917
Operation(al) Order(s)	40th Divisional R.A.M.C. Operation Order No. 31	02/08/1917	02/08/1917
Miscellaneous	Medical Services War Diaries Of A.D.M.S. 40th Division Field Ambulance For Month Of September 1917 Vols XVI		
War Diary	Sorel-Le-Grand (V.18.d.5.7) Map Reference	01/09/1917	01/09/1917
War Diary	France 57c 1-20000	03/09/1917	29/09/1917
Miscellaneous	Medical Arrangements 40th Division.	05/09/1917	05/09/1917
Miscellaneous	Medical Arrangements 40th Division	09/09/1917	09/09/1917
Heading	A.D.M.S. 40th Division		
War Diary	Sorel-Le-Grand	01/10/1917	05/10/1917
War Diary	Fosseux Map. France 51c P.10 d.9.9	09/10/1917	28/10/1917
War Diary	Lucheux (map France 51c T.16.a. Central)	29/10/1917	29/10/1917
Operation(al) Order(s)	40th Division R.A.M.C. Order No. 33	02/10/1917	02/10/1917
Miscellaneous	Addendum To 40th Division R.A.M.C., Order No33	03/10/1917	03/10/1917
Operation(al) Order(s)	40th Division. R.A.M.C. Order No. 34	28/10/1917	28/10/1917
Miscellaneous	March Table Issued With 40th R.A.M.C. Div./ Operation Order No. 34	28/10/1917	28/10/1917
Heading	Medical Services War Diary Of A.D.M.S. 40th Division For The Month Of November 1917 Volumes XVIII		
War Diary	Lucheux (map France 57c T.16.d. Central)	01/11/1917	15/11/1917
War Diary	Fosseux	16/11/1917	16/11/1917
War Diary	Achiet-Le-Petit	18/11/1917	18/11/1917
War Diary	Haplincourt (1.34.a.3.5. Map France 57c 1/40000	19/11/1917	23/11/1917
War Diary	Havrincourt Map Reference throughout 57c. 1/40,000	23/11/1917	30/11/1917
Operation(al) Order(s)	40th Division R.A.M.C. Operation Order No. 35	14/11/1917	14/11/1917

Type	Description	Date From	Date To
Operation(al) Order(s)	40th Division R.A.M.C. Operation Order No. 37	20/11/1917	20/11/1917
Operation(al) Order(s)	40th Division R.A.M.C. Operation Order No. 40	22/11/1917	22/11/1917
Miscellaneous	40th Division R.A.M.C. Operation Order No. 42	25/11/1917	25/11/1917
Miscellaneous	40th Divn R.A.M.C. O O. No. 43	26/11/1917	26/11/1917
Heading	Medical Services War Diaries of 40 Division For Month Of December 1917 Volumes XIX		
War Diary	Basseux	01/12/1917	01/12/1917
War Diary	Behagnies	03/12/1917	13/12/1917
War Diary	Gomiecourt	14/12/1917	31/12/1917
Operation(al) Order(s)	40th Division R.A.M.C. Order No. 44	01/12/1917	01/12/1917
Miscellaneous	March Table		
Miscellaneous	A.D.M.S. 40th Division No. 85 (M)	01/12/1917	01/12/1917
Operation(al) Order(s)	40th Division R.A.M.C. Order No. 45	12/12/1917	12/12/1917
Operation(al) Order(s)	40th Division R.A.M.C. Order No. 46	12/12/1917	12/12/1917
Miscellaneous	Evacuation Scheme		
Miscellaneous	Addendum No. 1 To 40th Division R.A.M.C. Order No. 46	14/12/1917	14/12/1917
Operation(al) Order(s)	40th Division R.A.M.C. Order No. 47	24/12/1917	24/12/1917
Miscellaneous	Evacuation Scheme Issued With Reference To 40th Div. R.A.M.C. Order No. 47	29/12/1917	29/12/1917
Heading	Medical Services War Diaries Of A.D.M.C. 40th Division For Month of January 1918 Volume XX		
War Diary	Gomiecourt	01/01/1918	31/01/1918
Heading	Medical Services War Diaries Of A.D.M.S. 40th Division For Month Of February 1918 Vols XXI		
War Diary	Behagnies	02/02/1918	12/02/1918
War Diary	Gomiecourt	13/02/1918	27/02/1918
War Diary	Basseux	28/02/1918	28/02/1918
Operation(al) Order(s)	40th Division R.A.M.C. Order No. 49	07/02/1918	07/02/1918
Operation(al) Order(s)	40th Division R.A.M.C. Order No. 50	24/02/1918	24/02/1918
Miscellaneous	Table To Accompany 40th Division R.A.M.C. Order No. 50		
Miscellaneous	A.D.M.S. 40th Div., No. 85 (D)	25/02/1918	25/02/1918
Miscellaneous	40th Division Defence Scheme Medical Arrangements When Division Is In Vith Corps Reserve	24/02/1918	24/02/1918
Heading	A.D.M.S. 40th Div		
War Diary	Basseux	01/03/1918	27/03/1918
War Diary	Lucheux	28/03/1918	28/03/1918
War Diary	Chelers	30/03/1918	30/03/1918
War Diary	Merville	31/03/1918	31/03/1918
Operation(al) Order(s)	40th Division R.A.M.C. Order No. 53	02/03/1918	02/03/1918
Miscellaneous	Addendum No 1 To 40th Division R.A.M.C. Order No. 54	18/03/1918	18/03/1918
Miscellaneous	Table to accompany Addendum No. 1 to 40th Division. R.A.M.C. Order No. 54 Table 'A'		
Miscellaneous	Herewith 40th Division R.A.M.C. Order No. 54	08/03/1918	08/03/1918
Operation(al) Order(s)	40th Division R.A.M.C. Order No. 54	08/03/1918	08/03/1918
Miscellaneous	To accompany 40th Division R.A.M.C. Order No. 54 Table "A"		
Miscellaneous	To accompany 40th Division R.A.M.C. Order No. 54 Table "A" (i)		
Miscellaneous	To accompany 40th Division R.A.M.C. Order No. 54 Table "A" (ii)		
Miscellaneous	To accompany 40th Division R.A.M.C. Order No. 54 Table "A" (iii)		

Miscellaneous	To accompany 40th Division R.A.M.C. Order No. 54 Table "B"		
Miscellaneous	Reference Para 6 40th Division R.A.M.C. Order No. 54	08/06/1918	08/06/1918
Operation(al) Order(s)	40th Division. R.A.M.C. Order No. 55	11/03/1918	11/03/1918
Miscellaneous	Table to accompany 40th Division R.A.M.C. Order No. 55	11/03/1918	11/03/1918
Operation(al) Order(s)	40th Division R.A.M.C. Order No. 56	20/03/1918	20/03/1918
Miscellaneous	Table to accompany 40th Division R.A.M.C. Order No. 58	20/03/1918	20/03/1918
Operation(al) Order(s)	40th Division R.A.M.C. Order No. 63	31/03/1918	31/03/1918
Heading	Medical Services War Diaries Of A.D.M.S. 40th Division For Month Of April 1918 Vols XXIII		
War Diary	Croix Du Bac	02/04/1918	09/04/1918
War Diary	Vieux Berquin	10/04/1918	11/04/1918
War Diary	La Motte	12/04/1918	12/04/1918
War Diary	Au Souverain	13/04/1918	13/04/1918
War Diary	Renescure	14/04/1918	14/04/1918
War Diary	Wizernes	15/04/1918	29/04/1918
War Diary	St Omer	30/04/1918	30/04/1918
Miscellaneous	Addendum to War Diary of ADMS 40th Division	28/04/1918	28/04/1918
Heading	A.D.M.S. 40th Divl May 1918		
War Diary	St Omer	03/05/1918	31/05/1918
Operation(al) Order(s)	40th Division R.A.M.C. Order No. 69	09/05/1918	09/05/1918
Operation(al) Order(s)	40th Division R.A.M.C. Order No. 70	27/05/1918	27/05/1918
Operation(al) Order(s)	40th Division R.A.M.C. Order No. 71	29/05/1918	29/05/1918
Heading	A.D.M.S. 40th Div June 1918		
War Diary	St Omer	01/06/1918	03/06/1918
War Diary	Lederzeele	04/06/1918	22/06/1918
War Diary	Renescure 27/T20d.8.6	23/06/1918	26/06/1918
War Diary	Renescure	27/06/1918	30/06/1918
Operation(al) Order(s)	Appendix 1 40th Division R.A.M.C. Operation Order No. 74	15/06/1918	15/06/1918
Miscellaneous	Amendment No. 1 To 40th Division R.A.M.C. Order No. 74	19/06/1918	19/06/1918
Operation(al) Order(s)	40th Division R.A.M.C. Order No. 75	22/06/1918	22/06/1918
Operation(al) Order(s)	40th Division R.A.M.C. Order No. 76	27/06/1918	27/06/1918
Heading	A.D.M.S. 40th Div July 1918		
War Diary	Renescure 27./T.20d.3.6	01/07/1918	02/07/1918
War Diary	Renescure	02/07/1918	03/07/1918
War Diary	Renescure 27/T.20.d.8.6	03/07/1918	18/07/1918
War Diary	Renescure T.20.d.8.6	18/07/1918	23/07/1918
War Diary	Renescure 27/T.20.d.8.6	24/07/1918	29/07/1918
Miscellaneous	Renescure T.20.d.8.6/27	30/07/1918	31/07/1918
Operation(al) Order(s)	40th Division R.A.M.C. Order No. 77	03/07/1918	03/07/1918
Operation(al) Order(s)	40th Division R.A.M.C. Order No. 78	17/07/1918	17/07/1918
Miscellaneous	Amendment No.1 to R.A.M.C. Order No. 78	17/07/1918	17/07/1918
Miscellaneous	40th Division R.A.M.C. Order No. 79	18/07/1918	18/07/1918
Operation(al) Order(s)	40th Division R.A.M.C. Order No. 80	29/07/1918	29/07/1918
Heading	Medical Services War Diaries Of A.D.M.S. 40th Division For Month Of August 1918 Vol. XXVII		
War Diary	Renescure 27/T.20.d.8.6	01/08/1918	20/08/1918
War Diary	Renescure	21/08/1918	22/08/1918
War Diary	Wallon Cappel 27/U.30.c.0.7	23/08/1918	31/08/1918
Operation(al) Order(s)	40th Division R.A.M.C. Order No. 82	10/08/1918	10/08/1918
Operation(al) Order(s)	40th Division R.A.M.C. Order No. 83	21/08/1918	21/08/1918
Operation(al) Order(s)	40th Division R.A.M.C. Order No. 84	30/08/1918	30/08/1918

Operation(al) Order(s)	40th Division R.A.M.C. Order No. 85	31/08/1918	31/08/1918
Heading	Medical Services War Diaries Of A.D.M.S. 40th Division Officer Commanding 135th Field Ambulance For Month Of September 1918 Volumes XXVIII		
War Diary	Wallon-Cappel 27/U.30.c.0.7	01/09/1918	01/09/1918
War Diary	La Motte 36 A /D.30c.9.7	02/09/1918	30/09/1918
Operation(al) Order(s)	40th Division R.A.M.C. Order No. 86	01/09/1918	01/09/1918
Operation(al) Order(s)	40th Division R.A.M.C. Order No. 87	05/09/1918	05/09/1918
Operation(al) Order(s)	40th Division R.A.M.C. Order No. 88	17/09/1918	17/09/1918
Operation(al) Order(s)	40th Division R.A.M.C. Order No. 89	22/09/1918	22/09/1918
Operation(al) Order(s)	40th Division R.A.M.C. Order No. 90	25/09/1918	25/09/1918
Heading	ADMS 40th Div Oct 1918		
War Diary	La Motte 36A/D 30.c.9.7	01/10/1918	01/10/1918
War Diary	36/A 21b 2.7	02/10/1918	17/10/1918
War Diary	Armentieres	18/10/1918	19/10/1918
War Diary	Mouvaux (36/7.c.7.7)	20/10/1918	26/10/1918
War Diary	L'Anway 37/G 15. Cent	27/10/1918	31/10/1918
Operation(al) Order(s)	40th Division R.A.M.C. Order No. 91	01/10/1918	01/10/1918
Operation(al) Order(s)	40th Division R.A.M.C. Order No. 92	05/10/1918	05/10/1918
Operation(al) Order(s)	40th Division R.A.M.C. Order No. 93	12/10/1918	12/10/1918
Operation(al) Order(s)	40th Division R.A.M.C. Order No. 94	16/10/1918	16/10/1918
Operation(al) Order(s)	40th Division R.A.M.C. Order No. 95	17/10/1918	17/10/1918
Operation(al) Order(s)	40th Division R.A.M.C. Order No. 96	18/10/1918	18/10/1918
Operation(al) Order(s)	40th Division R.A.M.C. Order No. 97	22/10/1918	22/10/1918
Operation(al) Order(s)	40th Division R.A.M.C. Order No. 98	23/10/1918	23/10/1918
Operation(al) Order(s)	40th Division R.A.M.C. Order No. 99	25/10/1918	25/10/1918
Operation(al) Order(s)	40th Division R.A.M.C. Order No. 100	26/10/1918	26/10/1918
Heading	ADMS 40th Divn Nov 1918		
Miscellaneous			
War Diary	Lannoy 37/G 15. Central	01/11/1918	24/11/1918
War Diary	Roubaix 36/L.5.a. 4 Rue des Arts	25/11/1918	30/11/1918
War Diary	Roubaix 4 Rue Des Artes	30/11/1918	30/11/1918
Operation(al) Order(s)	40th Division R.A.M.C. Order No. 102	23/11/1918	23/11/1918
Heading	A.D.M.S. 40th Div Dec 1918		
War Diary	Roubaix 4. Rue Des Artes	01/12/1918	31/12/1918
Heading	A.D.M.S. 40th Divn Jan 1919		
War Diary	Roubaix 4 Rue Des Artes	01/01/1919	31/01/1919
Miscellaneous	Officer Commanding. Appendix 1	15/01/1919	15/01/1919
Miscellaneous			
Miscellaneous	Field Ambulance Notes		
Miscellaneous	Officer Commanding. Appendix 2	30/01/1919	30/01/1919
Heading	A.D.M.S. 40th Division Feb 1919		
War Diary	Roubaix 4 Rue Des Artes	01/02/1919	22/02/1919
War Diary	Roubaix	23/02/1919	28/02/1919
Heading	ADMS 40th Division Mar 1919		
War Diary	Roubaix No 4 Rue Des Arts	01/03/1919	31/03/1919

woas/25 97/1/

40TH DIVISION

ASST DIR. MEDICAL SERVICES

JUN 1916 - ~~DEC 1918~~
1919 MAR

A.D. M.S. 40th Division

June 1916

COMMITTEE FOR THE
MEDICAL HISTORY OF THE WAR
Date 31 APR 1915

WAR DIARY of A.D.M.S. 40th Division

or INTELLIGENCE SUMMARY

Army Form C. 2118

Vol 1

Place	Date	Hour	Summary of Events and Information	Remarks and references to Appendices
BLACKDOWN CAMP	2.6.16	3 PM	Head Quarters left for SOUTHAMPTON.	
SOUTHAMPTON	"	6 PM	Arrived at SOUTHAMPTON.	
"	"	7.40 PM	Left SOUTHAMPTON. G.J. Burtchaell Col. A.M.S. A.D.M.S. 40th Division	
HAVRE	3.6.16	8 A.M	Arrived at HAVRE. G.J.B.	
"	4.6.16	2.49 PM	Left HAVRE. G.J.B.	
LILLERS	5.6.16	10.30 AM	Arrived at LILLERS. (Reference map. HAZEBROUCK. S.A 100,000, F.6.) G.J.B.	
"	5.6.16	11 AM	Proceeded to NORRENT. FONTES. (Same map F.6.) G.J.B.	
NORRENT.FONTES	"	12 noon	Arrived. Also 135 Field Ambulance at I.A. COULEE - NORRENT. FONTES. which has opened to receive the sick from the Division.	
"	6.6.16	2 P.M	Proceeded to A.A. & Q.M.G. Office at LABUISSIERE. 136 F.A arrived last night at HURIONVILLE. L.	
"	"	6 P.M	137 F.A arrived this day at FONTES. 21 Motor Ambulance wagons arrived + were posted at F.A's G.J.B	
"	7.6.16	1 A.M.	83rd Sanitary Section arrived at LILLERS. Inspected 137 + 135 F.A's G.J.B.	
"	8.6.16	10 A.C.	O.C. M.A.W.U. reported the arrival of his unit at LILLERS.	
"	"	7 PM	Inspected Dressing Station 135 F.A. G.J.B.	
"	9.6.16	11.30 AM	A.D.M.S. 1st Corps visited my office and subsequently inspected 135 and 137 F.A.	
"	"	5 P.M	Visited Town Major + ADMS 12" Divn re bath and laundry.	
"	"	7 P.M.	Interviewed D.C. with regard to anti-gas measures + instructions to be given by In O? G.J.B.	
"	10.6.16	2 P.M	Accompanied A.A. & Q.M.G. and visited baths at LILLERS. and BELLERY; and also inspected 136 F.A at HURIONVILLE. G.J.B.	
"	11.6.16	8 A.M	A. Section of 135 - 6 + 7 F.A. left their units for a ten days course of instruction will 15", 16" ST.	
"	"	7 P.M	Inspected Billets + Sanitary arrangements of Signal Company + Mobile Veterinary Section. G.J.B.	
"	12	5.30 PM	Attended Conference at Divisional Head Quarters G.H.	
"	14.6.16	10.30 AM	Visited A.D.M.S. 12" Division to arrange for Advance parties to take over stores etc from his F.A. on vacating their billets.	
"	15.6.16	7 A.M.	Advance parties from 135 + 136 F.A. proceeded to ALLOUAGNE + AUCHEL respectively to take over from 36 + 37 F.A. G.J.B.	

1875 Wt. W593/326 1,000,000 4/15 J.B.C. & A. A.D.S.S./Forms/C. 2118.

Army Form C. 2118

WAR DIARY of A.D.M.S. 40TH Division
or
INTELLIGENCE SUMMARY
(Erase heading not required.)

Instructions regarding War Diaries and Intelligence Summaries are contained in F.S. Regs., Part II. and the Staff Manual respectively. Title Pages will be prepared in manuscript.

Place	Date	Hour	Summary of Events and Information	Remarks and references to Appendices
NORRENT-FONTES	16.6.16	10.A.M	O. Sect. of 135 F.A. proceeded to ALLOUAGNE to take over sick, stores etc from 36 F.A. 12th Division. O. Sect. of 136 F.A. proceeded to AUCHEL to take over sick, stores etc from 37 F.A. 12th Division.	
"	17.6.16	3.P.M.	Attended conference of A.D.M.S. 1st Corps at BETHUNE	C.9. Luther Col Army A.D.M.S
"	"	6.P.M.	Accompanied A.D.M.S. to ALLOUAGNE & AUCHEL were we inspected the Medical arrangements. O.K.	
BRUAY	19.6.16	12 noon	Divisional No. Qr. 136.F.A. and 83rd Sanitary Section Due today. (Q.I.L) high Reference Sheet 36.B 1:40,000.	
"	"	"	135 F.A. at DIVION, SITE 18, J. 30.B. and 137 F.A. at RUITZ, K.19.d, same hrs.	
"	"	7 P.M.	A.D.M.S. 1st Corps visited this office and conferred on Sanitary and Medical matters. O.K.	
"	20.6./6	10.30.A.M	Visited 135 F.A. at DIVION - Everything very satisfactory	
"	"	12 noon	Visited 137 F.A. at RUITZ. Accommodation and billeting very bad. Ordered O.C. to proceed at once & interview Proper proper 121st Brigade who allotted the billets, to procure better accommodation.	
"	"	3.30 PM	Visited 136 F.A at BRUAY - O.K.	
"	21.6.16	11.A.M	D.A.M.S. 1st Corps called at my Office + discussed medical + Sanitary matters - We then visited 135 + 137 F.A.	
"	"	2.30 PM	Visited the Divisional Gas School at PONT DE REVEILLON + discussed with O.C. arrangements for coming classes. O.K.	
"	22.6.16	3 PM	Held a conference at my office with the O.Cs F.As. O.K.	
"	23.6.16	11 A.M	Visited 137 F.A. at RUITZ. No better accommodation being available this unit has opened out empty canvas as	
"	24.6.16	11 A.M.	R.A.D.M.S. inspected Divisional Laundry at BETHUNE - all correct. O.K.	
"	25.6.16	11 A.M.	D.A.D.M.S. inspected Divisional Clothing Store at BETHUNE - all correct. O.L. D.A.D.M.S visited office.	
"	"	1 P.M.	In accordance with 1st Army instructions I issued orders to O.Cs 135 - 6 and 7 F.A. to earmark 3 Officers, 3 N.C.Os. and 24 men for duty, if necessary to blend the personnel of a Reserve Bearer Division to be made up as on the same Authority.	
"	26.6.16	1.P.M.	follows - A + C Bearer Subdivisions of 136 F.A. and Bearer subdivision of A section of 135 F.A. B. Sections of both F.As constituting instruction with other Divisions. all	
"	27.6.16	4.P.M.	Inspected billeting area of 11th Kings own Regt. O.K.	
"	28.6.16	3.P.M.	Inspected camp of 120th machine Gun Company + No 3 Coy. A.S.C. all	
"	29.6.16	5.P.M.	Inspected billeting area H.L.J. all	
"	30.6/16	4.P.M	Inspected 136 F.A. all correct. O.K.	

C.J. Luther
Col.
A.D.M.S. 40th Division.

1875 Wt. W593/826 1,000,000 4/15 J.B.C. & A. A.D.S.S./Forms/C.2118.

Confidential

Medical Services.

War Diary.

of

A.D.M.S. 40th Division.

For month of July, 1916.

(Volume II)

COMMITTEE FOR THE
MEDICAL HISTORY OF THE WAR
Date   5-SEP 1916

Secret

Vol. II

WAR DIARY of A.D.M.S. 40th Division.

INTELLIGENCE SUMMARY

(Erase heading not required.)

Army Form C. 2118

Instructions regarding War Diaries and Intelligence Summaries are contained in F.S. Regs., Part II. and the Staff Manual respectively. Title Pages will be prepared in manuscript.

Place	Date	Hour	Summary of Events and Information	Remarks and references to Appendices
BRUAY.	1.7.16	10 A.M	B. Sections of 135, 136 and 137 F.A. returned this day from 10 days instruction in Trenches with 1st, 13th and 16th Divisions respectively. C. Sections to of above F.A. proceed today to undergo a similar course. O.I. Lieut. Col Aumy	
"	2.7.16	2.30 P.M	Proceeded to NOEUX. LES. MINES to confer with A.D.M.S. 1st Division as to taking over from him hospital billets, Dressing & Advanced Dressing Stations, Dumps of Stores etc at an early date. A.L.	Reference hosps BETHUNE (combined shelf) 1/40, OOD.
"	3.7.16	4 P.M.	Visited 136 F.A. Everything Satisfactory. O.L.	A.O.
"	4.7.16	12 noon	137. F.A. Arrived from at NOEUX LES MINES. BRAQUEMONT.	A.O.
			137. F.A. Arrived from at NOEUX LES MONT from RUITZ and took over all medical arrangements from 1st F.A. 1st Division. Vig. Head Quarters and Main Dressing Station at 36.B. L.23.b.6.2.S. — open. Advanced Dressing Stations at 36.B.L.35.a.8.S. — open — 36.C.M.2.a.4.7. open — and 36.C.M.2.6.1.4 — open.	A.O.
NOEUX.LES. MINES.	5.7.16		Remainder of Medical Units etc. arrived last night and and distributed as follows — A.D.M.S. Office at BRAQUEMONT. 36.B.-L.19.a.2.4. — 135. F.A. BRAQUEMONT Huts 36.R-2.23.c.1.3.4. — Advanced Dressing Station at GRENAY. 36.C.M.1.a.7.2. and CALONNE. 36C.M.14.a.8.1.(also open.) 136.F.A. open as Corps Rest Station at BRAQUEMONT. 36.B.D.17.a.4.4. 83rd Sanitary Section at BRAQUEMONT — 36.B. L.25.a. 7.9. O.L.	
"	6.7.16	3 P.M.	Visited the Dressing Station & Advanced Dressing Station of 135 F.A. all correct. Also the Rgtl A.I.D. Posts of 16th Welsh Rgt and Hut of 19th R.W. Fusiliers. O.L.	
"	7.7.16	3 P.M	Inspected the Advanced Dressing Station of 137. F.A. Everything very satisfactory. O.L.	
"	8.7.16	3 A.M.	Attended conference held by D.A.M.S. 1st Corps at 113 F.A. O.L.	
"	9.7.16	11 A.M.	Inspected Mt Qrs 135. F.A. Everything very satisfactory. O.L.	
"	"	3. A.M.	Inspected 1st Corps Rest Station for Officers and men at LABOUVIERE, with a few minor exceptions Everything satisfactory. O.L.	
"	11.7.16	2 P.M.	Inspected all R.B.'s - min. all	
"	11.7.16	3 P.M	Inspected Divisional Laundry at BETHUNE, all satisfactory with the exception of minor Sanitary defects etc.	
"	12.7.16	3. P.M.	Inspected 137 F.A. Everything Very Satisfactory. O.L.	
"	13.7.16	2.30 P.M	D.D.M.S. 1st Corps visited my office and conferred on medical arrangements. O.L.	
"	14.7.16	2 P.M.	Visited the Advanced Dressing Station of 135 F.A. and the Regimental Aid Posts Stations in the COLONNE sector all O.K.	
"	15.7.16	5. P.M.	Inspected Billets and Horse lines 185 Battery R.F.A. wrote to O.C. asking for report from M.O. as to his sanitary arrangements. Everything Satisfactory. O.L.	
"	16.7.16	3. P.M.	Inspected Billets of Divisional Police and Band. Everything satisfactory. O.L.	
"	17.7.16	6. P.M.	Visited the Divisional Gas School at HOUCHIN. Everything very Satisfactory. O.L.	

Secret

Vol. II

WAR DIARY of A.D.M.S. 40th Division.

INTELLIGENCE SUMMARY

(Erase heading not required.)

Army Form C. 2118

Instructions regarding War Diaries and Intelligence Summaries are contained in F.S. Regs., Part II. and the Staff Manual respectively. Title Pages will be prepared in manuscript.

Place	Date	Hour	Summary of Events and Information	Remarks and references to Appendices
BRAQUEMONT (NOEUX-LES MINES)	19.7.16	5. P.M.	Visited the main Dressing and Head Quarters of 137 F.A. Everything very satisfactory. A.D.M.S. Lukin Col. of 113 F.A.	
"	20.7.16	5. P.M.	Visited do. do. of 113 F.A. do. A.D.M.S. 16th Division	
"	21.7.16	9. P.M.	Accompanied A.D.M.S. 16th Division to PHILOSOPHE, FORT GLATZ and ST. PATRICK at LOOS with a view to taking over the places tomorrow, as Advanced Dressing Stations from 113 F.A. 16th Division. C.L.	
"	22.7.16	2. P.M.	137 F.A. took over from 113 F.A. the Advanced Dressing Stations at PHILOSOPHE, FORT GLATZ and ST. PATRICK. C.L.	
"	23.7.16	7. P.M.	Accompanied G.O.C. Division to CORPS. REST. STATION at LAROUVIERE and to the Advanced Dressing Station of 137 F.A. at LES BREBIS. C.L.	
"	24.7.16	5. P.M.	Inspected Head Quarters 137 F.A. all correct. C.L.	
"	25.7.16	3. P.M.	Inspected main Dressing Station 135 F.A. Everything very satisfactory. C.L.	
"	26.7.16	5. P.M.	Proceeded to Head Quarters 121st Infantry Brigade to confer with G.O.C. re Stretcher bearers (Regtl), considered unfit for the work, arrangements made to select & train stronger and more suitable men. C.L.	
"	27.7.16	3 P.M.	Inspected Advanced Dressing Station 136 F.A. also Regtl. Aid Posts. COLONNE Section. C.L.	
"	28.7.16	5:30 P.M.	Attended Conference at Divisional Head Quarters. C.L.	
"	29.7.16	3. P.M.	Inspected Main Dressing Station 136 F.A. Everything very satisfactory. C.L.	
"	30.7.16	4. P.M.	Inspected main Dressing Station 137 F.A. Everything very satisfactory. C.L.	
"	31.7.16	2:30 P.M.	Held Conference with O.C.s Field Ambulances. A.J. Luther Col. A.D.M.S. 40th Division	

A.J. Luther
Col.
A.D.M.S. 40th Division

A.D.M.S., 40th Division

August 1916

COMMITTEE FOR THE
MEDICAL HISTORY OF THE WAR
Date -9 OCT. 1916

Secret.

Vol. III.

WAR DIARY of A.D.M.S. 40th Division.

or

INTELLIGENCE SUMMARY

(Erase heading not required.)

Army Form C. 2118.

Place	Date	Hour	Summary of Events and Information	Remarks and references to Appendices
BRAQUEMONT (36.B.2 & 6.2.6)	1.8.16	3. P.M.	Forwarded original copies of my War Diary and those of 135, 136 and 137 Field Ambulances to A.A. & Q.M.G. & Anglican. Admitted from 9.A.M. yesterday to 9.A.M. today :- 1 Officer wounded, other ranks 20. Sick admissions for ration strength total 50.- P.C. 22. Sick evacuations 20.- P.C. 09.- 2 Returned to duty from Casualty Clearing Station. Inspected Regt. Aid Posts and Advanced Dressing Station CALONNE Section.	A.T. Sutton A.R.M.S. 40th Divsion.
"	"	4. P.M.		A.T.L.
"	2.8.16		Admitted OR wounded 19. Sick for ration strength 32.- P.C. 22. Sick evacuations 28.- .13.	A.T.L.
"	3.8.16		Admitted Officers sick 3, other ranks, sick 38, wounded 36. P.C. admission to ration strength. 19. evacuation 12.- P.C. b5. Returned from Casualty Clearing Station 2. Inspected all R.B. men in Divisional Area. Three found fit to return to duty.	A.T.L.
"	4.8.16	10.A.M.	Admitted O.Rs sick 1, wounded 2. O.R.s sick 30, wounded 16. Total admissions 31. P.C. 13. Evacuations 19.- 09. Returned from C.C.S. 2. hosp. Ryley R.A.M.C. A.A.D.M.S. Transferred to Corps Rest Station. Diagnosis D.A.H. Inspected H.Q. Div. 137. F.A. ???	
"	"	3.P.M.	Attended A.D.M.S' Conference at 24 F.A. at LABOURSE.	
"	"	5.30 M.	Attended G.O.C.s Conference at Adv. H.Q. Div.	A.T.L.
"	5.8.16		Admitted Officers sick 1. O.R.s 24. Wounded 16. Evacuated OR sick 1. OR's 12. wounded 15. Percentages admitted and evacuated .11 and .06. Returned from C.C.S. B. O.T.L.	
"	6.8.16		Admitted Officers sick 3, OR.s 17, wounded 13. Evacuated OR sick 1, OR.s 14, wounded 17. P.C. admitted and evacuated .09 and .08. 5- returned from C.C.S. Inspected Regt. Aid Post. Billets etc of 13 Yorkshire Regt at LES BREBIS. O.T.L.	
"	7.8.16	3 P.M.	Wounded Officers sick 1, wounded 30, OR's sick 26 wounded 36. Percentages admitted and evacuated .13 and .04. Capt. HUTCHISON R.A.M.C. M.O. Divisional Train granted me two hours of absence to arrange about his brother at home.	
"	8.8.16	5.30 A.M.	Attended G.O.C.'s conference at Divisional Head Quarter.	
"	"	8 P.M.	Admitted O's Sick 1, OR's Sick 46, wounded 36. Percentage admitted + evacuated .23 and .02 Visited Corps Rest Station at LABEUVRIERE.	A.T.L.
"	9.8.16		Admitted O's Sick 2, Wounded 1, OR's Sick 31 wounded 18. Percentage of admitted and evacuated .16 and .08 Inspected 2 R.F.A. and Train Lorne Lines.	A.T.L.
"	10.8.16	3 P.M.	Admitted OR's Sick 21, wounded 18. P.C. of admitted and evacuated .1 and .05. Inspected Regt. Aid Posts and Advanced Dressing Station CALONNE Section.	
"	"	5 P.M.	Inspected Regt. 135 F.A. proceeded on 14 days leave of absence. LIEUT GIBSON R.A.M.C. arrived at LABEUVRIERE. H.Q. Div. 136 F.A. on return from being attached to 137 F.A. C Sectn 136 F.A.	A.T.L.

Secret

Vol III.
WAR DIARY of A.D.M.S. 40th Division
or
INTELLIGENCE SUMMARY
(Erase heading not required.)

Army Form C. 2118

Place	Date	Hour	Summary of Events and Information	Remarks and references to Appendices
BRAQUEMONT	11.8.16	2 P.M.	Admitted O.Rs Sick 1, O.Rs Sick 26, wounded 13. P.C. of Admitted & evacuated .13 and .07. Proceeded to CALONNE and made a thorough Sanitary inspection of Kitchens, billets and cellars and latrines all the latter have now been conveyed into covered in deep pits – Much was much to be desired in the cleanliness of streets, billets and surroundings, I gave instructions to the various Regimental Medical Officers as to what was required to put the place in a clean and sanitary condition. A.L.	
"	12.8.16		Admitted Officers Sick 2, wounded 1. O.Rs Sick 30, wounded 14. P.C. .16 and .04. Visited Head Quarters 137 F.A. Everything very satisfactory. O.L	
"	13.8.16	3 P.M.	Admitted O.Rs Sick 1, wounded 4. O.Rs Sick 34, wounded 41. P.C. .18 and .09. Visited Corps Rest Station and Divisional Laundry. O.L	
"	14.8.16		Admitted O.Rs Sick 2, wounded 1, O.Rs Sick 26, wounded 17. Sick percentage of admitted & evacuated .14 & .08. Attended G.O.C. Conference at Div. Head Quarters.	
		5.30 P.M.	A.D.M.S. I. Corps visited this office and conferred on sanitary matters. O.L	
		6 P.M.	the Div. Sanc. Officer admitted to 137 F.A. – N.Y.D.	
"	15.8.16	11 A.M.	Admitted Officers Sick 1, O.Rs 22, wounded 13. P.C. of Sick admitted and evacuated .12 and .07. R.A.M.S. 1st Army arrived and inspected H.Q. and Advanced Dressing Stations at PONT BRENAY, CALONNE, and LES BREBIS, of 135- and 137 F.A.) at LES BREBIS, which was being shelled at the time, the R.A.M.S. was much pleased at the work being done with the Casualties by the M.O. and staff. O.L	
"	16.8.16	5 P.M.	Admitted Officers Sick 2. O.Rs 68 (26 Sick). Wounded 21. Sick admissions per ration strength .35 – Inspected R.T.G. + Train Lines A.L	
"	17.8.16	3 P.M.	Proceeded to Corps Rest Station at LABEUVRIERE and inspected them of 40th Division. and mass 13 of them T.U.S (temporary unfit)	
			Admitted O.Rs Sick 4, O.Rs 14, wounded 15. Sick admissions per ration strength .09. All CAPT BALFOUR-BROWNE R.A.M.C. T. evacuated sick to 1.C.C.S. Diagnosis N.Y.D. Lt. ALLINGHAM R.A.M.C 21st Middlesex Regt. admitted, gunshot wound of chest. O.L	
"	18.8.16	3 P.M.	Admitted O.Rs Sick, wounded 2. O.Rs Sick 33, wounded 6. Sick admissions per ration strength .17. Inspected CALONNE village & made a minute inspection of RUE BERTHELOT the cellars, Trench and Surroundings of which were in a very dirty + insanitary condition, taps, food Refuse, empty tins etc lying about, Divisional orders issued making units responsible for their respective areas.	
		5.30 P.M.	Attended conference at G.O.C Division Head Quarters." G.J. Luther Col A.D.M.S 40th Division

1875 Wt. W593/326 1,000,000 4/15 I.B.C. & A. A.D.S.S./Forms/C.2118.

Secret

Vol III.

WAR DIARY of A.D.M.S. 40th Division.

III.

or

INTELLIGENCE SUMMARY

(Erase heading not required.)

Army Form C. 2118

Instructions regarding War Diaries and Intelligence Summaries are contained in F. S. Regs., Part II. and the Staff Manual respectively. Title Pages will be prepared in manuscript.

Place	Date	Hour	Summary of Events and Information	Remarks and references to Appendices
BRAQUEMONT	19.8.16	3 P.M.	Admitted to Sick 1, wounded 1, ORs Sick 36, wounded 19. Sick admissions for ration strength .19. Q.L. Luthi, Col. Attended A.D.M.S's conference at 137. F.A. ADMS. 3. 40th Division.	
"	20.8.16	10.A.M.	Admitted officers wounded 4. ORs Sick 39, wounded 4. Sick admissions for ration strength . 2.	
		6.P.M.	Made a thorough Sanitary inspection of LES BREBIS, accompanied by the Town Major and the acting Sanitary Officer. Inspected R.F.A. billets, cookhouse lines etc.	a.l.
"	21.8.16	11.A.M.	Admitted officers sick 1. ORs Sick 27, wounded 2.6. Sick admissions for ration strength .13. Inspected billets, cookhouses, latrines etc in BRAQUEMONT.	
		5.30.P.M.	Attended Conference of G.O.C. at Divisional Head Quarters.	Q.L.
"	22.8.16		Admitted officers sick 1. wounded 1. ORs Sick 34, wounded 13. Sick admissions for ration strength . 18.	
		2.P.M.	Proceeded to MAROC and inspected advanced dressing Stations and Aid Posts, all very satisfactory, also made Sanitary inspection of NORTH and SOUTH MAROC.	Q.L.
"	23.8.16		Admitted officers Sick 1. ORs 37, wounded 18. Sick admissions for ration strength . 2. Capt. T.G. Shand Renée S.R arrived to take over command of 83rd Sanitary Section.	
		5. P.M.	Made Sanitary inspection of PETIT SAINS	
		9. P.M.	137 F.A. handed over MAROC Section to 135. F.A and took over 2008 section from the 18th Division. Jura Section of 90 Field Ambulance 32 Brigade arrived. One Section attached to 135. F.A. He other to 137. F.A.	Q.L.
"	24.8.16		Admitted officers wounded 2. ORs Sick Sick 36, including 9 2 self inflicted wounds. Sick admissions for ration strength . 18.	
		3.P.M.	Made a sanitary inspection of HOUCHIN and HESDIGNEUL	A.L.
"	25.8.16		Admitted officers sick 1. wounded 2. ORs Sick 15, wounded 2. Sr. Sick admissions for ration strength . 08.	
		5.30.A.M.	Attended G.O.C's conference at Div. Hd Qrs.	A.L.
"	26.8.16		Admitted officers Sick 2. wounded 2. ORs Sick 42, wounded 21. Sick admissions for ration strength . 23.	
		10.P.M.	Inspected advanced dressing Station at PHILOSOPHE, Fort GLATZ and St PATRICK, every thing very satisfactory.	Q.L.
"	27.8.16		Admitted officers Sick 3, wounded 1. ORs Sick 27, wounded 12. Sick admissions for ration strength . 12.	A.L.
		3.P.M.	Inspected A.S.C. billets, sanitary arrangements and horse lines.	
"	28.8.16		Admitted officers sick 1, wounded 3. ORs Sick 41, wounded 29. Sick admissions for ration strength . 17.	
		5.30.P.M.	Attended G.O.C's conference at Div. Hd Qrs.	

Q.L. Luthi, Col.
A.D.M.S. 40th Division.

Secret

Vol IV

WAR DIARY of A.D.M.S. 40th Division
or
INTELLIGENCE SUMMARY
(Erase heading not required.)

Army Form C. 2118

Place	Date	Hour	Summary of Events and Information	Remarks and references to Appendices
BRAQUEMONT	29.8.16	10 A.M.	Admitted officers Sick 1, wounded/. OR's Sick 36, wounded 12. Sick admissions per ration strength - 15.	
		2.30 P.M.	Inspected all R.O's and T.U's attached to the Division. O.K.	
			Inspected the Sanitation of LES 13 R.E. R.I.S. O.K.	
"	30.8.16	3. P.M.	Admitted officers Sick 3. OR's 36, wounded 6. Sick admissions per ration strength - 2.5.	
			Inspected Main Dressing Station 135 F.A. O.K.	
"	31.8.16	3 P.M.	Admitted officers Sick 3. OR's 25, wounded 6. Sick admissions per ration strength - 11.	
			Inspected Main Dressing Station 137 F.A. O.K.	
			A. J. Butler	
			Col.	
			A.A.M.S. 40th Division.	

No/134

A.D.M.S. 40th Div.

COMMITTEE FOR THE
MEDICAL HISTORY OF THE WAR
Date 30 OCT. 1916

Vol IV

Secret

WAR DIARY of A.D.M.S. 40th Division

or

INTELLIGENCE SUMMARY

(Erase heading not required.)

Army Form C. 2118

Instructions regarding War Diaries and Intelligence Summaries are contained in F.S. Regs., Part II. and the Staff Manual respectively. Title Pages will be prepared in manuscript.

Place	Date	Hour	Summary of Events and Information	Remarks and references to Appendices
BRAQUEMONT. (36.B.25-6.25.)	1.9.16		Forwarded War Diaries of A.Nos. 135, 136 + 137 F.A.s to Divisional Head Quarters. Admitted Officers sick 2, OR's 38, wounded 10. Sick admissions per ration strength. 16.	Q
		5.30 AM	Attended G.O.C's conference at Divisional Head Quarters.	A.L
"	2.9.16		Admitted Officers sick 4, wounded 1. OR's sick 43, wounded 9. Sick admissions per ration strength. 10. Made a sanitary inspection of LES BREBIS, noted improvement in general cleanliness of town. The provision of deep pit latrines in la Cuins, & the disposal of non humable refuse in mine pit craters by Mines Corps.	A. Asst. 40th Div. Sct. Q.
		3. P.M		Sufts Set.
"	3.9.16		Admitted Officers sick 1. OR's Sick 24, wounded 12. Sick admissions per ration strength. 13.	A.L
		3. P.M.	Visited Rest Station at LABEUVRIERE and Shelted 14 men chiefly staff shocked - as temporary invalids.	Q.L.
"	4.9.16		Admitted Officers Sick 2. OR's 34, wounded 13. Sick admissions per ration strength. 2.	
			The Officers Rest Station was moved from LABEUVRIERE today to AIRE, and is being administered by the Corps.	Q.L.
		3. P.M	Inspected HALLICOURT and HOUCHIN - Sanitation Satisfactory.	
"	5.9.16		Admitted Officers Sick 1. OR's Sick 32, wounded 12. Sick admissions per ration strength. 17.	G.L
		3. P.M.	Inspected Advanced Dressing Stations and Reg'tl Aid Posts MAROC Section. Everything very satisfactory.	
"	6.9.16		Admitted Officers Sick 2. OR's 48, wounded 7. Sick admissions per ration strength. 26.	
		3. P.M.	Inspected 135- F.A. main Dressing Station. Everything very satisfactory.	A.L
"	7.9.16		Admitted Officers Sick 3. Other ranks 21, wounded 17. Sick admissions per ration strength. 12.	
		10. A.M	Visited LES BREBIS. billets are being sprayed with cresol + millcons line washed, surroundings & pyplos & sanitary Statr.	
"	8.9.16		Admitted Officers sick 1, other ranks 35, wounded 19. Sick admissions per ration strength. 19	
		11 A.M.	Visited main Dressing Station 137. F.A. very very very satisfactory.	Q.L
		5.30. P.M.	Attended G.O.C. Conference at Div. H.H. Qrs.	
"	9.9.16		Admitted Officers sick 1, OR's 28, wounded 7. Sick admissions per ration strength. 15.	
		3. A.M.	Inspected Advanced Dressing Stations + Reg'tl Aid Posts MAROC Section. all Satisfactory.	Q.L
"	10.9.16		Admitted OR's sick 20, wounded 11. Sick admissions per ration strength. 15.	
		3. P.M.	Inspected R.F.A. horse lines, billets, cookhouses, latrines etc. all Satisfactory.	Q.L
"	11.9.16		Admitted Officers sick 1, OR's 25, wounded 12. Sick admissions per ration strength. 14.	
		3. P.M.	Inspected A.S.C. lines, all Satisfactory.	G.P.L
"	12.9.16		Admitted OR's 30, wounded 9. Sick admissions per ration strength. 16.	Q.L.

Secret

WAR DIARY of A.D.M.S. 40th Division.

Vol. II   Army Form C. 2118

or

INTELLIGENCE SUMMARY

(Erase heading not required.)

Place	Date	Hour	Summary of Events and Information	Remarks and references to Appendices
BRAQUEMONT 36.A.L.28.d.2.5.	13.9.16		Admitted Officers Sick 2, OR's Sick 46, wounded 1. Sick admissions per ration strength . 2.6 Accompanied G.O.C. R.A. to HOUCHIN and inspected proposed billeting accommodation for D.A.C. with the exception of one which had no sanitary surroundings, all could be turned into suitable billets.	A.J. Luther ADMS 40th Div 2
"	14.9.16	3.P.M.	Admitted Other ranks Sick 22, wounded 6. Sick admissions per ration strength . 1.2 Inspected billets and surroundings at PETIT SAINS. Everything satisfactory.	A.D.M.S. 40th Div Sgd.
"	15.9.16	3.30 A.M.	Admitted Officers Sick 1, wounded 1. OR's Sick 38, wounded 6. Sick admissions per ration strength - 2.1. Attended G.O.C.'s conference at Divisional Head Quarters.	G.J.L A.L
"	16.9.16	3.P.M.	Admitted Officers Sick 1, OR's 37, wounded 12. Sick admissions per ration strength - 2.1. Inspected Divisional Laundry at BETHUNE, work has carried on satisfactorily. Capt Williams, Lt Morgan and Lt Byrne went on instruction from First Army Lieut-Colonel for the Army at the SOMME	O.I.L all
"	17.9.16		Admitted Officers Sick 3, OR's 60, wounded 39. Sick admissions per ration strength . 2.3. Admitted OR's Sick 2, wounded 1, OR's Sick 39, wounded 7, 137 F.A. .0.14 Inspected ALMAINT dressing Station 13.5 - and 137 F.A.	.014
"	18.9.16	4.P.M. 5.30P.M	Admitted Officers Sick 1, OR's 26, wounded 7. Sick admissions per ration strength . 15 Attended G.O.C. Conference at Div. H.Q. Qrs.	.O.I.L
"	19.9.16		Admitted Officers wounded 1. OR's Sick 33, wounded 8. Sick admissions per ration strength . 19	.A.L
"	20.9.16		Admitted Officers Sick 1. OR's 32, wounded 8. Sick admissions per ration strength . 18. Visited LES BREBIS and inspected billets and sanitary arrangements generally - all satisfactory.	.A.L
"	21.9.16	3.P.M. 2.P.M. 8.P.M.	Admitted Officers wounded 1. OR's Sick 26, wounded 17. Sick admissions per ration strength . 14. Visited all Advanced Dressing Stations and Regimental Aid Posts MA.R.O.C. - all satisfactory. 137 F.A. took over from 3rd Division Advanced Dressing Stations 14.13.15 Section.	G.J.L. A.L
"	22.9.16	4.30P.M	Admitted OR's Sick 30, wounded 5. Sick admissions per ration strength . 17. Attended G.O.C.'s Conference at Divisional Head Quarters.	A.L
"	23.9.16		Admitted Officer Sick 1, OR's 19, wounded 14. Sick admissions per ration strength . 1. Visited all Advanced Dressing Stations and Regtl Aid Posts in 14.13.15 Section, all satisfactory. Gave instructions for the Battle Posts in this area which are in course of construction to be gone on with.	a.l.
"	24.9.16	5.30P.M	Admitted Officers Sick 1, OR's 44, wounded 12. Sick admissions per ration strength . 2.5 Visited all Advanced Dressing Stations and Regtl Aid Posts in LOOS Section. All satisfactory.	A.L.
"	25.9.16		Admitted OR's Sick 31, wounded 20. Sick admissions per ration strength . 16	

C.J. Luther
A.D.M.S. 40th Division

Secret

Vol. IV
WAR DIARY of A.D.M.S. 40th Division.
or
INTELLIGENCE SUMMARY
(Erase heading not required.)

Army Form C. 2118

Place	Date	Hour	Summary of Events and Information	Remarks and references to Appendices
BRAQUEMONT. 36.B.L.25.1.2.5	26.9.16	3.P.M.	Admitted Officers wounded 2, OR's Sick 25, wounded 32, Sick admissions per ration strength - 13. Inspected Head Quarters 135. F.A. everything satisfactory. A. J. Luther Col. A.D.M.S 40th Division.	
	27.9.16	3.P.M.	Admitted OR's Sick 43, wounded 3. Sick admissions per ration strength - 2. Inspected Head Quarters 137. F.A. Everything Satisfactory. A.L.	
	28.9.16		Admitted Officers Sick 1, wounded 1. OR's Sick 5-2, wounded 5. Sick admissions per ration strength - 27. Inspected at 'R.R.' and 'T.U.' men in the Division. A.L.	
	29.9.16		Officers admitted Sick 2, OR's 38, wounded 3. Sick admissions per ration strength - 2.	
		5.30 P.M.	Attended C.O.C's Conference at Div. H.Q. Qrs. A.L.	
	30.9.16		Admitted Officers Sick 4, OR's 36, wounded 9. Sick admissions per ration strength - 2.	
		10 A.M.	Accompanied D.M.S. I Corps at his inspection of H.Q. Qrs. 137 Field Ambulance. Inspected all R.B. men in late 3rd Divisional Area - NEUX-LES-MINES.	

A. J. Luther Col.
A.A.M.S. 40th Division

140/1815

Oct. 1916

A.D.M.S. 40th Division

Secret

Vol. V.

WAR DIARY of A.D.M.S. 40th Division.

INTELLIGENCE SUMMARY
(Erase heading not required.)

Army Form C. 2118

Instructions regarding War Diaries and Intelligence Summaries are contained in F.S. Regs., Part II. and the Staff Manual respectively. Title Pages will be prepared in manuscript.

Place	Date	Hour	Summary of Events and Information	Remarks and references to Appendices
BRAQUEMONT. 36.B.1.2.3.4.2.5.	1.10.16	11.A.M.	Admitted Officers wounded 2. OR's Sick 36, wounded 10. Sick admissions per ration strength - 18. Forwarded War Diaries for month of September, and list of units under my command to Div. Hd. Qrs. A/L	
"	2.10.16		Accompanied Divisional Commander at his inspection of Main Dressing Stations 135 and 137 Field Ambulances. Admitted Officers sick 3, wounded 1. OR's Sick 27, wounded 10. Sick admissions per ration strength - 14. A/L Capt. A.J. Butler left A. and sent 40 Division.	
"	3.10.16	11.A.M.	Accompanied A.D.M.S I Corps at his inspection of 135 F.A. Received orders from I Corps for 2 R.A.M.C. Officers to proceed forthwith to 3rd Division. Attended GOC Conference at Div. Hd. Qrs. A/L	
"	"	3.30 P.M.	Admitted Officers Sick 2, wounded 1. OR's Sick 40, wounded 9. Sick admissions per ration strength - 21. Lieut Brown 136 F.A. and Lieut Black 137 F.A. left today for 3rd Division. A.L.	
"	4.10.16	11.A.M.	Admitted Officers sick 3, wounded 2, OR's Sick 63, wounded 9. Sick admissions per ration strength - 33. Inspected Advanced Dressing Station of 135 F.A. at LES BREBIS. Also Divisional Baths - all Satisfactory. A.L.	
"	"	3. P.M.	Admitted Officers Sick 3, wounded 1. OR's Sick 33, wounded 13. Sick admissions per ration strength. 18	
"	5.10.16	3. P.M.	Inspected all Advanced Dressing Stations, Regtl. Aid Posts, Soup Kitchens and Private Coffee Bar in MAROC. A/L	
"	6.10.16		Admitted Officers Sick 1, OR's 36. Sick admissions per ration strength - 2. Attended G.O.C. Conference at Div. Hd. Qrs. All A/L	
"	7.10.16	5.30 P.M.	Admitted Officers Sick 2, wounded 2. OR's Sick 47, wounded 13. Sick admissions per ration strength - 25. Inspected Camps and Baths at MAZINGARBE. A/L	
"	8.10.16	3. P.M.	Admitted Officers Sick 3, OR's 42, wounded 7. Sick admissions per ration strength - 24. Inspected Billets and Sanitation of PETIT SAINS. A/L	
"	9.10.16	3. P.M.	Admitted Officers Sick 4, wounded 2. OR's Sick 33, wounded 28. Sick admissions per ration strength. 19. Attended G.O.C. Conference at Div. H.Q. Quartier. A/L	
"	10.10.16	5.30 P.M.	Admitted Officers wounded 1. OR's Sick 37, wounded 30. Sick admissions per ration strength - 19. A/L	
"	11.10.16	3. P.M.	Inspected R.A. and A.S.C. Horse Lines - A/L	
"	"		Admitted Officers Sick 2, wounded 1. OR's Sick 30, wounded 13. Sick admissions per ration strength - 17. Under Corps instructions, two Officers R.A.M.C. were transferred to 32nd Division. Capt A.G. FISHER and LIEUT D.H. PATERSON and 2 Officers - CAPT W. SMITH & LIEUT P.G. FOULKES were transferred to this division from 21st Division. A/L	
"	12.10.16		Admitted Officers Sick 1, wounded 1, OR's Sick 73, wounded 11. Sick admissions per ration strength. 38. 136 and 137 Field Ambulances exchanged duties this day. The latter taking over the Corps Rest Station at LABEUVRIERE and Officers Rest Station at AIRE, the former the Main Dressing at BRAQUEMONT and Advanced Dressing Stations at PHILOSOPHE, LOOS, and ST GEORGE. Clearing the LOOS, 14 BIS and NORTH of the HULLOCH Station. Lt Col ROWAN-ROBINSON, OC 136 F.A. acting A.D.M.S. in my absence. Proceed on leave from noon 13th inst. to 22nd ins. C.V. Lester Col. A.D.M.S. 40th Division.	

Secret

WAR DIARY of A.D.M.S 40th Division
or
INTELLIGENCE SUMMARY

Army Form C. 2118

(Erase heading not required.)

Place	Date 1916	Hour	Summary of Events and Information	Remarks and references to Appendices
BRAQUEMONT 36.B.12.5&2.5	13.10.16	11 am	Admitted Officers Sick 3 O.R Sick 23 wounded 7 Sick Admissions per ration strength .13. Attended G.O.C's conference at Headquarters.	
	14.10.16	11 am	Admitted Officers Sick 1 wounded 1 O.R Sick 29 wounded 13. Sick admissions per ration strength. 15. The D.A.D.M.S and I visited the advanced dressing Station at St GEORGES the arrangement and host 14 Bn SUPPORT and present dug outs in use by 136 Field Ambulance in that part of the line.	J Howard Peyton Lt Col R.A.M. Actg A.D.M.S 40th Division
	15.10.16	11 am	Admitted Officers wounded 3 O.R Sick 35 wounded 9. Sick admissions per ration strength .19	YPRES
		9 am	The L.A.D.M.S and I visited the advanced dressing Station and Regimental aid posts in the RIGHT SUBSECTION LOOS	
	16.10.16	11 am	Admitted Officers Sick 2 O.R Sick 25 wounded 12. Sick admissions per ration strength .14 YPRES	
	17.10.16	11 am	Admitted Officers Sick 1 wounded 1 O.R Sick 26 wounded 3. Sick admissions per ration strength .13	
		9 am	Visited the advanced dressing Station at PHILOSOPHE, & StGEORGES and the Regimental aid posts in the HULLUCH SECTOR.	YPRES
	18.10.16	11 am	Admitted Officers wounded 2 O.R Sick 64 wounded 14. Sick admissions per ration strength .33 Under instructions from G.O.C to order parties of men working to construct a trench at No Mans nursery to build ten new huts for a Divisional Sanitary from of view.	YPRES
	19.10.16	11 am	Admitted Officers Sick 4 O.R Sick 35 wounded 14. Sick admissions per ration strength. 2	YPRES
	20.10.16	11 am	Admitted Officers Sick 1 O.R Sick 43 wounded 10. Sick admissions per ration strength 23	YPRES

Secret
Vol I

WAR DIARY of ADMS 40th Division
or
INTELLIGENCE SUMMARY

Army Form C. 2118

(Erase heading not required.)

Place	Date 1916	Hour	Summary of Events and Information	Remarks and references to Appendices III
BRAQUEMONT 36.B.95.62.5	21.10.16	11 am	Admitted Officers nil. O.R. sick 31 wounded 8. Sick admission per ration strength .16	
		3.30	Visited Advance Dressing Station at PHILOSOPHES ST GEORGES	Y.R.2
	22.10.16	11 am	Admitted Officers Sick 1 wounded 1. O.R. sick 35 wounded 11. Sick admission per ration strength .19	Y.R.2
	23.10.16	11 am	Admitted Officers Sick 1 wounded 1. O.R. sick 22 wounded 12. Sick admissions per ration strength .12	Y.R.2
		3. P.M.	Returned from leave this day. A.L. Butler Col. A.M.S. 40th Division.	
"	24.10.16		Admitted Officers Sick 1, wounded 1. O.R.s sick 38, wounded 29. Sick admissions per ration strength .2. Issued operation orders re vacating our present front and going into G.H.Q Reserve. A.I.L	
"		6. P.M.		
"	25.10.16		Admitted Officers Sick 1. O.R.s 5-7. Wounded 11. Sick admissions per ration strength .3.	
		3. P.M.	Inspected Advanced Dressing Stations 135 and 136 F.A.s at BRAQUEMONT. Everything very satisfactory. A.I.L	
		5.30 P.M.	Attended G.O.C.s conference at Divisional Head Quarters.	
"	26.10.16		Admitted O.R.s Sick 30, wounded 10. Sick admissions per ration strength .15. Inspected all P.B. men in Divisional area. A.I.L	
"	27.10.16		Admitted Officers Sick 2. O.R.s Sick 24. wounded 14. Sick admissions per ration strength .14.	
		1. P.M.	135. F.A. left BRAQUEMONT for BRUAY and is attached to 120th Infantry Brigade during move to Reserve Army. A.I.L	
		5. P.M.	Attend G.O.C.s conference at Divisional Head Quarters.	
"	28.10.16		Admitted Officers Sick 4. O.R.s 24. wounded 9. Sick admissions per ration strength .15	
"	29.10.16		Admitted Officers Sick 2. O.R.s 43 wounded 4. Sick admissions per ration strength .29	
			137. F.A. Left LAREUVRIERE for BRUAY and is attached to 121 Infantry Brigade. A.I.L	
"	30.10.16	11. A.M.	Left Will Av. Hd. Qrs. for ROELLECOURT. (Sheet 36.13. 1/40,000 T.20. C.2.8). Heavy rain for the last 48 hours. Very wet and muddy. A.I.L	
ROELLECOURT Sheet 36.13. 1/40,000 T.20.C.2.8.	"	12. noon	Arrived at ROELLECOURT.	
"	31.10.16		Visited 135th F.A. at Sheet 36. B.13. T.9. N.2.5. Visited 14 Argyll & Sutherland Highlanders and inspected billets and Sanitary arrangements - all satisfactory	

C.J. Butler Col.
A.D.M.S. 40th Division

140/862

A.D.M.S. 40th Division

Secret.

Vol. VI.

Vol X 6

WAR DIARY of A.D.M.S. 40th Division.

or

INTELLIGENCE SUMMARY

(Erase heading not required.)

Army Form C. 2118

Instructions regarding War Diaries and Intelligence Summaries are contained in F. S. Regs., Part II. and the Staff Manual respectively. Title Pages will be prepared in manuscript.

Place	Date	Hour	Summary of Events and Information	Remarks and references to Appendices
ROELLECOURT Shed 26 B.1.40.00 T20 C.2.8 FROHEN-LE-GRAND	1.11.16 2.11.16 3.11.16 4.11.16		Sick evacuated during the last 24 hours. 14 Brigade = T.9. D.2.3 - 136 - T.9. D.3.9 137 - W.13.2.4 " " " O.R.s 4.5. " A.3. SIBIVILLE " E.2. NEUVILLE " E.3 orry G.1 Loftus Gl " " O.R.s 16 " " " " VILLERS-L'HÔPITAL " BOFFLES " CLOREEL. Q.1.2. " " O.R. 31 " " LANCHES. " FROHEN-LE-PETIT. GORGES. G.11. " " O.R. 21	
BERNAVILLE (June 1, 1/10, OTR LENS. Sheet) " " " "	5.11.16 6.11.16 7.11.16 8.11.16 9.11.16	4.P.M. 3.P.M. 3.P.M. 2.30 P.M.	Sick Admitted 10 Offrs 32 O.R. Evacuated 1 O & 24 O.R. R.E. admitted . 23 Evacuated . 18. Visited 136 F.A. Everything satisfactory. A.1.2. Sick admitted 3 Officers, 33 O.R.s. Evacuated 3 Officers 22 O.R.s Sick. = . 25. Visited 135 F.A. Everything satisfactory. A.1.2. Sick admitted O.R.s 20, evacuated O.R.s 121 = . 15. Visited 137. F.A. Everything satisfactory. A.1.1. Sick admitted O.R.s 28. Evacuated officer sick 1 O.R.s 26. = . 2 Inspected 6 men 21st Middlesex Regt. Recommended them for Permanent Base, also Hospital billets and sanitary arrangements of the Regt. All.	
" " " " FROHEN-LE-GRAND " " " BOUQUEMAISON " "	10.11.16 11.11.16 12.11.16 13.11.16 14.11.16 15.11.16 16.11.16 17.11.16 18.11.16 19.11.16 20.11.16 21.11.16	3.P.M. 2.30 P.M 3.30 P.M 12 noon 12 noon 3.P.M	Admitted O.R.s Sick 30 Evacuated O.R.s Sick 22. = . 22. Inspected billets and Sanitary arrangements of 14 A. & S. H. satisfactory. All Admitted Officers sick 4. O.R.s 23 - Evacuated Officers sick 4. O.R.s sick 10. Evacuation. 15. O.11 " " " 2 - " 38 - " 2 - " 25 - " 18. O.11 " " " 1 - " 13 - " 1 - " 10 - " 07. O.11 " " " 1 - " 32 - " 1 - " 22 - " 24. All Inspected billets of 17 Welsh Regt. Good arrangements have been made to billet 20 men at a time. hot water provided. 12" South Wales Borderers - they have 4 Pumps since Bath & hot water provided. Sanitation satisfactory. A.12 Divisional H.Q. arrived here at 12 noon today. Admitted Officers Sick 4. O.R.s 17 = . 18, Evacuated = . 44. A.11 " " " 4. " 46 = . 04. Inspected A. & B. C billets and sanitation - satisfactory. A.12. " " " 3. " 33 = . 3. " 2 Inspected H.Q.Dn billets and sanitation - satisfactory. All. " " " 1. " 13 = . 09. " O.B. Inspected R.E. (signals) billets & sanitation - satisfactory. A.12 Divisional H.Q. arrived here at 12 noon today. Admitted Officers Sick 4. O.R.s 23, wounded 2. Evacuated officers sick 4. O.R. sick 6 wounded 2. = 3. Evacuating = . 14. All Inspected Heart drafts of 20. Middlesex Regt-on the whole they are a good well developed lot of men, also inspected 4 men for Permanent Base. A.11 Admitted O.R.s sick 36, wounded 10 evacuated O.R.s sick 12, wounded 3 = . 14. A.12	

Vol. VI.
Serial

WAR DIARY of A.D.M.S. 40th Division.

INTELLIGENCE SUMMARY

(Erase heading not required.)

Army Form C. 2118

Instructions regarding War Diaries and Intelligence Summaries are contained in F.S. Regs., Part II. and the Staff Manual respectively. Title Pages will be prepared in manuscript.

Place	Date	Hour	Summary of Events and Information	Remarks and references to Appendices
DOULLENS.	22.11.16	12 noon	Arrived at DOULLENS. Admitted ORs Sick 28, wounded 1, per ration strength 1,25 = and 3 OH	
CANAPLES	23.11.16	12 noon	Admitted Officer 28, wounded 1. Evacuated ORs Sick 29, wounded 1, per ration strength, 3 OH	
AILLY-LE-HAUT CLOCHER.	24.11.16	12 noon	Arrived from DOULLENS. Admitted officers Sick 1. ORs Sick 32, not admissions per ration strength 1, 4 evacuations, 3 all	
"	25.11.16		Arrived from CANAPLES. Admitted ORs Sick 56, wounded 5. Evacuated ORs Sick 36 " = .33 " = 3 all	
"		M.A.M.	" = .24. hit = .07 per ration strength	
"	26.11.16	M.A.M.	Visited A.D.M.S. office at LONG and conferred on Medical & Sanitary arrangements this Division came under the command of XV Corps. Fourth Army yesterday. O.K.	
"	27.11.16	3.P.M.	Admitted 1 officer, 37 men = 25. Evacuated 1 officer, 29 men = 2	
			Inspected billets and Sanitation of AILLY-LE-HAUT CLOCHER all Satisfactory O.K.	
		M.A.M.	Admitted 1 officer, 23 ORs = 18. Evacuated 10 officer, 19 = 14.	
			Visited 135 F.A. at FAMECHON and 137 F.A. at LETOILE. Little accommodation at 137 a building capable of accommodating 100 patients to be taken over tomorrow. O.K.	
"	28.11.16		Admitted ORs 38 = .26%. Evacuated 18 ORs = .1% per ration strength. O.K.	
"	29.11.16		" Officers 1. ORs 22 = .18% " 19 " = .13% per ration strength.	
		3.P.M.	Inspected Head Quarters 136 F.A. at VAUCHELLES only poor accommodation for 16 by big storm doors O.K.	
"	30.11.16		Admitted ORs 18 = .13%. Evacuated officers 1.	
			Inspected recent drafts and men proposed for permanent Base of the 12th South Wales Borderers and 14th Argyll + Sutherland Highlanders.	

A. J. Duke
Col.
A.D.M.S. 40th Division.

14/192

A.D.M.S. 40th Division

COMMITTEE FOR THE
MEDICAL HISTORY OF THE WAR
Date 31 JAN. 1917

Vol. VII

Secret.

WAR DIARY of A.D.M.S. 40th Division.
or
INTELLIGENCE SUMMARY.
(Erase heading not required.)

Army Form C. 2118

Vol 7

Place	Date	Hour	Summary of Events and Information	Remarks and references to Appendices
AILLY-LE-HAUT-CLOCHER. (Sheet ABBEVILLE 1/100,000)	1.12.16	3 P.M.	Admitted OR's sick 36. Evacuated S. = .25 and .03 respectively per ration strength 133rd F.A. Everything satisfactory.	
"	2.12.16	2 P.M.	Admitted OR's 40 sick. Evacuated OR's 16 = .28 and .1 per ration strength respectively. A.M.C. Lowthian.	
"	3.12.16		Inspected men proposed for Permanent Base of the 18th Royal Welsh Fusiliers, 17th Welsh Regt and 20th Middlesex Regt. A/2.	
"		11.A.M.	Admitted Officers 2 - OR's 41. Evacuated 1 Officer and 14 OR's = .3 and .1 respectively per ration strength. Inspected men of 13th East Surrey Regt. proposed for transfer to Permanent Base. A./L	
"	4.12.16	11 A.M.	Admitted Officers 1, OR's 23 - Evacuated officers 2, OR's 14 = .15 and .1 per ration strength respectively. Inspected men 12th Suffolk Regt. proposed for permanent base. All.	
"	5.12.16	11 A.M.	Admitted Officers 1, OR's 33 - Evacuated Officers 1, OR's 21 = .2 and .15 per ration strength respectively. Inspected P.B.'s at Form'n Camp School at FIXECOURT.	
"		12 noon	Inspected 137 F.A. at L'ETOILE. Everything satisfactory. A/L	
"	6.12.16	H.A.M.	Admitted OR's 32. Evacuated OR's 20 = .2 and .15 per ration strength respectively.	
"		3. P.M.	Inspected men of 11th Kings Own 21st Lancs Regt proposed for Permanent Base	
"			Inspected billets and Sanitary arrangements of 13th York Regt. Everything very satisfactory. A/L	
"	7.12.16		Admitted OR's 18. Evacuated OR's 26; percentage per ration strength .1 and .1 respectively. A/L	
"		3. A.M.	Inspected men of the 14th H.L.I. proposed for Permanent Base. A/L	
"	8.12.16		Admitted Officers 2. OR's 27. Evacuated Officers 3. OR's 12 - percentage per ration strength .2 and .1 respectively. Inspected men of the 18th Welsh and 119 Machine Gun Company proposed for Permanent Base. A/L	
"	9.12.16	3.P.M.	Admitted Officers 1. OR's 22. Evacuated officers 5. OR's ? 8 - percentage per ration strength .2 and .1 respectively. A/L	
"	10.12.16		" 1. " 5-9 " 1 " 77 percentage per ration strength .1 and .6 " A/L	
"	11.12.16		Admitted OR's 19. Evacuated OR's 22, percentage per ration strength .14 and .07 respectively. A/L	
"	12.12.16		Admitted officers 2 - OR's 12. Evacuated officers 2. OR's 4, percentage per ration strength .1 and .04 respectively. A/L	
"	13.12.16		" " 2. " 25. " " " 2 " 16. " " " .2 " .1 " a/L	
"	14.12.16		" " 2. " 25. " " " 2 " 38 " " " .2 " .2 " a/L	
"	15.12.16		" " 1. " 28. " " " 1 " 3 " " " .2 " .03 " a/L	
CHIPILLY (AMIENS Sh.J. 1/100,000)	15.12.16	2 P.M.	Head Quarters 40th Division and 83rd Sanitary Section arrived at CHIPILLY. 135 F.A. at Camp 112 - Sheet ALBERT 1/40,000, L.2.A., Camp 19, 15.33.b, and 137 F.A. at SAILLY-LAORETTE, J.36.D.H. Admitted Officers 2, OR's 38. Evacuated officers 2, OR's 30, percentage per ration strength 3 and 28 respectively.	
"	16.12.16	11 A.M.	Visited 136 and 137 F.A., with the Président of the Sea of sand, and the field left by the troops who have just vacated the Camps. The huts and accommodation for patients and personnel are fairly good, and are capable of accommodating 40 patients each. The latrines are doing good work in clearing up, making incinerators, latrines, refuse dumps etc. A/L	

VOL. VII
Sec^t. WAR DIARY of A.D.M.S. 40th Division
or INTELLIGENCE SUMMARY

Army Form C. 2118

(Erase heading not required.)

Place	Date	Hour	Summary of Events and Information	Remarks and references to Appendices
CHIPILLY (AMIENS Sheet 1,000,000)	17.12.16	2.P.M.	Admitted Officers 2, OR's 27. Evacuated Officers 2, OR's 10 - Percentage for ration strength .22 and .08 respectively. Visited Camp 312 occupied by 119th Inf. Battn. and recommended sites for Sanitary arrangements etc.	A.12
"	18.12.16		Admitted officers 1, OR's 10. Evacuated OR's 1, percentage for ration strength .09 and .008 respectively.	A.12
"	19.12.16		" 3, " 30; " 20; Inf. Bde and inspected huts, sanitation etc, all satisfactory	a.12 a.12
"	20.12.16	2.P.M	Visited Camp 112 occupied by 120th Inf. Bde and inspected huts, sanitation etc, all satisfactory.	a.12
"	21.12.16		Admitted Officers 1, OR's 36. Evacuated Officers 1, OR's 12, percentages for ration strength 3 and 1 respectively.	a.12
"	22.12.16		" " 32 " " 22 " .25 " .17	a.12
"	23.12.16		" " 23 " " 16 " .18 " .13	a.12
"	24.12.16		" " 42 " " 21 " .34 " .17	a.12
"	25.12.16		" 3, " 34 " 2, " 21, " 3 " .25	a.12
"	26.12.16		" " 35 " 1, " 27 " .27 " .27	a.12
"	27.12.16		" 2, " 29 " " 22 " .38 " .27	a.12
"			" 3, " 28 " " 21 " .49 " .36	a.12
MAR. ALBERT 1,400,000 1.16 d 1.9	28.12.16	12 Noon	The Field Ambulances moved up to the Front Line, position as follows. Reference map ALBERT 1,400,000. 135, 136 and 137 Field Ambulances at Camp 17 SUZANNE. G.8.b. Admitted officers 5, other ranks 67. Evacuated Off. 5, OR's 18, percentages for ration strength .3 and .16 respectively. Divisional H.Q. Can. 13. Echelon arrived in Camp. Personnel accommodated in dug-outs.	G.8.b.
"	29.12.16	10.A.M.	Admitted officers 1, other ranks 58. Evacuated 1 officer and 9 OR's - percentage for ration strength 4 Comp.t .06 respectively. Visited the Advanced Dressing Station of 135th F.A. at LE CRANIER. B 16.c. 87. Also Bearer Posts at B15.a.64 - B16.a.4.8. - C13.a.8.o. - C8,c,6,6 and Relay Post at C8, c.1.4. G.T.L.	A.12
"	30.12.16	10.A.M	Admitted officers 2, other ranks 197-68 being Trench Foot. Evacuated Officers 2. OR's 74. percentage for ration Strength 9 and .35 respectively. Visited Advanced Dressing Station. 136 F.A. at LE PRIE FARM, 13. b.a. 4.1. - Reserve Bearer Post at MAUREPAS B.14.c and Advanced Bearer Post at C.7, b.9,8.	A.12 G.1.
"	31.12.16	11.A.M	Admitted officers 2, OR's 183 (Trench Foot 46). Evacuated 65. OR's - percentage for ration strength .88 and .31 respectively. Visited Head Quarters of 135, 136 and 137 Field Ambulances at Camp 17. SUZANNE, G.8.b.	

C.J. Buller
Col.
A.D.M.S. 40th Division.

40/942

A.D.M.S. 40th Division

COMMITTEE FOR THE
MEDICAL HISTORY OF THE WAR
Date 13 MAR. 1917

Vol. VIII.
Secret
WAR DIARY of A.D.M.S. 40th Division
or
INTELLIGENCE SUMMARY
Army Form C. 2118

Place	Date	Hour	Summary of Events and Information	Remarks and references to Appendices
MAP. ALBERT AMIENS Sheet (1/100,000) 1,16, & 1,9.	1.1.17	3.P.M.	Admitted 3 officers and 121 O.R. Evacuated 3 officers and 88 O.R. % per ration strength, 3.6 and .40 respectively.	
"	2.1.17		Visited Head Quarters of 135th F.A. and inspected billeting and Sanitary arrangements in Camp. A.D.M.S., A.A. & Q.M.G. of Division.	
"	3.1.17	3.P.M.	Admitted 4 officers and 142 O.R. Evacuated 4 officers and 105 O.R. % per ration strength, .66 and .49 respectively.	
"	4.1.17		129 3.9 O.R. Visited Head Quarters of 136 F.A. and inspected billeting and Sanitary arrangements in Camp.	
"	5.1.17		Admitted 2 officers and 134 O.R. Evacuated 2 officers and 77 O.R. % per ration strength .65 and .32 respectively.	
"	6.1.17	10.P.M.	Visited Advanced Dressing Stations of 135th F.A. at PINNEY'S POST, CRANIÈRE and ANDOVER, all satisfactory. Admitted officers 3, O.R.'s 87. Evacuated 2 officers and 24 O.R.s % per ration strength .44 and .13 respectively. Capts. Rooton and Richardson returned from 14 days Course at Bear.	
"	7.1.17		Admitted officers 5, O.R.s 89, evacuated officers 4, O.R.s 40. % per ration strength .45 and .2 respectively.	
"	8.1.17		" 0 " 72 " 0 " 35 " - " .14 "	
"	9.1.17		" 4 " 94 " 4 " 46 .6% per ration " 5 " .25 "	
"	10.1.17		" 2 " 44 " 1 " 14 % " .22 " .07 "	
"	11.1.17	2.30 A.M.	Inspected Camp 21, Detention hut, and hut being prepared for the prophylactic treatment of Trench feet. This is being run by 135th F.A. Enough 100 men will have what but meals with cooked food whole billed and Tents & Camps provided; at a Enum, it is hoped that this number will supply to be diminished. Admitted officers 2, O.R.s 73. Evacuated 2 officers and 31 O.R.s percentage per ration strength, .36 and .16 respectively.	
"	12.1.17		" 4 " 78 " " " " " .48 " .1 "	
"	13.1.17		" 5 " 86 " 3 " 30 " .30 " .12 "	
"	14.1.17	2.30 P.M.	A.M.S. Trench Army visited Camp 21 and inspected the arrangements for Trench Foot prevention. Admitted officers nil. O.R.s 62. Evacuated 31 O.R.s percentage per ration strength .20 and .10 respectively.	
"	15.1.17		" " " 74 " 40 " " " " " .25 " .14 "	
"	16.1.17	11.A.M.	Visited Advanced Dressing Stations at LE FOREST and PRIES FARM. Everything Satisfactory. Admitted officers 4, O.R.s 157 (82 trench feet), Evacuated 79 O.R.s percentage per ration strength .51 and .26 respectively. Lt. Col. Rowan Robinson, D.G. 136 F.A. Sent to Corps Main Dressing Station suffering from P.U.O. Capt. Griffiths Senior Officer of the Unit ordered to assume Charge.	
"	17.1.17		Admitted 3 officers 3, O.R.s 77, Evacuated O.R.s 65, percentage per ration strength .35 and .29 respectively.	
"	18.1.17	2.P.M. 4.P.M.	" officers 1, O.R.s 69, " officers 1, O.R.s 22, " .24 " Visited Advanced Head Quarters and conferred with G.O.C. re Trench feet. Visited Head Quarters 135th F.A. at Camp 17.	
"	19.1.17		Admitted officers 1, O.R.s 77. Evacuated O.R.s percentage per ration strength .37 and .16 respectively. Issued Divisional Order No. 15.	

Secret Vol. VIII.

WAR DIARY of A.D.M.S. 40th Division

INTELLIGENCE SUMMARY

Army Form C. 2118

(Erase heading not required.)

Place	Date	Hour	Summary of Events and Information	Remarks and references to Appendices
MAP ALBERT. (AMIENS Sheet 1,100,000) L.16, d.1.9.	20.1.17	3. P.M	Admitted 2 Officers and 69 O.Rs. Evacuated 1 Officer and 2.0 O.Rs. Percentage per ration strength = 2.0 and .95. Inspected the Sanitation of Camp 17, 20 and 21; manual good work has been done by 83rd Sanitary Section.	
"	21.1.17		Admitted 2 Officers and 66 O.Rs. Evacuated 2 Officers and 45 O.Rs. Percentage per ration strength. 35 and .2 J.	
"	22.1.17	3.P.M.	Visited Head Quarters of 135–136 and 137 F.A. at Camp 17.	
"	22.1.17		Admitted 2 Officers and 105 O.Rs. Evacuated 3 Officers and 66 O.Rs. Percentage per ration strength .57 and .36.	
"	23.1.17		Admitted 5 Officers and 75 O.Rs. Evacuated 4 Officers and 35 O.Rs. Percentage per ration strength .33 and .16.	
"	24.1.17		Admitted 1 Officer and 50 O.Rs. Evacuated 47 O.Rs. Percentage per ration strength .22 and .20.	
"			66 O.Rs. " .31 and .11	
"	25.1.17		24 "	
"	26.1.17		137 F.A. moved from Camp 17 to Camp 12. K.33.L.	
"	26.1.17		Admitted 3 Officers and 45 O.Rs. Evacuated 1 Officer and 10 O.Rs. Percentage per ration strength .25 and .05	
"	27.1.17		" 37 O.Rs. " 2 " 17 O.Rs. " .34 " .17	
CORBIE	28.1.17		135 and 136 F.A. proceeded from Camp 17 to CORBIE and SAILLY LORETTE respectively. Divisional Head Quarters moved today from L.16, d.1.9 to CORBIE. 83rd Sanitary Section to SAILLY LORETTE	
"	29.1.17		Admitted 13 O.Rs. Evacuated 3 O.Rs. Percentage per ration strength .11 and .01 respectively.	
"	30.1.17		Admitted 3 Officers and 34 O.Rs. Evacuated 1 Officer and 26 O.Rs. Percentage per ration strength .31 and .24.	
"	30.1.17	11 am	2 " 43 O.Rs. " 1 " 22 O.Rs. " .47 " .24	
"			Visited Head Quarters 135 F.A. Stationed in CORBIE. Everything satisfactory.	
"	31.1.17		Admitted 3 Officers and 50 O.Rs. Evacuated 2 Officers and 37 O.Rs. respectively. Strength .52 and .37 percentage per ration	

C. J. Butler
Col.
A.D.M.S. 40th Division.

A.D.M.S., 40th Division

COMMITTEE FOR THE
MEDICAL HISTORY OF THE WAR
Date 4.- APR.1917

Secret   VOL. IX
WAR DIARY of A.D.M.S. 40TH Division.
Army Form C. 2118

INTELLIGENCE SUMMARY
(Erase heading not required.)

July

Place	Date	Hour	Summary of Events and Information	Remarks and references to Appendices
CORBIE. AMIENS SHEET 1/100,000.	1.2.17	12 NN	Admitted officers 4, O.R. 44. Evacuated officers 1, O.R. 34. Percentage per ration strength .45 and .38 respectively. Inspected 135 F.A. at CORBIE — everything satisfactory. Q.1. Dutton Col. A.P.M.S. 40 Division.	
	2.2.17	3 P.M.	Visited SAILLY LORETTE and inspected 136 F.A. 83rd Sanitary Section and baths. The baths started today and are of the French Spray Pattern, capable of bathing 1000 men per day, clean clothing is supplied and the outer clothing ironed.	
	3.2.17		Admitted 3 officers, 48 O.R: Evacuated 2 officers and 9 O.R: percentages per ration strength .47 and .1 respectively.	
	4.2.17		" 4 " 45 O.R " " " 0 " .45 and .09 "	
	5.2.17		" 1 " 37 O.R " " " 0 " 8 " .36 and .08 "	
			" 3 " 28 O.R " " " 2 " 6 " .34 and .08 "	
	6.2.17		I am proceeding on 10 days leave tomorrow and am handing over duties of A.D.M.S. to Major Ripley Range D.A.D.M.S. G. J. Dutton Col. A.D.M.S. 40 Division. Visited 136 FA, 157 FA and 83 San. Sec. admitted 1 officer 52 O.R.; evacuated 0 officers 15 O.R. percentage per ration strength .48 and .14. Ripley, May, for A.D.M.S.	
	7.2.17		A.D.M.Ss of 4th & 8th Division called with reference to handing over the RANCOURT SECTOR.	
	8.2.17		Issued operation orders with reference to taking over RANCOURT SECTOR. admitted 4. O. 67 O.R.; evacuated 4. O. 31 O.R. percentage 12. Lt COL R. ROBINSON returned to duty from Hospital. admitted 6. O. 67 O.R. ; evacuated 4. O. 31 O.R. percentage .2.	
	9.2.17		" " O. 64 O.R. " - O. 39 O.R. " .21	
	10.2.17		" 6. O. 90 O.R. " 4. O. 86 O.R. " .49	
			135 FA marched from CORBIE to Camp 112 137 FA marched from Camp 12 to BRAY.	
	11.2.17		Took over the RANCOURT SECTOR from 8th Division; 137 F.A. clearing the line. 136 F.A. marched from SAILLY LAURETTE to Camp 21. Took over French foot bait and commenced treatment of 119th Bde. Lt Col. DUNKERTON returned from leave. admitted 4. O. 76 O.R.; evacuated 3 O. 52 O.Rs percentage .5	
	12.2.17		" " " - " 2 " " .01	
L.16 21 9.	13.2.17		Provost officer from CORBIE to L.16.d.1.9. Visited 135 FA at camp 112 reference to starting trench foot prevention. admitted 1 officer 45 O.R. evacuated 21 O.R. percentage .11. Visited 136 FA, MAUREPAS RAVINE Baths, 12th S.W.B., PINNEYS POST LA FOREST. 119th Bde.H.Q. and Advanced H.Q. and 137 FA.	

1875 Wt. W593/826 1,000,000 4/15 J.B.C.&A. A.D.S.S./Forms/C.2118.

SECRET

WAR DIARY of A.D.M.S. 40th Division
Vol IX
Army Form C. 2118

or

INTELLIGENCE SUMMARY

(Erase heading not required.)

Place	Date	Hour	Summary of Events and Information	Remarks and references to Appendices
L.16.d.1.9. AMIENS SHEET 1,40,000	14.2.17		Interviewed O.C. 3A San Sec. as to the work in hand in divisional area	
	15.2.17		Visited DDMS XV Corps. Admitted O's 3 O.R. 61, evacuated O's 3, O.R. 24 percentage ·15	
	16.2.17		Admitted O's 3 O.R. 52 evacuated O's 2 O.R. 15 percentage ·09. Visited PRIEZ FARM, B.R.s and R.A.P.s of RANCOURT SECTOR. Admitted O.I. O.R. 72, evacuated O.I. O.R. 45 percentage ·25'.	
	17.2.17		Admitted O.I. O.R. 35 evacuated O.I. O.R. 22. percentage ·12.	
	18.12.17		Visited A.D.M.S. 8th Division. Handed over duties of A.D.M.S. to Col. A.J. LUTHER. A.M.S. Ryley Maj Reserve	
	19.2.17		Returned from leave at 6.30 P.M. last night. Admitted officers 2, O.R.s 154. Evacuated O's 2, O.R.s 17. % 32 and ·11	
	20.2.17	10 AM	Visited advanced HQ Quarters to confer with A.A. + Q.M.G. A.Q. Luther Col Amb. Admitted O's 4 - O.R.s 79. Evacuated 37 O.R.s %·49 and ·22 respectively.	
	21.2.17	10. AM.	Visited Camp 21 and inspected 126 F.A. Trench Foot Prevention Hut and Detention Hut - all satisfactory.	
	22.2.17		Kept by D.A.D.M.S. Ryley. Proceeded on ten days leave. Admitted Officers 3, O.R.s 69. Evacuated officers 3, O.R.s 21. % 43 and ·13 respectively.	
	23.2.17	2.30 AM	Visited Camp 112 and inspected sanitary arrangements, also 135 F.A. Sick Detention Hut and Trench Foot Prevention Hut. Admitted 1 officer and 82 O.R.s. Evacuated 1 officer and 48 O.R.s % ·49 and ·29 respectively	
	24.2.17		With A.A.+Q.M.G. visited officers Rest House. Clothing Store and Laundry in BRAY. 3 " 57 " 30 " · 18 "	
	25.2.17	2.PM	Admitted 2 officers and 59 other ranks. Evacuated 39 O.R.s % ·36 and ·23. Attended Conference at Divisional Wired Quarters.	
			135 Field Ambulance left Camp 112 & took over Corps Rest Station at SAILLY LORETTE. Camp 125. J.36.A. Bearing a party at Camp 112 to look after British Sick and Venereal Foot treatment Hut. Admitted 40 other ranks, evacuated 1 officer and 22 O.R.s % ·26 and ·14.	
	26.2.17		Admitted 3 officers and 40 O.R. Evacuated 2 officers and 25 O.R.s % ·26 and 1·16.	
	27.2.17	2.30 PM	Inspected 65 men of 11th pioneers 12" Infy inspected as P.B.; result 19 fit, 41 recommended as P.B.; 3 L-a-m a.p.U (17). two sent to hospital.	
	28.2.17	3.P.M.	Visited A.F.M.S. 33. Division. Medical arrangements showed me take over Hut area. Admitted 1 officer and 48 O.R.s, evacuated 1 officer and 22 O.R.s % ·27 and ·13	

A.J. Luther Col.
A.D.M.S. 40th Division.

CONFIDENTIAL.

MEDICAL SERVICES.

WAR DIARIES.

OF

A.D.M.S. 40TH. DIVISION.

135TH. FIELD AMBULANCE.

136TH. FIELD AMBULANCE.

137TH. FIELD AMBULANCE.

83RD. SANITARY SECTION.

FOR MONTH OF

MARCH.

1917.

VOLUMES

X.

A.F. Luther
Lt. Col.
A.D.M.S. 40th Division

Secret VOL. X

WAR DIARY of A.D.M.S. 40th Division.

INTELLIGENCE SUMMARY
(Erase heading not required.)

Army Form C. 2118

Place	Date	Hour	Summary of Events and Information	Remarks and references to Appendices
L16.L.1.9. AMIENS, Sdst 1.40.60.0	1.3.17		Admitted Officers 4, other ranks 53. Evacuated 3 Officers and 22 other ranks. O/o .3 and .16 Forwarded Weekly Progress of Medical Units to A.D.M.S. 40th Division.	G.Q. Latter A.D.M.S. 40th Division
	2.3.17	3.P.M.	Visited 136 F.A. at Camp 21.	
		10.A.M.	Attended Conference at A.D.M.S. XVth Corps.	
	3.3.17		Admitted Officers 1, O.R. 36. Evacuated 1 Officer and 20 O.R. O/o .22 and .12	
		3.P.M.	Issued Operation Order No. 18.	
			Visited Camp 21.	
	4.3.17		Admitted 1 officer and 41 O.R. Evacuated 1 officer and 21 O.R. O/o .25 and .12	
	5.3.17		" 49 " " " " " " " " .3 " .9 "	
			Major Ryley R.A.M.C. A.D.M.S. returned from leave.	
			Admitted 1 Officer and 45 O.R. Evacuated 1 Officer and 24 O.R. O/o .27 and .27	
	6.3.17		" 14 O.R. " 10 O.R. O/o .09 " .06	
			Visited detachment 135 F.A. running Ablution Hut and Foot-treatment Hut at Camp 112. Forwarded Recommendations for Honours & Rewards for Kings Birthday Gazette.	
	7.3.17		Interviewed A.D.M.S. 33rd Division re taking over this Divisional Area.	
			Admitted 1 Officer and 61 O.R. Evacuated 33 O.R. O/o .3 and .16	
SUZANNE G.8.d.	8.3.17		" 1 " " 39 " " 10 O.R. O/o .18 and .09	
	9.3.17		The 40th Division today took over the Divisional Area from the 33rd Division. Position of Medical Units:- A.D.M.S.- SUZANNE G.8.d. 135th F.A. running XVth Corps Rest Station at SAILLY LORETTE. 136.F.A. SUZANNE. 137. F.A. HEM H.8.a.2.7. Open and Clearing the Front line held by 2 Brigades. 83rd Sanitary Section – SUZANNE.	
			Admitted 1 officer and 24 O.R. Evacuated 1 officer and 14 O.R. O/o .19 and .09.	
			" " 53 O.R. " 28 O.R. O/o .37 " .19	
	10.3.17	10 A.M.	Visited HOWITZE wood camp. Advanced Dressing Station HEM (137 F.A.) and LINGER Camps.	
	11.3.17		Admitted 2 officers and 58 O.R. Evacuated 3 officers and 25 O.R. O/o .36 and .17	
	12.3.17		Visited 136 F.A. SUZANNE. Have in accommodation for some 100 patients in the various tented.	
	13.3.17		Admitted 61 O.R. Evacuated 28 O.R. O/o .36 and .17.	
			Inspected LINGER CAMP and Camp 1 and 19.	
	14.3.17		Admitted 1 officer and 70 O.R. Evacuated 3 officers and 34 O.R. O/o .42 and .21	
			" 5 " " " " " 34 O.R. O/o .33 and .22	
	15.3.17		Inspected the 13 Baths and foot bath at SUZANNE and CURLU	
	16.3.17		Admitted Officers 3, other ranks 38. Evacuated 1 Officers and 17 other ranks. O/o .2 and .1	
	17.3.17		" 2 " " 72 " " " " 38 " " .41 and .25	
			" " 37 " " " 24 " " O/o .19 and .13	
			Inspected 136 F.A. and Arrangements for bathes and General Foot Preventative treatment Baths at SUZANNE and CURLU	

Secret WAR DIARY Vol X of A.D.M.S. 40th Division
INTELLIGENCE SUMMARY

Army Form C. 2118

(Erase heading not required.)

Instructions regarding War Diaries and Intelligence Summaries are contained in F.S. Regs., Part II. and the Staff Manual respectively. Title Pages will be prepared in manuscript.

Place	Date	Hour	Summary of Events and Information	Remarks and references to Appendices
SUZANNE Q.8.d.	18.3.17	10 A.M	Visited 137 F.A. Dressing Station at HEM and Advanced Dressing Station at CLERY. Also Divisional Rest Camp and Quarters at P.C. CHAPEAU.	
AMIENS Shed 1,40,0.0.0.	19.3.17		Admitted 3 officers and 65 men, Evacuated 1 officer and 51 men. O/o - 4 and - 31. O.R. later at Adv. 40 Division. O/o - 4 and - 36. " - 34	
	20.3.17		Reconnoitred HAUT ALLAINES and MOUNT ST QUENTIN with a view of establishing an Advanced Dressing Station. Admitted 2 officers and 69 O.R. Evacuated 1 officer and 44 O.R. O/o - 42 and - 27. 137 F.A. moved forward from HEM to CLERY. establishing an Advanced Dressing Station at HAUT ALLAINES.	
	21.3.17		136 F.A. moved forward from SUZANNE to HEM. Admitted 1 officer and 41 O.R. Evacuated 19 other ranks - O/o - 25 and - 11	
	22.3.17		" " 18 " - " " O/o - 22 and - 11	
	23.3.17		Visited 137 F.A. at CLERY and Advanced Dressing Station at ALLAINES. Admitted 1 H1 O.R. Evacuated 17 O.R. O/o - 25 and - 1 Visited 136 F.A. at HEM	
	24.3.17		Admitted 1 officer and 30 O.R. Evacuated 1 S - O.R. O/o - 18 and - 03 Advand	
	25.3.17		40 Division to go into Corps Reserve today. 137 F.A. having an Dressing Station at ALLAINES & 6 Division moving back to Camp 163. B/14.C.(Central) and Evacuating sick from 119th Brigade Area, 136 F.A. forming an Advanced Dressing Station at CLERY and Evacuating sick from 120 + 121 Brigade Area. Admitted 1 officer and 3 2 O.R. Evacuated 8 O.R. O/o - 2 and - 05 " 2 8 " " 6 " O/o - 17 and - 06 " " " " O/o - 08 - 04	
CRANIERE. B16.d.38	26.3.17		2 officers " " to CRANIERE (B/16, d.3.8)	
	27.3.17		A. Echelon moved today to P.C. JEAN (H.1.C.1.9)	
	28.3.17		Admitted 3 Officers and 25. O.R. Evacuated 2 officers and 9 O.R. O/o - 17 and - 07 Visited 136 F.A. Main Dressing Station at HEM, and Advanced Dressing Station at CLERY.	
	29.3.17		Admitted 25 other ranks, Evacuated 19 O.R. percentage - 15 - and - 1 Visited 137 F.A. at Camp 163	
	30.3.17		Admitted 1 Officer and 23 O.R. Evacuated 17 O.R. O/o - 15 and - 1 Visited Advanced Dressing Station 137 F.A. at PRIEZ FARM.	
	31.3.17		Admitted 5 officers and 25 O.R. Evacuated 4 officers and 23 O.R. O/o - 18 and - 18. Made a Sanitary Inspection of CRANIERE and LE FOREST	

A.J. Luther
Col
A.A.M.S. 40th Division.

140/2025

A.D.M.S., 40th Division.

COMMITTEE FOR THE
MEDICAL HISTORY OF THE WAR
Date — 6 JUN.1917

Secret Vol XI

WAR DIARY of A.D.M.S. 40th Division

Army Form C. 2118

INTELLIGENCE SUMMARY
(Erase heading not required.)

Instructions regarding War Diaries and Intelligence Summaries are contained in F. S. Regs., Part II and the Staff Manual respectively. Title Pages will be prepared in manuscript.

Place	Date	Hour	Summary of Events and Information	Remarks and references to Appendices
GRANIERE B16.d.3.8.	1.4.17		Admitted 2 Officers and 36 Other Ranks Evacuated 2 Officers and 32 ORs. O/o 23 and .21 Forwarded War Diaries of Unit units to A.D.M.S 40th Division	
"	2.4.17	2.P.M.	Admitted 2 Officers and 35 ORs. Evacuated 2 officers and 28 ORs. Percentage .22 and .18 Visited 137 F.A. at MAUREPAS	
"	3.4.17		Admitted 2 officers and 38 ORs. Evacuated 2 officers and 10 ORs. O/o .24 and .07 Visited Advanced Dressing Stations at PRIEZ FARM and LE FOREST.	
"	4.4.17		Admitted 2 officers and 37 ORs. Evacuated 1 officer and 14 ORs. O/o .24 and .09 Issued Operation Order no. 23	
"	5.4.17		Admitted 1 officer and 45 ORs. Evacuated 10 ORs. O/o .28 and .07	
"	6.4.17		" 27 " " 2 Officers/10 ORs. O/o .2 and .06.	
"	7.2.17		136 F.A. moved from HEM to MOISLAINS. 83rd Sanitary Section to same place Admitted 1 officer and 53 ORs. Evacuated 2 officers and 14 ORs. O/o .33 and .12 136 F.A. moved from MOISLAINS to MANANCOURT. MAP FRANCE 1/40,000 sheet 57.D — V19.a.9.3, 83rd San. sect to Sand place. 137 F.A. moved from MAUREPAS to MOISLAINS. C/2,C.,7.7.	
"	8.4.17	12 noon	136 F.A. established an Advanced Dressing Station at PINS. Visited 136, 137 and 83rd San. Sect. sect 7.A. 2no accommodation for S.O Lying down cases.	
"	9.4.17		Admitted 2 officers and 43 ORs. Evacuated 1 officer and 19 ORs. O/o .28 and .12. 17 ORs. O/o .24 .11	
"	10.4.17		Received telephone message from D.D.M.S. XVth corps to take over his duties temporarily, Lt. Col. Rowan Robinson. OC. 136 FA relieving me. G.O.L Luther. Col. A.D.M.S 40th Division	
"			Assumed duties of acting A.D.M.S. 10th Division H Blencowe Lt Col	
"	11.4.17		Admitted officers Ord: OR 10 Evacuated officers Ord: OR 43 Evacuated Officers Nil OR 12 % .11 and .07 "Admitted Officers Ord: OR 21D Evacuated Officer Ord: OR 10 % .12 and .06 gbm	
"	12.4.17		Visited Sanitary arrangements of 19-17" Welsh Regiment Admitted Officers 2 OR 32 Evacuated Officers 1 OR 12 % .21 and .08 H/os	
"	13.4.17		Office of A.D.M.S moved to MANANCOURT hut. Ord. 57e V.13.C.44 Admitted adequate baths front of 136 Y Amb. Bath is situated in a barn at Q 32 d.33. The Infirmary and home of the Bn. in the line at W.2.d.33.	
MANANCOURT V.13.C.44			20th Battalion is in a hut on the METZ-COUZEAUCOURT ROAD at Q.28.C.53 Admitted officers nil OR 50 Evacuated officers out OR 9 % .31 and .05 YPR	

Army Form C. 2118

Sent Vol XI

WAR DIARY of A.D.M.S. 40th Division
or
INTELLIGENCE SUMMARY
(Erase heading not required.)

Instructions regarding War Diaries and Intelligence Summaries are contained in F.S. Regs., Part II. and the Staff Manual respectively. Title Pages will be prepared in manuscript.

Place	Date 1917	Hour	Summary of Events and Information	Remarks and references to Appendices
MANANCOURT V13c44	14.4.17		Admitted Officers and O.R. 74. Evacuated Officers and O.R. 14. % 4.5 and .09 YRR	
"	15.4.17		Admitted Officers 3. O.R. 55. Evacuated Officers 2. O.R. 11 % 35 and .08. Visited the R.A.P's in the line the brown hut and the A.D.S. and arranged with the O.C. 136 F Amb the methods of evacuating sick - wounded YRR	
"	16.4.17		Admitted Officers 6. O.R. 94. Evacuated Officers 6. O.R. 12. % .6 and .11 YRR	
"	17.4.17		Admitted Officers 2. O.R. 47. Evacuated Officers 2. O.R. 27. % .29 and .17 YRRR	
"	18.4.17		Admitted Officers OR. Evacuated Officers OR. Arrangements for the evacuation of sick - wounded from Beauz Goc 119th Brigade and made arrangements for the evacuation of sick - wounded from his front line held by 119th Brigade	
"	19.4.17		Admitted Officers 1. O.R. 23. Evacuated Officers 2. O.R. 16. Percentage .24 and .11 Handed over duties of A.D.M.S. to Colonel A J Seton A.D.S. and assumed command of 136 F. Amb.	F Howard Otfinyton Lt Col R.A.M.C.
"	20.4.17	2 P.M.	Resumed duties as A.D.M.S. 40th Division A J Luther, Col. A.M.S. Admitted 1 Officer and 42 OR's. Evacuated 14 OR's. percentage .26 and .08. Visited 136 F.A. at MANANCOURT.	
"	21.4.17	2 P.M.	Admitted 5 Officers and 82 OR's. Evacuated 4 Officers and 20 OR's percentage .51 and .14. Visited 137 F.A. at MOISLAINS.	
"	22.4.17	3 P.M.	Admitted 5 OR's. Evacuated 1 Officer and 12 OR's ⁰⁄₀ .03 and .08 MANANCOURT. Inspected billets and sanitary arrangements in and about MANANCOURT.	
"	23.4.17		Admitted 2 Officers and 22 OR's. Evacuated 1 Officer and 8 OR's. ⁰⁄₀ .13 and .05. Issued Ronne Order no. 24. 136 FA to move to FINS. 137 FA to MANANCOURT. moves to be completed by 6 P.M. 83 Sanitary Section under Army instructions to move forward to VILLERS BRETTONEUX for duty under 4th Army.	
"	24.4.17	11 A.M.	40 Division arrived at VILLERS PLOUICH and BEAUCAMP at 4 A.M. this morning and joined their objectives	
"		10 A.M.	Visited A.D.S. opened at evening Wilson FINS bill 6 P.M. Arrangements for collection, treatment and putting wounded worked most satisfactorily. Sick Admission 2 Officers and 20 OR. Evacuation 9 OR's - ⁰⁄₀ .33 and .05.	

VOL. XI

Secret WAR DIARY of A.D.M.S. 40th Division.
or
INTELLIGENCE SUMMARY
(Erase heading not required.)

Army Form C. 2118

Instructions regarding War Diaries and Intelligence Summaries are contained in F. S. Regs., Part II. and the Staff Manual respectively. Title Pages will be prepared in manuscript.

Place	Date	Hour	Summary of Events and Information	Remarks and references to Appendices
MANANCOURT V.13.c.4.4.	25.4.17	5 AM	Sick admissions 2 officers and 20 OR. Evacuations 7 OR's - O/o .13 and .04 wounded admitted since 5 AM yesterday, 2 officers lying, 6 sitting, other ranks 113 lying 300 sitting. He myself being bullet & shrapnel wounds, a very small percentage of penetrating wounds of abdomen. Chest or head.	
"	26.4.17		Sick admitted 3 officers, 37 OR's. Evacuated 10 OR's - O/o .23 and .06 wounded admitted since 5 AM yesterday 3 officers lying 1 sitting, other ranks 41 lying 24 sitting.	
"	27.4.17	11 AM	Sick admitted 2 officers and 34 OR's. Evacuated 2 officers and 20 OR's - O/o .23 and .14. Visited 136 Field Ambulance	
		3 PM	Inspected Water Points in Divisional Area	
"	28.4.17		Sick admitted 2 officers, 38 OR's. Evacuated 1 officer + 14 OR - O/o 23 and .09	
		2. PM	Inspected 137 F.A and Divisional Baths at MANANCOURT.	
"	29.4.17		Sick admitted 1 officer and 34 OR's. Evacuated 10 OR's - O/o .22 and .06. Inspected billets and sanitary arrangements at ETRICOURT and EQUANCOURT	
"	30.4.17		Sick admitted 32 other ranks, Evacuated 16 other ranks. O/o .2 and .1.	
		3 P.M.	Inspected 136 F.A at FINS, water supply and billets at same place – all satisfactory	

C. J. Luther Col.
ADMS 40th Division.

May 1917

Detached Appendix E (Medical Arrangements 140/2453) and placed with first copy of summary

O.D.m.S., 40th Division

COMMITTEE FOR THE
MEDICAL HISTORY OF THE WAR
Date 10 JUL. 1917

Vol. XII.

WAR DIARY of A.D.M.S. 40th Division
Army Form C. 2118

INTELLIGENCE SUMMARY
(Erase heading not required.)

Vol 12

Place	Date	Hour	Summary of Events and Information	Remarks and references to Appendices
MANANCOURT V.13.C.4.4. MAP FRANCE Sheet 57c	2.5.17		The Division occupies a front Q.11.6.27 & G.12.C.7.8. - R.7.d.0.9 - R.14.b.7.0 - R.14.d.2.2. - R.21.a.7.1 - R.21.C.8.2. Having the 8th Division on our right, 20th Division on our left. Things are fairly quiet since taking BEAUCAMP and VILLERS PLOUICH with the exception of the normal intermittent shelling. GOUZEAUCOURT receiving particular attention. The 40th Division still keeps up the reputation of having the lowest casualties for casualties in the British Army.	R.A.M.C. Instruction order N°25 dated 4.5.17 attached
	4.5.17		"G" operation order received ordering an interior raid on LA VACQUERIE to inflict loss on enemy, & his moral and to secure prisoners. "ZERO" hour 11P.M. on 5th May. Issued R.A.M.C. Operation order N°25. 136.F.A. opens 3 horse ambulances and 4 medical officers from 137.F.A art. during the Bourmoil front. 136.F.A. Main Dressing Station at FINS. advanced Dressing Station in the Sunken road at Q.22.d.central and at METZ-EN-COUTURE. Bearer posts at Q.30.6.63 - R.14.d.5.8 - R.20.a.88 - R.19.c.9.3 - R.25.d.4.4. R.19.a.8.3 - Line of evacuation - From Regimental Aid Posts to A.D.S. Stretcher and hand carriage - Stretcher cases to be evacuated to FINS by horse and motor ambulances wagons - Walking wounded and sitting to Division & Main Dressing Station, FINS. Advanced Dressing Station are equipped with Gas Stoves for the apply gassed and not capable. Major C. RYLEY R.A.M.C. A.D.M.S. was temporarily moved from Medical Transit to 137.F.A. MANANCOURT. Ryley and helpers for ambulances - Unity was arrested at the Chateau Grounds at MANANCOURT. 4 N.CO.s	
	5.5.17	5:30pm	Major RYLEY'S funeral took place at the Church in MANANCOURT. R.A.M.C. A.S.C. etc. will attended by Divisional Hd.Qrs Staff.	
	7.5.17	6pm	Captain F.G. THATCHER R.A.M.C. assumed duties of acting D.A.D.M.S. Operation on 5th May was successfully carried out - Brigade entering LA VACQUERIE and remaining there about two hours. Medical arrangements worked invariably all wounded being evacuated in four hours. Total Casualties were - 2 Officers, 30 O.R. killed. 7 officers 161 O.R. wounded and 49 O.R. missing, plus. W.I.a. Central and W.2.C Central Main Creativature points at FINS.	
	9.5.17		Visited Field Ambulance and inspected new water points, and the others two are to open tomorrow. The gas at FINS is working.	

Vol. XII.

Secret

WAR DIARY of A.D.M.S. 40th Division

INTELLIGENCE SUMMARY

(Erase heading not required.)

Army Form C. 2118

Instructions regarding War Diaries and Intelligence Summaries are contained in F.S. Regs., Part II. and the Staff Manual respectively. Title Pages will be prepared in manuscript.

Place	Date	Hour	Summary of Events and Information	Remarks and references to Appendices
	10.5.17		Received warning order No. G.S. 2/47 dated 10.5.17., regarding relief of 8th Division and readjustment of Corps front. The relief of the Left Brigade 40th Division by one Brigade 20th Division, and relief of 8th Division by two Brigades 40th Division to commence on night 12/13 May, & to be completed by 14 May.	
	11.5.17		Received 40th Division Operation order No. 79, dated 11.5.17. The left Divisional boundary will be:– R.21.c.3.7 – R.14.d.6.1. – R.19.b.4.0. – Q.32.d.6.0. – W.2.a.4.2. – W.1.a.9.1. – V.6.a.1.0. – along Road through V.6. Central – P.35 Central to the present boundary P.35.a.7.3. The right boundary will be the Right Corps Boundary. Issued 40th Division R.A.M.C. Operation order No. 26. dated 11.5.17. 136 Field Ambulance will remain at FINS, and be responsible for the evacuation of sick and wounded from the left and Centre Brigades, taking over from 24th Field Ambulance, 8th Division, the A.D.S. at X.1.a.5.9. and Many Posts clearing to that point, by 6 p.m. 13th May. 137 Field Ambulance (less Bearer personnel to run a detachment Hospital at MANANCOURT, will take over from MANANCOURT to HEUDECOURT on 14th May, and the Baths at ÉTRICOURT) will take over from 24th Field Ambulance, 8th Division, and take over Bearing Stations and Bearer Posts from Right Brigade. ½ Responsible for Evacuation of sick and wounded from Right Brigade. Divisional Headquarters will remain at MANANCOURT. Para: 10. of Operation order was Cancelled, and Divisional Headquarters will remain at MANANCOURT.	R.A.M.C. Operation order No. 26. dated 11.5.17. attached
	12.5.17		An inspection was carried out today by A/D.A.D.M.S. and party of the Old vacated trenches East of a line from COMBLES & LE CRANIÈRE, found to be a vertical line just west of MANANCOURT. Falk & Vaux to finding and localizing any dead bodies which might be still thereabouts. None were found west of RANCOURT. Several French parties were not completing the burial of a large Numbers of bodies which had been found between RANCOURT and Sheeton edge of ST. PIERRE VAAST WOOD. In this Wood fourteen bodies were found, and in VAUX WOOD two were found. They were all German. Report sent A.D.M.S. XV Corps. 6 D.D.M.S.	

VOL. XII.

Secret

WAR DIARY of A.D.M.S. 40th Division

or INTELLIGENCE SUMMARY

(Erase heading not required.)

Army Form C. 2118

Place	Date	Hour	Summary of Events and Information	Remarks and references to Appendices
	13.5.17		For week ending May 12th. Sick wastage was only '24%. This is the lowest in the Fourth Army.	
	14.5.17		Today an Officer and Tent Subdivision 9/136 Field Ambulance left our Officers Corps Rest Station, BOIS DE L'ABBEYE, ABBEVILLE for an ffer and tent subdivision 25th Field Ambulance, 8th Division.	
	15.5.17		Captain F.G. THATCHER R.A.M.C. assumed appointment of D.A.D.M.S. (authority G.H.Q. ⁴⁹/⁴⁶. 483 15/5/15) visited 136 and 137 Field Ambulances.	Headquarters 40th Division dated 17.5.17 attached
	17.5.17		Issued Medical Arrangements 40th Division, giving position & Regimental Aid Posts, Bearer Posts, advanced dressing Stations and the method of evacuation from each. Received 8th Division R.A.M.C. Formation order No.194 dated 17.5.17. Regarding the settlement of the Division from XV corps and the handing over of the Corps Main Dressing Station by 26th Field Ambulance, 8th Division to 105th Field Ambulance, 35th Division. Also 20th Division R.A.M.C. formation order No.95, dated 17/5/17 regarding the withdrawal of two R.A.M.C. Officers and its transfer to I ANZAC Corps. It is being relieved by the 42nd Division. Division from this Corps, and consequently the reorganization of the XV corps which and consequently be on the left of the 40th Division when the reorganization of the XV corps takes place. Also received 35th Division R.A.M.C. formation order No. 10, dated 17.5.17. Regarding the entrance of the Division into XV corps. This Division will be on the right of the 40th Division. The 35th Division will take over that portion	
	18.5.17		Received 40th Division formation order No. 80, dated 18.5.17. The 35th Division will take over that portion of the line now held by the 120th and 121st Brigades, 40th Division. The 119th Brigade will remain in its present position. The provisional boundaries of the Divisional Area, which will come into force at 10 A.M. May 26th will be as follows:- Northern Boundary:- LE PAVE - GOUZEAUCOURT Road inclusive to 40th Division to Q.36.5.7.7. Q.36.6.0.0.- Q.35.d.5.0.- W.14.C.0.5.- W.25.C.0.5.- D.3.c.0.0.- D.10.C.2.7.- D.8.d.0.4.- C.18.d.9.9.- C.24.a.6.6.- C.23.a.8.8.- C.17.a.3.9.- C.18.a.0.3.- C.20.6.0.8.	

1875 Wt. W593/826 1,000,000 4/15 J.B.C. & A. A.D.S.S./Forms/C.2118.

Vol. XII.

Army Form C. 2118.

Secret WAR DIARY of A.D.M.S. 40th Division.
or
INTELLIGENCE SUMMARY.
(Erase heading not required.)

Place	Date	Hour	Summary of Events and Information	Remarks and references to Appendices
			Northern Boundary :-	
			L.32.d.4.5. – Q.12.d.0.9 – Q.11.d.8.6. – Q.11.d.10.4 – Q.12.b.9.5 – Q.23.a.1.9. – R.25.c.6.3.	
			P.35.b.0.0. – V.4.C.1.1. – V.2.c.6.4 – V.15.00 – V.10.d.0.0. – U.15.d.0.5. – U.20.a.0.7.	
	19.5.17		Issued R.A.M.C. Operation Order No. 27. dated 19.5.17.	
			Headquarters 136 Field Ambulance, with Main dressing station – will remain at FINS, and have	
			advanced dressing stations at Q.22.c.0.5. and Q.29.c.6.0. It will be responsible for the collection	R.A.M.C.
			of sick wounded from the Divisional Front to FINS, inclusive, and will hand over the	Operation order
			A.D.S. at X.1.a.2.2. to 105 Field Ambulance, 35th Division, on the 25th inst.	No. 27
			137 Field Ambulance will hand over the 23rd inst. to 103 Field Ambulance, 35th Division, – 35th Division	dated 19.5.17
			the dressing station at HEUDECOURT and lines posts at X.13.C.2.1. and X.9.C.9.8.	attached.
			and return to take all sick at MANANCOURT. It will then be responsible for	
			the collection of sick from the Divisional Back area west of FINS.	
			Divisional Headquarters will not move.	
	21.5.17		Received 40th Division Operation Order No. 81 dated 21.5.17. Ordering No. 30 dated 16.5.17	
			Agrees to previous arrangement to that 35th Division will take over the line west and held	
			by the 120th and 121st Brigades, 40th Division, up to R.33.b.6.7 – and that the 121st	
			Brigade will take over the line of the 125th Brigade, 42nd Division up to R.7.d.3.8.	

VOL. XII.

Army Form C. 2118.

WAR DIARY of A.D.M.S. 40th Division
or
INTELLIGENCE SUMMARY.
(Erase heading not required.)

Place	Date	Hour	Summary of Events and Information	Remarks and references to Appendices
WOOD.			The 119th Brigade will be in divisional Reserve — two Battalions at EQUANCOURT and two in DESSART	Ruth's Orders No 28 attached
			Issued R.A.M.C. operation order No 28. The 138th Field Ambulance will now retain the Advanced Dressing	
			Station at X.1.a.2.8. and the other A.D.S. will remain at Q.29.a.6.0. 137th Field Ambulance will	
			Carry on as ordered in Operation order No 27 dated 19-5-17.	
			From 26th May, the 40th Division will have the 59th Division on its left and the 35th Division	
			on its right.	
			The Inter Divisional boundaries will:—	
			Northern boundary — R.19.a.30.95 — R.29.c.0.0. — R.34.a.0.9. — R.33.central. — X.1.central.	
			— W.12.6.80.95. — W.12.a.0.4. — W.11.d.0.6. — W.9.c.8.2. — W.20.c.5.6. — V.30.d.3.7. —	
			D.11.c.0.0. — D.10.a.8.6. — D.15.6.5.5. — D.14.a.0.2. — D.19.a.3.7. — C.24.a.2.7. — C.25.6.2.2.	
			Southern boundary — R.8.a.3.9. — R.13.a.5.5.70. — R.10.a.2.6. — Q.24.a.2.0. — Q.23.d.2.4. —	
			Q.34.a.7.0. — Q.32.central. — V.6.a.6.2. — V.17.9.8.8. — V.10.c.3.1. — along road (inclusive	
			to 40th Division). — V.14.a.15.10. — V.13.a.6.9. along road (inclusive to 40th Division)	
			— U.26.a.4.0.	

VOL. XII.

Scott

WAR DIARY of A.D.M.S. 40th Division
or
INTELLIGENCE SUMMARY.
(Erase heading not required.)

Army Form C. 2118.

Place	Date	Hour	Summary of Events and Information	Remarks and references to Appendices
	22.5.17		Two Raids were carried out last night by 119th & 121st Brigades. Other Casualties were 21 wounded which were cleared from Field Ambulances by 9 A.M.	
	23.5.17		A.D.M.S. 59th Division visited H.Q.	
			Inspected 137 Field Ambulance - MANANCOURT	
	24.5.17		R.A.M.C. operation order N.º 18. 59th Division relieved	
	25.5.17		Attended conference at D.D.M.S. of the XV Corps, between medical arrangements of the Corps.	
	26.5.17		Inspected 136 Field Ambulance at FINS, and also discussed a number of men of 20th Hussars were kept with a view to equipping them "P.B." Issued "Standing Orders for Regimental Medical Officers".	
	27.5.17		Visited Advanced Dressing Stations to much arrangements regarding the evacuation of sick and wounded from Advanced Dressing Stations - known Dressing Station FINS. Is DEcauville Railway; the latter is not yet in working order however, guaranteed that the existing accommodation in advanced dressing stations is to be considerably increased and signals such as soap as possible.	
	28.5.17		Issued Medical Arrangements to 40th Division. 136 Field Ambulance with Headquarters at FINS will be responsible for the evacuation of the sick and wounded from the Divisional Front to FINS and will *Advanced dressing stations are at Q.30.d. 8.8 and at X.19.c.2.9. two forwards are in the line*	Medical arrangements 40th Division dated 28.5.17. 2 Enclosed.

A6945 Wt. W11422/M1160 350,000 12/16 D. D. & L. Forms/C./2118/14.

Vol. XII.

Scott WAR DIARY of A.D.M.S. 40th Division
or
INTELLIGENCE SUMMARY.
(Erase heading not required.)

Army Form C. 2118.

Place	Date	Hour	Summary of Events and Information	Remarks and references to Appendices
	29.5.17		137 Field Ambulance has Headquarters at MANANCOURT and a Tent Subdivision at NURLU and is responsible for the Evacuation of sick from the Divisional front area from FINS exclusive. Visited NURLU. Inspected dressing station and Baths. The latter requires a Pump as being arranged with the C.R.E. Tables, a duty linen store and an ironing room.	
	30.5.17		Visited SOREL-LE-GRAND. 2 yards area generally, also the Baths which are taken over yesterday, a store for both clean and dirty clothing is required there, also an ironing room. Amendment to Medical arrangements dated 28.5.17 issued. The subdivision of 137 Field Ambulance at NURLU will collect sick from Medical Inspection rooms in SOREL.	
	31.5.17		Sick parades of the Division remained low, as for week ending May 28th it was again the lowest in the Corps. Opening Strength this week 2913 Constituting sick and eligible, remainder returned to duty by Field Ambulances of the Division. This number is lowest of 62nd from the Corps Week Return.	

C.Y. LUKE
A.D.M.S. 40 Division

App. A

SECRET.   Copy. No...15..

40th. Division R.A.M.C. Operation Order No. 25.

Reference Map 57c. 1.40.000.   3/5/17.

1. The 40th. Division will attack the LA VACQUERIE position in conjunction with the 8th. Division on the 5th. May. Zero hour will be 10.30 p.m.

2. The attack will be carried out by the 119th. and 121st. Infantry Brigades. The 120th. Inf. Bde. will continue to hold its present line.

3. 137th. Field Ambulance will attach 3 bearer sub-divisions to 136th. Field Ambulance on the 4th. inst.

4. 136th. Field Ambulance with Headquarters at FINS will establish Advanced Dressing Stations in the sunken road at Q.29.d.central and at METX-EN-COUTURE.

5.
    A   Line of Evacuation - From Regimental Aid Posts to Advanced (Dressing Stations at METZ and Q.29.d.central by wheeled (stretchers and hand carriage. Bearer Posts will be (established as required.

    B   (Walking wounded will be directed to Main Dressing Station (FINS.

    C   (Stretcher cases from Advanced Dressing Stations will (be evacuated to FINS by horsed and Motor Ambulance (wagons.

Acknowledge.

Issued at 7.30. p.m.

```
Copy No.  1   "G"
   "    "  2   "Q"
   "    "  3   D.D.M.S.
   "    "  4   A.D.M.S. 8th. Division.
   "    "  5   A.D.M.S. 20th. Division.
   "    "  6   119t. Infantry Brigade.
   "    "  7   120th.      "         "
   "    "  8   121st       "         "
   "    "  9   135th. Field Ambulance.
   "    " 10   136th.   "        "
   "    " 11   137th.   "        "
   "    " 12   C.R.A.
   "    " 13   O.C. 20th. M.A.C.
   "    " 14   40th. Div. Train.
   "    " 15   Office ✓
   "    " 16   Diary.
```

(sd) A.J.Luther,
Colonel,
A.D.M.S. 40th. Division.

SECRET.   Copy No. 15

40th. Division R.A.M.C. Operation Order No. 26.
Reference Map 57c. 1/40.000.

The Corps front will be readjusted as follows :-

1. (a) Night 12th/13th. May.
   120th. Infantry Brigade will be relieved by the 60th. Infantry Bde., 20th. Division in its present area (less EQUANCOURT)

   (b) The present Southern boundary of the 120th. Infantry Bde. is R.7.d.5.9. - Q.23.c.7.2. - Q.22.d.0.0. - Q.27.c.3.5.

   (c) Command to pass 10 a.m. 13th. instant.

   (d) After relief, the 120th. Infantry Bde. will become Brigade Reserve to the 8th. Division in place of the 24th. Brigade and will be accommodated as follows :-
   SOREL   - Brigade Headquarters and 1 Battalion.
   HEUDECOURT   - 2 Battalions, T.M.Battery and M.G.Coy.
   DESSART WOOD - 1 Battalion.

2. (a) Night 13th/14th. May.
   120th. Infantry Bde. will relieve the 23rd. Infantry Bde. in the left Bde. Sector of the 8th. Divisional Front.

   (b) Command to pass on completion of relief.

3. (a) Night 13th/14th May.
   The 121st. Infantry Bde will be relieved by the 60th. Infantry Bde 20th. Division in its present area.

   (b) Command to pass on completion of relief.

   (c) The Southern boundary up to which the 60th. Infantry Bde. will take over will be R.14.d.0.1. - R.14.c.3.1. - R.19.b.4.0. - Q.36.d.6.0. - W.2.a.5.5. - W.2.a.4.2. - W.1.a.9.1. V.6.d.1.0. - along road through V.6.central - P.35. central to the present boundary P.35.a.7.3.
   This will then be the boundary between the 20th and 40th. Divisions.

   (d) After relief, the 121st. Infantry Bde. will become Reserve Brigade to the 8th. Division and will be accommodated as in paragraph 1. (d). except that Brigade Headquarters may remain in DESSART WOOD

4. The command of the whole front taken over by the 20th. will pass to the G.O.C., 20th. Division at 10.a.m. 14th.May.

5. (a) Night 14th/15th. May
   The 121st. Infantry Bde. will relieve the 25th. Infantry Bde. in the Right Bde. Sector of the 8th. Division.

   (b) Command to pass on completion of reliefs

6. The command of the 8th. Division Front will pass to the 40th. Division at 10 a.m. 15th. May.

7. 136th. Field Ambulance will remain at FINS and be responsible for the evacuation of sick and wounded from the left and centre Brigades, taking over from 24th. Field Ambulance, 8th. Division, the Advanced Dressing Station in X.1.a.5.9. and Bearer Posts, clearing to that point ; by 6 p.m. 13th. inst.

8. 137th. Field Ambulance (less sufficient personnel to run a detention hospital at MANANCOURT and the baths at ETRICOURT) will move from MANANCOURT to HEUDICOURT on 14th. instant, and take over Dressing Station and Bearer Posts from 24th. Field Ambulance, 8th. Division ; and be responsible for the evacuation of sick and wounded from the Right Brigade.

9. Details of relief to be arranged between O.C's concerned.

10. Divisional Headquarters will close at MANANCOURT at 10 a.m. 15th. May. and open at GUELU WOOD at the same hour.

11. Acknowledge.

Issued at 8. p.m.

A. J. Cutler.
Colonel,
A.D.M.S. 40th. Division.

11/5/17.

Copy No. 1. "G"
2. "Q"
3. D.D.M.S. XVth. Corps.
4. A.D.M.S. 8th. Division.
5. A.D.M.S. 20th. Division.
6. 119th. Infantry Brigade.
7. 120th. Infantry Brigade.
8. 121st. Infantry Brigade.
9. 135th. Field Ambulance.
10. 136th. Field Ambulance.
11. 137th. Field Ambulance.
12. C.R.A.
13. 20th. M.A.C.
14. Divisional Train.
15. Office.
16. Diary.   18. 14th. Sanitary Section.
17. C.R.E.   19. 53rd. Sanitary Section.

* Reference para. 3 (c), in front of R.14.d.0.1. the boundary between the 20th. and 40th. Divisions will be the road to R.21.b.3.7. inclusive to the 40th. Division.

SECRET

App. C.

Copy No. 20

40th. Division R.A.M.C. Operation Order No. 27.

Reference Map. 57c. S.E. 1/20.000.   19/5/17.

1. The following reliefs will take place —

 (a) The 42nd. Division is relieving the 20th. Division in the line.

 (b) The 35th. Division will take over that portion of the line now held by the 121st. and 120th. Infantry Brigades, in accordance with the attached Table A.

 (c) After relief the 121st. Inf. Bde. will take over the front held by the 125th. Inf. Bde., 42nd. Division, in accordance with Table A.

 (d) One Battalion of the 120th. Inf. Bde. will be attached to the 121st. Inf. Bde. for the relief of 125th. Inf. Bde. It will come under command of G.O.C. 121st. Inf. Bde. at 9 p.m. 25th. May and will relieve the left battalion of 125th. Inf. Bde.
 It will come under orders of G.O.C. 120th. Inf. Bde. on the rearrangement of the line about which orders will be issued later.

2. The provisional boundaries of Divisional Area which come into force at 10 a.m. 26th. May will be as follows :—
 Southern Boundary. LE PAVE - GOUZEAUCOURT ROAD exclusive to 40th. Division to Q.33.b.7.7 - Q.36.b.9.0. - Q.35.d.5.0. - W.14.c.0.5. - W.25.c.0.5. - D.5.c.0.0. - D.10.c.2.7. - D.8.d.0.4. - C.18.d.9.9. - C.24.a.6.6. - C.23.a.8.8. - C.17.d.3.9. - C.16.a.0.3. - C.20.b.0.8.
 Northern Boundary. L.32.d.4.5. - Q.12.d.0.9. - Q.11.d.8.6. - Q.11.d.10.4. - Q.17.b.0.5. - Q.23.a.1.9. - Q.25.c.0.6. - P.35.b.0.0. - V.4.c.1.1. - V.2.c.6.4. - V.1.c.0.0. - U.10.d.0.0. - U.15.d.0.5. - U.20.a.0.7.

3. (a) G.O.C. 35th. Division will assume command of the front now held by 120th. and 121st. Inf. Bdes. at 10 a.m. 26th. May, at which time the G.O.C. 40th. Division will assume command of the front now held by the 125th. Inf. Bde.

 (b) Command of Infantry Brigade Sectors will pass on completion of reliefs.

4. Headquarters 40th. Division do not move.

5. H.Q. 119th. Inf. Bde. will move into the new H.Q. which are being built in DESSART WOOD, by noon 23rd. May. 121st. and 120th. Inf. Bdes will return to their old H.Q. in DESSART WOOD, after relief.

 In conformity with above the following will be the Medical Arrangements.

A. 136th. Field Ambulance with Main Dressing Station at FINS and and Advanced Dressing Stations at Q.22.c.0.5. and Q.29.a.6.0. will be responsible for the collection of sick and wounded from the Divisional Front to FINS inclusive, and will hand over the Advanced Dressing Station at X.1.a.8.8. to 106th. Field Ambulance 35th. Division on 25th inst.

B. 137th. Field Ambulance will hand over on the 23rd. inst. to 106th. Field Ambulance 35th. Division. the Dressing Station at HEUDECOURT and Bearer Posts at X.13.c.2.1. and X.9.c.0.8., and return to its old site at MANANCOURT ; and be responsible for the collection of sick from the Divisional Back Area west of FINS.

Details of above reliefs to be arranged between O.C's concerned.

Acknowledge.

Issued at 7.30 p.m.

A. J. Luther.
Colonel,
A.D.M.S. 40th. Division.

Copy.
1. "A"
2. "Q"
3. D.D.M.S. XVth. Corps.
4. A.D.M.S. 35th. Division.
5. A.D.M.S. 42nd. Division.
6. 119th. Infantry Brigade.
7. 120th.   "   "
8. 121st.   "   "
9. 135th. Field Ambulance.
10. 136th.   "   "
11. 137th.   "   "
12. C.R.A.
13. C.R.E.
14. 12th. Yorks Regt.
15. 20th. M.A.C.
16. Divisional Train.
17. 14th. Sanitary Section
18. 33rd.   "   "
19. Diary. ✓
20. Office. ✓

TABLE A.

To accompany 40th. Division F.A.i.C. Operation Order No. 27. dated 19/5/17.

Item.	Date.	Formation.	Moves from	Destination	Time	Remarks.
1.	23/24th.	121st. Inf. Bde.	Right Sector.	EQUANCOURT Area.	After relief by 105th. Inf. Bde.	
2.	23/24th.	105th. Inf. Bde. (35th. Div)	GUYENCOURT Area.	Right Sector.	Not to be East of PEIZIERE - VAUCELLETTE FARM railway before 9 p.m.	To relieve 121st. Inf. Bde.
3.	23rd.	104th. Inf. Bde. (35th.Div)	PERONNE.	GUYENCOURT Area.	To be arranged direct with 105th. Bde.	
4.	25/26th.	121st. Inf. Bde.	EQUANCOURT Area.	Right Sector. 42nd. Div.	To be arranged between 121st. and 125th. Bdes.	To relieve 125th. Bde. 42nd. Div.
5.	25/26th.	120th. Inf.Bde.	Centre Sector.	EQUANCOURT Area.	After relief by 104th. Inf. Bde.	
6.	25/26th.	104th. Inf. Bde.	GUYENCOURT Area	Centre Sector.	Not to be East of REVELON before 9p.m.	To relieve 120th. Bde.
7.	25th.	105th. Inf. Bde.	PERONNE	GUYENCOURT Area.	To be arranged between 104th. & 105th. Bdes.	

SECRET.   Copy. 20

40th. Division R.A.M.C. Operation Order No. 28.

Reference Map 57c S.E. 1/20,000.   21/5/17.

40th. Division R.A.M.C. Operation Order No. 27. dated 19/5/17. is cancelled with the exception of para 5 (b).

1. (a) The 42nd. Division is relieving the 20th. Division in the line.

   (b) The 35th. Division will take over the line now held by the 121st. and 120th. Infantry Brigades, up to R.33.b.8.7. on 23/24th. inst.

   (c) After relief the 121st. Infantry Brigade will take over the front of the 125th Infantry Brigade, 42nd. Division, as far West as R.7.d.3.8. on 25/26th. inst.

2. The provisional boundaries of the Divisional Area which come into force at 10 a.m. 26th. May, will be as follows :-
   Northern Boundary. - R.8. c.9.1. - R.7.d.2.4. - R.13.a.cent.- R.19.a.2.8. - Q.23.d.5.4. - Q.34.d.0.9. - Q.33.a.0.0. - Q.32.c. 0.5. - W.1.b.0.9. - V.6.a.7.3. - V.17.a.9.8. - V.10.c.3.1. - V.14.b.6.2. - V.13.a.8.8.
   Southern Boundary. - X.29.d.10.0. - X.29.c.0.0. - X.34.a.1.9. - X.33.c.8.8. - X.1.b.5.4. - W.12.b.0.8. - ? - W.9.c.9.1. - W.28.c.5.3. - V.30.c.5.0. - D.17.c.1.9. - D.10.c.6.9. - C.24. d.0.6. - C.20.d.1.9.

3. (a) Command will pass between Divisions at 10 a.m. on 26th. May, in both cases.
   (b) Command of Infantry Brigade Sectors will pass on Completion of reliefs.

4. Headquarters 40th. Division do not move.

5. Headquarters, 119th. Infantry Brigade will move into the new Headquarters which are being built in DESSART WOOD, by noon 23rd. May.

   The 121st. Infantry Brigade will return to its old Headquarters in DESSART WOOD, after relief.

   Headquarters, 120th. Infantry Brigade will not move.

6. 136th. Field Ambulance with Main Dressing Station at FINS and Advanced Dressing Stations at Q.29.a.6.0. and X.1.a.2.8. will be responsible for the collection of sick and wounded from the Divisional Front to FINS inclusive.

7. Details of reliefs to be arranged between O's.C. concerned.

8. Acknowledge.

   Issued at 11 p.m.

   A. J. Luther.
   Colonel,
   A.D.M.S. 40th. Division.

Copy 1. "G"
2. "Q"
3. D.D.M.S. XVth. Corps.
4. A.D.M.S. 35th. Division.
5. A.D.M.S. 59th. Division
6. 119th. Infantry Brigade.
7. 120th.   "   "
8. 1 1st.   "   "
9. 135th. Field Ambulance.
10. 136th.   "   "
11. 137th   "   "
12. C.R.A.
13. C.R.E.
14. Divisional Train.
n15. 12th. Yorks Regt.
16. 20th. M.A.C.
17. A.P.M.
18. 28th. Sanitary Section.
19. 33rd.   "   "
20. Office. ✓
21. Diary.

app. F

SECRET.   COPY.No........

MEDICAL ARRANGEMENTS 40th. DIVISION.

Map reference. 1.20.000. Sheet.57c.S.E.

Two Brigades in the line.

1.   138th. Field Ambulance with Headquarters at FINS, will be responsible for the evacuation of sick and wounded from the Divisional front to FINS inclusive.

   137th. Field Ambulance, Headquarters at MANANCOURT and one Tent-Subdivision at NURLU, will be responsible for the evacuation of sick from the Divisional Back Area from FINS exclusive.

2.   Lines of Evacuation.
   A.   Left Brigade.
   R.A.P. Left Batt.   R.19.a.5.4.
   R.A.P. Right "   R.20.a.2.9.

   From both these aid posts evacuation is by wheeled stretcher to Bearer Post. Q.30.d.8.8. thence by wheeled stretcher by day, and by car at night, to A.D.S. Q.29.b.2.9. From here evacuation is by horsed or motor ambulance to Main Dressing Station, FINS via QUEENS CROSS and METZ.

   B.   Right Brigade.
   Regimental Aid Post. Left Batt.   R.25.d.2.9.
   Regimental Aid Post. Right "   R.31.b.8.9.

   From both these aid posts evacuation is by wheeled stretcher to Advanced Dressing Station X.1.a.2.9. thence by hand carriage to W.6.a.2.6. on the GOUZEAUCOURT - REVELON Road, and then by wheeled stretchers along the road to W.11.c.6.5. where the cases are loaded into ambulance wagons and evacuated via HEUDECOURT to Main Dressing Station, FINS. At night horsed and motor ambulances can proceed to W.6.a.2.6.

3.   At present the accommodation at Advanced Dressing Stations is as follows :-

   Q.29.b.2.9. - 12 lying and 20 sitting cases.
   X.1.a.2.9. - 6   "   " 10   "   "

   and the work of extending this considerably is proceeding as rapidly as possible.

4.   From Headquarters of 138th. Field Ambulance at FINS serious wounded cases are evacuated direct to Casualty Clearing Station at PERONNE by Motor Ambulance Car, all other cases to XVth. Corps Main Dressing Station at V.18.c.

5.   When the Decauville is in working order, all lying cases will be evacuated by this means.

                                                 A. J. Luther

D.H.Q.
28/5/17.   Colonel,
                                                 A.D.M.S. 40th. Division.

AMENDMENTS TO MEDICAL ARRANGEMENTS 40th. DIVISION
85 (M) DATED 28/5/17.

Para 1.   Tent sub-division of 137th. Field Ambulance, NURLU, will be responsible for collection of sick from Medical Inspection Rooms, SOREL from May 30th Inclusive.

Acknowledge.

D.H.Q.
30/5/17.

Colonel,
A.D.M.S. 40th. Division.

140/229.

O.D.M.S, 4 O. H. Div.

COMMITTEE FOR THE
MEDICAL HISTORY OF THE WAR
Date   -7 AUG. 1917

VOL. XIII.

WAR DIARY of A.D.M.S. 40th Division

or

INTELLIGENCE SUMMARY

Army Form C. 2118.

Vol 13

Place	Date	Hour	Summary of Events and Information	Remarks and references to Appendices
MANANCOURT	1.6.17.		Presided at a Medical Board at Hdqrs. 137 Field Ambulance, with O.C. 137 Field Ambulance and an Officer selected by him as Member, with a view to classifying a Warrant Officer "B" for duty with Divisional Company. Selected men at present employed in duties behind the line, for return to their units.	
			Shortage for this Division for week ending May 26th was again the worst in the Corps.	
	2.6.17.		Today the III'rd Corps took over from the XV Corps and this Division now consists of the following Divisions – 35th, 40th, 42nd and 59th.	
			Medical Board again held at Hdqrs. 137 Field Ambulance.	
	3.6.17.		Medical Board held at Hdqrs. 136 Field Ambulance with O.C. 136 Field Ambulance and an Officer detailed by him as Member.	
			Called on D.D.M.S. III'rd Corps.	
	4.6.17.		Medical Board held as yesterday.	
	5.6.17.		O.C. 48th Sanitary Section reported his arrival. This section has headquarters at MANANCOURT and is responsible for 40th Divisional area.	
			Inspected Baths at NURLU and SOREL. Certain improvements, erection of dressing rooms better hot water supply etc. are being carried out.	
			Two Officers of 136 Field Ambulance transferred Sick to III Corps Main Dressing Station.	

VOL. XIII.
Army Form C. 2118.

WAR DIARY
or
INTELLIGENCE SUMMARY.
(Erase heading not required.)

Place	Date	Hour	Summary of Events and Information	Remarks and references to Appendices
	7.6.17.		Inspected 138 Field Ambulance. Considerable extension of front accommodation for patients is being carried out. Visited advanced dressing stations. Also the both gauge line of dug outs to dressing and will shortly be finished. Decauville Railway not yet ready for use.	
	9.6.17.		Inspected 137 Field Ambulance. Excellent accommodation has now been provided for 150 patients. Two Officers evacuated sick, and struck off the strength.	
	11.6.17.		Accompanied D.D.M.S. III Corps to an inspection of advanced dressing stations. Decauville is now ready for use and a trial run was successfully carried out. The Division will have 3 horse each capable of carrying 8 lying & 6 sitting cases drawn by a petrol engine. All evacuations from advanced dressing stations to main dressing station will be by this means, and GS wagons for sitting cases. The line will be drawn up.	
	13.6.17.		Sick wastage for week ending June 9th was again very low - being 1.37%.	
	15.6.17.		Lt. Colonel Leviston Power, O.C. 137 Field Ambulance proceeded on leave to England.	
	17.6.17.		Captain Linnell R.A.M.C. assumed temporary command. Issued Medical Arrangements - 40th Division. The use of the right A.D.S. has been discontinued. Latrines are at the A.D.S. at Q.29.d.29. Latrines & Decauville for walking wounded at Q.27.2.5.8.	Medical arrangements dated 17.6.17 received

A6945. Wt. W1442/M1160 350,000 12/16 D. D. & L. Forms/C/2118/14.

Vol. XIII.

Army Form C. 2118.

Secret

WAR DIARY of A.D.M.S. 40th Division.

or

INTELLIGENCE SUMMARY.

(Erase heading not required.)

Instructions regarding War Diaries and Intelligence Summaries are contained in F. S. Regs., Part II. and the Staff Manual respectively. Title pages will be prepared in manuscript.

Place	Date	Hour	Summary of Events and Information	Remarks and references to Appendices
	18.6.17		Visited F.A.s and selected a site for a Field Ambulance, in case it may be necessary to move up 137 Field Ambulance from MANANCOURT.	
	19.6.17		Sick wastage for week ending 16-6-17 is abt '29% - again the worst in the Corps.	
	21.6.17		Inspected the G.M. Stores, wagon lines etc. of all units in SOREL, in company with the D.A.D.M.S. Recommended that the one general sanitary fatigue should be discontinued, and Men employed in Units. Captain SMITH R.A.M.C. M.O. 20/ Middlesex Regt. admitted to Corps Main Dressing Station with slight multiple shell wounds, of face and arm.	
	22.6.17		Inspected 137 Field Ambulance MANANCOURT. There is now sufficient accommodation there for 150 patients.	
	24.6.17		Attended Conference at D.D.M.S. office III Corps.	
	25.6.17		Am proceeding on 10 days leave to England tomorrow. Lt Colonel Ravens Robinson O.C. 136 Field Ambulance will take over duties of A/A.D.M.S.	A.J. Dobbs Col ADMS 40th Division
	26.6.17		Resumed duties of A/A.D.M.S.- Office of Medical Officer in Charge Medical Corps Postes to 137 Field Ambulance posting Lt. Col. Ambulton O.C. 137 Field Ambulance retained pending his arrival from leave.	H.F. Ravenscroft Robinson Lt Col
	27.6.17		40th Divisional Orders received regarding the taking over of the 35th Divisional front by the 121st Infy. Bde.	

VOL XIII.   IV

WAR DIARY of A.D.M.S. 40th Division

or INTELLIGENCE SUMMARY

Army Form C. 2118.

(Erase heading not required.)

Place	Date	Hour	Summary of Events and Information	Remarks and references to Appendices
	30.6.17		Brigade H.Q.s Division on nights 1/2 and 2/3 July. Further details to be issued later.	R.A.M.C. op. orders No 29 attached
			Issued R.A.M.C. operation order No. 29.	
			Arrangements for the evacuation sick and wounded from the left and centre Brigade	
			6 Fins inclusive. 137 Field Ambulance will move to HEUDECOURT on July 3rd takes over	
			main dressing station there, and Advanced Dressing Station at VILLERS GUISLAIN from 106	
			Field Ambulance. 35th Division. Detachments will remain at MANANCOURT and at	
			NURLU until further orders. The 35th Division will evacuate sick and wounded of the	
			121st Infantry Brigade for the nights 1/2 July until noon 3rd July.	
			The Decauville Railway will be used for evacuating cases from VILLERS GUISLAIN	
			to HEUDECOURT, and will also take wounded cases direct to GOUZEAUCOURT	
			Dressing Station, FINS.	

F Murray Paterson
Lt. Colonel. R.A.M.C.
A/ADMS. 40th Division.

SECRET.   COPY No 18

40TH. DIVISION R.A.M.C. OPERATION ORDER No. 29.

Map Reference 57.c.S.E 1:20.000.

1. 121st. Infantry Brigade will take over the 35th Divisional front as follows:-

   (a) On night 1st/2nd. July, the GAUCHE WOOD Sector from 105th. Infantry Brigade.

   (b) On night 2nd/3rd. July, the VILLERS GUISLAINS Sector from 104th. Infantry Brigade.

   (c) Headquarters, 121st. Infantry Brigade will move to W.23.b.3.1. on night 2nd/3rd. July.

   (d) 40th. Division will assume command of extended front at 10.a.m. 3rd. July.

2. 136th. Field Ambulance with Main Dressing Station at FINS, and Advanced Dressing Station at Q.29.d.2.9. will be responsible for the collection of sick and wounded of the Left and Centre Brigades to FINS, inclusive.

   137th. Field Ambulance, Headquarters, will move to HEUDICOURT on 3rd. July, leaving one tent sub-division (less one Officer) at MANANCOURT and at NURLU, until further orders. They will take over from 106th. Field Ambulance, 35th. Division, the Main Dressing Station at HEUDICOURT, and the Advanced Dressing Station at VILLERS GUISLAINS, and will be responsible for the collection of sick and wounded from Right Brigade; and from Divisional back area excluding FINS

3. Details of relief to be arranged between Officers Commanding concerned; relief to be completed by 12 noon 3rd. July.

4. 106th Field Ambulance, 35th. Division will evacuate sick and wounded of 121st. Infantry Brigade, until 12 noon 3rd July

5. Details of Medical evacuation scheme will be issued later.

6. 40th. Divisional Headquarters will move to SOREL-LE-GRAND, on a date to be notified later.

7. Acknowledge.

   Issued at 8.30.a.m.

Divisional Headquarters

30th. June, 1917.

S.J. Thatcher.
Captain, for
Lieut-Colonel, R.A.M.C.
A/A.D.M.S. 40th. Division.

```
Copy No.  1     "G"
  "   "   2     "Q"
  "   "   3     D.D.M.S.IIIrd.Corps.
  "   "   4     A.D.M.S.35th.Division.
  "   "   5     H.Qrs.119th.Infantry Brigade.
  "   "   6       "   120th.    "        "
  "   "   7       "   121st.    "        "
  "   "   8       "   135th.Field Ambulance.
  "   "   9       "   136th.    "       "
          10      "   137th.    "       "
          11      "   C.R.A.
          12      "   C.R.E.
          13      "   Divisional Train.
          14      "   O.C.12th.Yorks.Regt.
          15.     "   O.C.21st.M.A.C.
          16      "   A.P.M.
          17      "   O.C. 14th.Snaitary Section.
          18      "   Office.
          19      "   Diary.
          20      "       "
```

140/292

A.D.M.S. 40th Division

COMMITTEE FOR THE
MEDICAL HISTORY OF THE WAR
Date 10 SEP. 1917

VOL. XIV.

Secret

WAR DIARY of A.D.M.S. 40th Division
or INTELLIGENCE SUMMARY
(Erase heading not required.)

Army Form C. 2118.

Place	Date	Hour	Summary of Events and Information	Remarks and references to Appendices
MANANCOURT	1-7-17		Received 35th Division R.A.M.C. junction orders.	
			Received 40th Division junction orders No. 88. The Centre Brigade will extend its right to NEWTON POST in Chevron.	
			Boundary between the right and centre Brigades with the 35th Road R.28.c.9.9 to R.34.c.39 in Chevron to	
			the Centre Brigade, thence along 22 Ravine to R.33.c.5.5 – X.2.c.1.8. – GAUCHE WOOD inclusive to Right	
			Brigade – X.1.c.75.30. – W.17.a.3.9. The Left Brigade will extend its right and Lestertive Trench B.	
			The Boundary between left and centre Brigades will be R.15.d.8.1 – R.20.c.5.5 – R.20.c.6.8.0.25 –	
			R.25.b.2.0. along railway to R.25.d.05.25. thence main Cambrai – Finns Road.	
			Divisional Headquarters will move to SOREL-LE-GRAND at an early date.	
			Visited D.D.M.S. III Corps. Discussed medical arrangements. Shortly the Corps main dressing	
			Station will close, the site taken over by a Field Ambulance 40th Division as a	
			Divisional Main Dressing Station. Cars will be earmarked from the district of	
			C.C.Ss at TINCOURT.	
	2-7-17		Received hairdry over and rendered taking over atfecal to A.D.M.S. 35th Division.	
			Received orders regarding formation of a Divisional Main Dressing Station for 40th Division "G".	
			40th Division will be to the left of the 3 Divisions in the III Corps, and will take over the	
			Site of the present III Corps Main Dressing Station as the Divisional Dressing Station	

VOL XIV.

WAR DIARY of A.D.M.S. 40th Division.
INTELLIGENCE SUMMARY.
(Erase heading not required.)

Army Form C. 2118.

Place	Date	Hour	Summary of Events and Information	Remarks and references to Appendices
	3.7.17		Re taking over probably to be completed by 10th July. Telephoned D.D.M.S. III Corps regarding the return of 135 Field Ambulance to this division from Corps Rest Station MARICOURT, pointing out the difficulty of clearing a 9000 yard front and running a Divisional Main Dressing Station, with two incomplete Field Ambulances. 135 Field Ambulance will probably return to the division at an early date. 137 Field Ambulance moved to HEUDICOURT today. Issued Medical Arrangements dated 3-7-17.	Medical arrangement dated 3-7-17 attached
	4.7.17		Received wire from D.D.M.S. III Corps to the effect that Tent Subdivision of 136 Field Ambulance will report Headquarters on 6-7-17, from 135 Field Ambulance - MARICOURT.	
	5.7.17		Command of Fourth Army front passes to Third Army 10 a.m. today.	
	6.7.17		Received instructions from D.D.M.S. III Corps regarding taking over of sick of III Corps main dressing station - V.18.C. - on July 10th and copy instructions to O.C. 135 Field Ambulance regarding his handing over Tent Corps rest station MARICOURT to Ambulance of 58th Division, Fourth Corps, on July 9th after which 135 Field Ambulance will rejoin 40th Division.	
	7.7.17		Returned from leave today - Lt. Col. Norman Patterson relinquishes duties of D.A.D.M.S.	
	8.7.17		Issued R.A.M.C. Location order No 30.	R.A.M.C. location order No 30 attached

VOL. XIV.

WAR DIARY of A.D.M.S. 40th Division

INTELLIGENCE SUMMARY

Army Form C. 2118.

Place	Date	Hour	Summary of Events and Information	Remarks and references to Appendices
			136 Field Ambulance will open as Divisional Main Dressing Station on 10th July, and will continue	
			to clear Infantry Brigades until 135 Field Ambulance moves into present site of 136 Field	
			Ambulance about the 11th inst. when they will take over the evacuation of Infantry Brigades.	
			137 Field Ambulance will remain at HEUDICOURT where tent subdivision at NURLU and will	
			be responsible for right Brigade.	
			Tent subdivision of 137 Field Ambulance has been withdrawn for MANANCOURT.	
			Divisional Hdqrs. is now at SOREL-LE-GRAND, and A.D.M.S. Offices will move there	
			probably on the 11th inst.	
	9.7.17		Received Medical Arrangements III Corps No. 10. signalling the new arrangements regarding	
			Divisional M.D. Stations instead of Corps M.D.S. who hitherto regarding evacuating	
			of Daily States by the Officer in charge of DDMS Office - afte 10th inst.	
	10.7.17		Inspected 137 Field Ambulance - HEUDICOURT and Advanced Dressing Station, etc. in	
			VILLERS GUISLAIN	
	11.7.17		A.D.M.S. Office opened at SOREL-LE-GRAND at 10A.M. this morning. Instructed 135 Field Ambulance	
			who are now located at FINS and have taken over the evacuations from Left and Centre Brigades	
			from 136 Field Ambulance.	

IV

VOL. XIV.

Army Form C. 2118.

Scott WAR DIARY of A.D.M.S. 40th Division

or

INTELLIGENCE SUMMARY.

(Erase heading not required.)

Instructions regarding War Diaries and Intelligence Summaries are contained in F. S. Regs., Part II. and the Staff Manual respectively. Title pages will be prepared in manuscript.

Place	Date	Hour	Summary of Events and Information	Remarks and references to Appendices
SOREL-LE-GRAND V.18.a.5.7.	12.7.17		Attended Conference D.D.M.S. III Corps.	
	13.7.17		Accompanied D.D.M.S. on inspection of Divisional Main Dressing Station - Possibility of moving the latter to LIÉRAMONT to be considered.	
	14.7.17		Visited the Advanced Dressing Station, & inspected private site for another Advanced Dressing Station in GOUZEAUCOURT.	
	16.7.17		Advanced Dressing Station in VILLERS GUISLAIN destroyed by shellfire. Moved to excellent cellars near aid site. Two regimental medical officers who have been in the line for a prolonged period detailed for 3 weeks temporary duty with Headquarters of Field Ambulances, and this will be done in future as long as Battalions cannot get out for any length of time. Inspected 135 Field Ambulance - FINS. Lt. Colonel Roger Robertson, O.C. 136 Field Ambulance proceeded on leave to England.	
	17.7.17		Inspected 136 Field Ambulance - Divisional Main Dressing Station.	
	19.7.17		Visited new advanced dressing station in VILLERS GUISLAIN. This is an excellent deep cellar. Capable of holding about 40 stretcher cases. Issued medical arrangements No. 5.	Medical arrangements No. 5 attached

VOL. XIV.

Army Form C. 2118.

Secret WAR DIARY of A.D.M.S. 40th Division

or

INTELLIGENCE SUMMARY.

(Erase heading not required.)

Instructions regarding War Diaries and Intelligence Summaries are contained in F. S. Regs., Part II. and the Staff Manual respectively. Title pages will be prepared in manuscript.

Place	Date	Hour	Summary of Events and Information	Remarks and references to Appendices
	22.7.17		Inspected Divisional Main Dressing Station in company with D.D.M.S. III Corps. Arrangements discussed for the probable removal of the Field Ambulance to a new site at LIÉRAMONT, for which place has been prepared. Tent subdivision (minus one officer) rejoined 136 Field Ambulance from Officers Rest Station BOIS DE L'ABBEYE.	
	23.7.17		Orders received for D.D.M.S. to detail a tent subdivision (minus one officer) for temporary duty with No. 34 C.C.S. from 25th inst. 136 Field Ambulance to find the subdivision. Visited Advanced Dressing Station stuck to in process of construction in GOUZEAUCOURT. This will be a good safe dressing station, being mainly in cellars. accommodation for about 40 stretcher cases while this is completed the A.D.S. in Q.29.d.2.9. will be given up and the line of evacuation diverted accordingly.	
	25.7.17		Visited LIÉRAMONT and concluded arrangements for moving D.M.D.S. there if necessary.	
	27.7.17		Visited Advanced Dressing Station in VILLERS GUISLAIN in company with D.D.M.S. III Corps. Excellent accommodation in a short completed here - shellproof, and capable of accommodating 50 stretcher cases in one large cellar.	
	29.7.17		Amendment to Medical Arrangements No. 5 dated 19-7-17 issued. The detachment at NURLU and arrangements for reduced arrangements No 5 attached	
			Open Headquarters 137 Field Ambulance HEUDICOURT on August 1st.	

VOL. XIV.

Secret WAR DIARY of A.D.M.S. 40th Division
or
INTELLIGENCE SUMMARY.
(Erase heading not required.)

Army Form C. 2118.

VI

Place	Date	Hour	Summary of Events and Information	Remarks and references to Appendices
			Two Medical Officers sent by road to report to A.D.M.S. 40th Division – He questioned by how many M.O's could be spared from the Division who were named by D.D.M.S. and I replied that possibly one could be spared from either the Divisional Train or the D.A.C. and one from R.E.	
			G.O.C. III army compliments 14th A. & S. Highlanders on the excellent sanitary arrangements in the VILLERS PLOUICH Sector. Lt.Col. Reave Atkinson. O.C. 136 Field Ambulance, reported his return from leave. Since 25.7.17. over 50 cases of shell gas poisoning have been admitted to Divisional Rain Dressing Station, of which 2 cases died. The gas employed was Phosgene, no evidence of the new "Mustard" gas having been employed on this front.	
	31.7.17		Attended D.D.M.S. III Corps Conference Question of Evacuation of R.A.M.C. personnel with Divisions discussed. D.M.S. Third Army will visit Field Ambulances tomorrow.	
			G. G. Luther
Colonel
A.D.M.S. 40th Division.	

SECRET.   COPY No. 20

40TH. DIVISION R.A.M.C. OPERATION ORDER No. 30.

Map Reference 57c.S.E. 1:20.000.   8/7/1917.

1. 136th. Field Ambulance will move from present site at FINS, and take over site of IIIrd. Corps Main Dressing Station at V.18.c. from 105th Field Ambulance, 35th. Division, on July 10th., and will establish a Divisional Main Dressing Station.

   Pending arrival of 135th. Field Ambulance, 136th. Field Ambulance will continue to be responsible for the evacuation of sick and wounded from the Left and Centre Brigades, and also from SOREL-LE-GRAND.

2. Under Corps instructions, 135th. Field Ambulance will hand over IIIrd. Corps Rest Station MARICOURT, to 2/2 H.C. Field Ambulance, 58th. Division on July 9th. It will then move to FINS, and take over from 136th. Field Ambulance the evacuation of sick and wounded from the Left and Centre Brigades. 136th. Field Ambulance will continue to collect sick from SOREL-LE-GRAND.

3. 137th. Field Ambulance with Headquarters at HEUDICOURT, and with detachment at NURLU, will continue to collect sick and wounded from Right Brigade.

4. From 10th. July inclusive, all wounded will be evacuated direct to 40th. Division Main Dressing Station V.18.c. also all sick cases that are not likely to be fit for duty in 48 hours will be sent there from Field Ambulances clearing the line.

5. From Divisional Main Dressing Station, all wounded cases will be evacuated by M.A.C. to C.C.Ss. at TINCOURT, sick cases either to C.C.Ss. TINCOURT or to IIIrd. Corps Rest Station, MOISLAINS. (Cases to C.R.S. will be conveyed in cars of 136th. Field Ambulance.

6. Serious surgical and medical cases requiring immediate attention will continue to be sent direct to nearest C.C.S. from all Field Ambulances.

7. Details of reliefs to be arranged between Os.C. concerned.

8. Acknowledge.

   Issued at 10.30.a.m.

                                                    O.J. Luther
                                                       Colonel.
Rear D.H.Qrs.   A.D.M.S. 40th. Division.

              Copy No. 1 "G"
               "   "   2 "Q"
               "   "   3 D.D.M.S. IIIrd. Corps.
               "   "   4 A.D.M.S. 35th. Division.
               "   "   5 A.D.M.S. 58th.   "
               "   "   6 H.Qrs. 119th. Infantry Brigade.
               "   "   7   "   120th.   "   "
               "   "   8   "   121st.   "   "
               "   "   9 135th. Field Ambulance.
               "   " 10 136th.   "   "
               "   " 11 137th.   "   "
               "   " 12 C.R.A.
               "   " 13 C.R.E.
               "   " 14 Divisional Train.
               "   " 15 O.C. 12th. Yorks. Regt.
               "   " 16 O.C. 21st. M.A.C.
               "   " 17 A.P.M.
               "   " 18 O.C. 48th. Sanitary Section.
               "   " 19 Office.
               "   " 20 Diary.
               "   " 21   "

SECRET. Copy No. 18

MEDICAL ARRANGEMENTS 40TH. DIVISION.

Map Reference France 57c S.E. 1:20.000.

Medical Arrangements 40th. Division dated 17/9/17 is cancelled.

1. Three Brigades in the line.

136th. Field Ambulance with Headquarters at FINS will be responsible for the evacuation of the sick and wounded from Left and Centre Brigades to FINS inclusive.

137th. Field Ambulance with Headquarters at HEUDICOURT, 1 Tent Sub-Division (less 1 Officer each) at NANANCOURT and NURLU will be responsible for the evacuation of sick and wounded from Right Brigade, and from Divisional Back Area from FINS exclusive.

2. LINES OF EVACUATION.

(A) Left Brigade.

R.A.P. Left Battn.	R.13.a.8.3.
R.A.P. Right Battn.	R.20.a.2.9.

From both these evacuation is by wheeled stretcher to Bearer Post at Q.30.d.8.8. The cases from Left Battn. passing through Bearer Post R.19.a.5.4. Thence by wheeled stretcher by day and by car at night to Advanced Dressing Station at Q.29.d.2.9. From here by Ambulance Car to Loading Point at Q.27.d.5.8. and thence by Decauville Railway to Main Dressing Station at FINS.

(B) Centre Brigade.

R.A.P. Left Battn.	R.25.d.2.9.
R.A.P. Right Battn.	R.26.d.50.05.

From the Right evacuation is by wheeled stretcher through Bearer Post close to this Aid Post to Bearer Post at R.25.d.2.9. Thence cases from both R.A.Ps by wheeled stretcher to Bearer Post at Q.30.d.8.8. From here to Main Dressing Station as for Left Brigade.

(C) Right Brigade

R.A.P. Left Battn.	X.2.b.8.2.
R.A.P. Left Centre Battn.	X.2.b.9.0.
R.A.P. Right Centre Battn.	X.3.d.6.3. (Temporary)
R.A.P. Right Battn.	X.15.b.8.2.

At each of these R.A.Ps are Four R.A.M.C. bearers. Cases are brought by hand carriage or wheeled stretcher from R.A.Ps to Advanced Dressing Station at X.9.c.0.7. Thence by wheeled ...

wheeled stretcher by day and by ambulance car by night to
X.13.c.2.0. From here to Headquarters Main Dressing Station at
W.21.b.3.9. by ambulance car.

3. From Headquarters of both Field Ambulances serious
wounded cases are evacuated direct to Nearest C.C.Ss at ~~LECOURT~~ by
motor ambulance car. All other cases to IIIrd. Corps Main
Dressing Station at V.13.c.

4. Shortly, the Decauville Railway from VILLERS GUISLAIN
will be utilized to evacuate wounded cases direct to IIIrd. Corps
Main Dressing Station from Advanced Dressing Station at X.9.c.0.7.

Issued at 10.30 p.m.

J.G. Thatcher
Captain,
for Lieut-Colonel, R.A.M.C.
A/A.D.M.S. 40th. Division.

3/7/17.

```
Copy No.  1.   D.D.M.S.
  "    "  2.   "G"
  "    "  3.   "Q"
  "    "  4.   C.R.A.
  "    "  5.   C.R.E.
  "    "  6.   135th. Field Ambulance.
  "    "  7.   136th.    "       "
  "    "  8.   137th.    "       "
  "    "  9.   119th. Infantry Brigade.
  "    " 10.   120th.    "       "
  "    " 11.   121st.    "       "
  "    " 12.   12th. Yorks Regt.
  "    " 13.   A.P.M.
  "    " 14.   Divisional Train
  "    " 15.   21 M.A.C.
  "    " 16.   Office.
  "    " 17.   Diary.
  "    " 18.     "
```

SECRET.   COPY No. 17

MEDICAL ARRANGEMENTS 40TH. DIVISION.
No 5.

Map Reference 57c. S.E. 1:20.000   19th. July, 1917.

1.   Three Brigades in the line.

      135th. Field Ambulance with Headquarters at FINS will be responsible for the evacuation of sick and wounded from Left and Centre Brigades to FINS, inclusive.

      137th. Field Ambulance with Headquarters at HEUDICOURT, 1 tent sub-division (less 1 Officer) at NURLU, will be responsible for the evacuation of sick and wounded from Right Brigade.

2.   LINES OF EVACUATION.

(A) Left Brigade.

R.A.P.	Left Battalion.	R.13.a.8.3.
R.A.P.	Right "	R.20.a.2.9.
R.A.P.	Support "	R.19.a.5.4.
R.A.P.	Reserve "	Q.30.d.8.8.

      From the two Battalions in the line cases are evacuated to Bearer Post at Q.30.d.8.8.; cases from the Left Battalion passing through Bearer Post at R.19.a.5.4. Thence to A.D.S. at Q.29.a.2.9. From here to Loading Point at Q.27.d.5.8. and thence by Decauville Railway to Main Dressing Station, FINS.

(B) Centre Brigade.

R.A.P.	Left Battalion.	R.25.d.2.9.
R.A.P.	Right "	R.26.d.50.05.
R.A.P.	Support "	R.39.c.7.7.
R.A.P.	Reserve "	W.6.d.5.5.

      From the Right, evacuation is through Bearer Post close to this R.A.P. to Bearer Post at R.25.d.2.9. Thence cases from both R.A.Ps. in the line to Bearer Post at Q.30.d.8.8. From here to Main Dressing Station as for Left Brigade.

(C) Right Brigade.

R.A.P.	Left Battalion	X.2.b.8.2.
R.A.P.	Right "	X.15.b.8.5.
R.A.P.	Support "	X.3.d.30.15.
R.A.P.	Reserve "	X.13.c.1.3.

P.T.O.

Cases are evacuated from the two R.A.Ps. in the line and from the R.A.P. in Support to A.D.S. at X.9.a.2.2. Thence to Loading Point at X.13.c.2.0. From here to Headquarters Main Dressing Station at W.21.b.3.9.

3. From Headquarters of both Ambulances serious wounded cases are evacuated direct to nearest C.C.S. All other cases to D.M.D.S. (136th. Field Ambulance) at V.18.c.

4. Shortly, the Decauville Railway from VILLERS GUISLAIN will be utilized to evacuate wounded cases direct to D.M.D.S. from A.D.S. at X.9.a.2.2.

5. Acknowledge.

J.J. Thatcher
Captain, R.A.M.C.
for Colonel.
A.D.M.S. 40th. Division.

Divisional Headquarters

Copy No.	1	"G"	
" "	2	"Q"	
" "	3	D.D.M.S.	
" "	4	C.R.A.	
" "	5	C.R.E.	
" "	6	135th. Field Ambulance.	
" "	7	136th. " "	
" "	8	137th. " "	
" "	9	119th. Infantry Brigade.	
" "	10	120th. " "	
" "	11	121st. " "	
" "	12	12th. Yorks. Regt	
" "	13	A.P.M.	
" "	14	Divisional Train.	
" "	15	36th. M.A.C.	
" "	16	Office.	
" "	17	Diary.	
" "	18	"	

SECRET.

AMENDMENT TO MEDICAL ARRANGEMENTS 40TH. DIVISION
No 5 DATED 19TH. JULY, 1917.

    On August 1st. the tent subdivision at NURLU - less sufficient personnel to run the Baths and retain the Field Ambulance site, will rejoin Headquarters, 137th. Field Ambulance at HEUDECOURT. From that date, inclusive, sick from NURLU and vicinity, will be admitted to Divisional Main Dressing Station - 136th. Field Ambulance, at V.18.c.

A. J. Luther.
Colonel.
A.D.M.S. 40th Division.

D.H.Qrs.
29/7/17.

Distribution normal and 40th D.A.C.

Confidential.

Medical Services

War Diaries

of

A.D.M.S. 46th Division
~~O.C. 135th Field Ambulance.~~
~~O.C. 136th   "   "~~
~~O.C. 137th   "   "~~

For Month of

August 1917.

Vols. XV.

G. E. Luster
Colonel
A.D.M.S. 46th Division

1st September 1917.

VOL. XV.

Secret **WAR DIARY** of A.D.M.S. 40th Division.

or

INTELLIGENCE SUMMARY

(Erase heading not required.)

Army Form C. 2118.

Place	Date	Hour	Summary of Events and Information	Remarks and references to Appendices
SOREL-LE-GRAND	1-8-17		Received 40th Divisional Operation Order No. 91. The III Corps front is to be extended on the North up to the BEAUCAMP VALLEY. Q.5.d.9.2. and the 40th Division will extend its left to take in the new area. The 121st Brigade will hand over that portion of its trenches South of X.11.a.0.6. to the 104th Brigade. 35th Division. The 120th Brigade will extend its left and take over from the 27th Regt. 9th Division. All reliefs will be completed by 10AM. 8th August.	
	2-8-17		Issued R.A.M.C. Operation Order No. 31. 135 Field Ambulance - two sufficient personnel from 137 Field Ambulance and also casualties from 119th 120th and 1st Battalion of 121st Brigade. 137 Field Ambulance will clear the wounded of the 121st Brigade front.	Issued O.O. No. 31 attached
	4-8-17		The arta taken over by 9th Division was left in a dirty condition. Bucket latrines were in general use. In the division all latrines are pole deep-pit. Flyproof types, and will be kept constructed at once to change these. Had working arrangts.	
	6-8-17		Drew up appendix of Medical arrangements for a fourth attack of 3 Divisions on the front Divisional Front. phoning Advanced Dressing Stations which could be used.	Appendix Medical arrangts. dated 6-8-17 attached
	28-17		Each Division s routes of evacuation. Visited Wounded dressing station in GOUZEAUCOURT which is very nearly complete also spray baths. Interviewed G.O.C. 119 Bgd. arrange to have made that the battalion in reserve should get...	

VOL. XV.

Secret WAR DIARY of A.D.M.S. 40th Division

or INTELLIGENCE SUMMARY.

(Erase heading not required.)

Army Form C. 2118.

Instructions regarding War Diaries and Intelligence Summaries are contained in F. S. Regs., Part II. and the Staff Manual respectively. Title pages will be prepared in manuscript.

Place	Date	Hour	Summary of Events and Information	Remarks and references to Appendices
			Rather than Riot.	
	9-8-17		Visited A.D.S. VILLERS-GUISLAIN Valley, accompanied by A.A. & Q.M.G.	
	10-8-17		Inspected Divisional Main Dressing Station.	
	12-8-17		Attended D.D.M.S. Conference at III Corps Headquarters, and later accompanied D.D.M.S. on an inspection of Divisional Main Dressing Station.	
	14-8-17		Assumed duties of A/D.D.M.S. during absence on leave of D.D.M.S. III Corps.	
	19-8-17		Attended special lecture at the G.H.Q. S. on the effects & treatment of the new gas recently used by the enemy given by the Physiological adviser to the IInd Army	
	21-8-17		Secured Rm. C. Sanitation order No. 32. No. 135 Field Ambulance now relieves division [?] ambulance in type [?] the 111th Corps Rest Station now the 111th Corps Rest Station in the 23rd inst., on [?] furnishing a detachment	Rm. C. O.O. to 32. St to At
			on the 21st. Reinforced by an extra ambulance, 2 Motor [?] opposite from Field Ambulances of 35th Division. No. 137 Field Ambulance will advance with Divisional Stores at Headquarters - a [?] & motor will take over charge of	No. 137
			B.M.B.S. at VI.E.C from 136th Field Ambulance	
	23-8-17		Inspected 111th Corps Rest Station at Moislains which has been taken over by the 136th Field Ambulance	
	29-8-17		Inspected 135 Field Ambulance and 137 Field Ambulance (Divisional Main Dressing Station)	
			Another Officer of United States Medical Corps joined the Division as a Reinforcement	

Vol. XV

Secret WAR DIARY of A.D.M.S. 40th Division

Army Form C. 2118.

Place	Date	Hour	Summary of Events and Information	Remarks and references to Appendices
	31.8.17		Relinquished duties of acting D.D.M.S. Inspected Divisional Main Dressing Station. C.J. Lutton Colonel A.D.M.S. 40th Division	

APPENDIX......

MEDICAL ARRANGEMENTS.

Reference Map.1:20.000.
57c. S.E.

ADVANCED DRESSING STATIONS.

	Position.	Splinter or Shell Proof.	Capacity.
LEFT DIVISION.	Q.29.d.2.9.	Splinter.	28 lying cases / 14 sitting "
CENTRE "	Q.36.d.6.9. (Post Office)	Shell	28 lying cases / 20 sitting "
RIGHT "	X.9.a.2.2.	Shell	40 lying cases / 80 sitting "

EVACUATION ROUTES.

LEFT DIVISION. To Advanced Dressing Station at Q.29.d.2.9.
Thence by (a) Decauville from Loading Point at Q.27.cent. (approx) to Casualty Clearing Station via Dressing Station at V.12.b.8.8. or (b) by road to V.12.b.8.8 via METZ.

CENTRE " To Advanced Dressing Station at Q.36.d.6.9.
Thence by (a) Decauville to Casualty Clearing Station, TINCOURT, or (b) by FINS-GOUZEAUCOURT Road to V.28.d.3.5.

RIGHT " To Advanced Dressing Station at X.9.a.2.2.
Thence by (a) Decauville to Casualty Clearing Station, TINCOURT, via Dressing Station at HEUDICOURT W.21.b.2.9. or (b) by night by road via VAUCELLETTE FARM to W.21.b.2.9

SECRET.   COPY No. 19

40TH. DIVISION R.A.M.C. OPERATION ORDER No.32.

Reference Map 57c.S.E. 1:20,000.

21/8/1917.

1.   135th.Field Ambulance with Headquarters at FINS, and Advanced Dressing Station at Q.29.d.2.9. will continue to clear casualties from the front held by 120th., 119th. and Left Battalion of 121st.Infantry Brigade as heretofore.

2.   136th.Field Ambulance Headquarters, and one Section will proceed to MOISLAINS on 21st.instant, and take over charge of IIIrd.Corps Rest Station from 2/1 North Midland Field Ambulance, 59th.Division. On completion of handing over Divisional Main Dressing Station, the remainder of the Field Ambulance will join its unit.

         One Section including 2 Medical Officers from Field Ambulance of 35th.Division, will be attached for duty on the 23rd.inst.

3.   137th.Field Ambulance with Advanced Dressing Stations at HEUDICOURT and VILLERS GUISLAIN, will take over charge of the Divisional Main Dressing Station at V.18.c. from 136th.Field Ambulance.

4.   Taking over and handing over to be completed by 6.p.m. on the 23rd.instant

5.   Details to be arranged between Officers Commanding concerned.   Completion to be reported to this Office.

6.   Acknowledge.

         Distribution normal plus 59th.Division.

         Issued at 2.30 p.m.

                                                    Colonel.
                                            A.D.M.S.40th.Division.

SECRET. Copy No. 21

40th. Divisional R.A.M.C. Operation Order No. 31.

Reference Map 57c S.E. 1:20,000. 2/8/17.

1. The IIIrd. Corps Front is being extended Northwards.

    From to-day the Northern Boundary will be :-
    Q.5.b.9.9. - Q.5.d.9.2. - Cross Tracks at Q.17.b.0.7. - N.E.
    Corner of GOUZEAUCOURT WOOD, Q.22.c.3.4. - Cross Tracks at Q.27.
    c.3.5., joining present boundary at V.6.d.5.5.

    The Southern Boundary will be :-
    X.12.a.3.8. - X.11.a.0.6. - X.10.b.5.7. - X.10.a.2.0. -
    X.15.b.2.8. - X.20.a.9.8. - X.19.c.7.4. - X.25.a.1.6. - joining
    present boundary at W.30.c.0.4.

2. 135th. Field Ambulance (plus sufficient personnel from
   137th. Field Ambulance) will clear casualties from the fronts
   held by 120th., 119th. and the left Battalion of the 121st.
   Infantry Brigades, to the Advanced Dressing Station at Q.29.d.2.9.

    137th. Field Ambulance (less personnel attached to 135th.
    Field Ambulance) will clear the front held by 121st. Infantry
    Brigade (less that held by the left battalion) to Advanced
    Dressing Station at X.9.a.2.2.

3. Details to be arranged between Officer's Commanding, Field
   Ambulances concerned.

4. Acknowledge.

    Issued at 1 p.m.

                                    Colonel,
                                    A.D.M.S. 40th. Division.

```
Copy No.  1.   "G"
  "   "   2.   "Q"
  "   "   3.   D.D.M.S.
  "   "   4.   A.D.M.S. 9th. Division.
  "   "   5.   A.D.M.S. 35th.    "
  "   "   6.   119th. Infantry Brigade.
  "   "   7.   120th.    "         "
  "   "   8.   121st.    "         "
  "   "   9.   135th. Field Ambulance.
  "   "  10.   136th.    "      "
  "   "  11.   137th.    "      "
  "   "  12.   C.R.A.
  "   "  13.   C.R.E.
  "   "  14.   13th. Yorks Regt.
  "   "  15.   40th. Divisional Train.
  "   "  16.   A.P.M.
  "   "  17.   36 M.A.C.
  "   "  18.   48. Sanitary Section.
  "   "  19.   Diary.
  "   "  20.   Office.
  "   "  21.   DIARY
```

Vol 16

140/2426

Confidential.

Medical Services

War Diary

of

A.D.M.S. 40th Division.

O.C. 135th Field Ambulance.

O.C. 136th " "

O.C. 137th " "

For Month of

September

1917.

Vols. XVI.

COMMITTEE FOR THE
MEDICAL HISTORY OF THE WAR
Date -5 NOV. 1917

1st October 1917

A. J. Luther
Colonel
A.D.M.S. 40th Division

I.

VOL. XVI.

Army Form C. 2118.

Secret

WAR DIARY of A.D.M.S. 40th Division
or
INTELLIGENCE SUMMARY.
(Erase heading not required.)

Instructions regarding War Diaries and Intelligence Summaries are contained in F.S. Regs. v. art. II. and the Staff Manual respectively. Title pages will be prepared in manuscript.

Place	Date	Hour	Summary of Events and Information	Remarks and references to Appendices
SOREL-LE-GRAND (V.18.d.5.7) MAP REFERENCE FRANCE 57.C. 1-20,000.	1.9.17		Inspected 136 Field Ambulance at Tn Cope Post Station Horstems Constructin work proceeding but to be kept moist	
	3.9.17		Inspected 137 Field Ambulance accompanied A.D.M.S. TN Cope. ad labs inspected were discussed. Took us when in Ambulance team & stretcher cases to a board over	
	5.9.17		Board Medical Arrangements No 6. Mor Regiments and post & Lines, lines of evacuation Here been discussed but Medical Arrangements were formed	Medical Arrangements No 6 attached
			Visited New A.D.S. G.007 Am Cent This is nearing completion selected to hospital it was to about 10 days. Also visited existing A.D.S. at O.29 d.2.9.	
	6.9.17		Inspected Divisional Main Dressing Station	
	7.9.17		Attended D.D.M.S. Conference at Tn Cope Head Quarters Arrangements being made regarding Anti-Typhoid Fort Treatment. The Truck method will be fully mer The Use of the glass Prophylaxis (investing of Fort Hygiene (Exposure Fort to the atmosphere) and application of which rub. & also suggested when the treatment cam be carried out, including lether on the village close behind the front line	
	9.9.17		Inspected 136 Field Ambulance at Tn Cope Rest Station	

Vol. XVI.

Sent

WAR DIARY of A.D.M.S. 40th Division
or
INTELLIGENCE SUMMARY.

Army Form C. 2118.

Place	Date	Hour	Summary of Events and Information	Remarks and references to Appendices
	10.9.17		Found Medical Arrangements No 7 necessary as the evacuation routes have changed owing to the New A.D.S. at GOUZEAUCOURT being taken into use from tonight and the one in Q.29.a.2.9. being given up. The new A.D.S. has accommodation - shell and gun proof - for 45 stretcher and 25 sitting cases - and all the routes to it are along made roads thus doing away with the use of tracks when the bad weather sets in. Attended lecture by Colonel Gray C.B. Consulting surgeon Third Army. at D.M.D.S. Good attendance of Medical Officers.	Medical arrangements N°7 attached
	11.9.17		Scheme for French Foot Frostbite Treatment completed. There will be Eight Salle Lavoies at various places including small centres in BEAUCAMP and VILLERS PLOUICH. The French Treatment will not be done.	
	13.9.17		Accompanied D.M.S. Third Army and D.D.M.S. 3rd Corps in an inspection of Divisional Main Dressing Station and 10th Advanced Dressing Stations. Attended Divisional Commander's Conference this morning nothing affecting Medical Corps discussed.	
	14.9.17		Two U.S.A. Medical Officers joined the Division and too others for a months instruction. Two officers named to England for Inhalation for India. Commander an Army Medical Services visited D.M.D.S. but no infirmary steward held, though interview had been arranged to attend.	
	16.9.17			

Vol XVI.

Secret WAR DIARY of A.D.M.S. 40th Division

or

INTELLIGENCE SUMMARY.

(Erase heading not required.)

Army Form C. 2118.

Place	Date	Hour	Summary of Events and Information	Remarks and references to Appendices
	19.9.17		Inspected 138 Field Ambulance at MOISLAINS.	
	21.9.17		Inspected A.D.S. in GOUZEAUCOURT, and also Baths at various places regarding erection of trucks etc for Canti trench foot treatment. The Divisional area will have 8 such Baths ready for use by the 26th inst.	
	22.9.17		A very successful Minor Operation was carried out 8/9. 14th H.L.I. this evening. Nine prisoners were captured. For Casualties see light.	
	25.9.17		A Raid on a large Scale was carried out this evening but the 12 "Suffolk Regt. 3 "Prisoners were captured. Our Casualties were much heavier. 92 wounded during ten hours with. The Dressing was arranged to convey seriously wounded cases from no. 141 M.A.D.S. in VILLERS GUISLAIN separately, to C.C.S. at YPRES. This method of transport was very successful, and the cases had a very comfortable transit - taking about 2 hours.	
	26.9.17		The Military Medal has been awarded to two NCOs and a man of 137 Field Ambulance for gallantry near the A.D.S. VILLERS GUISLAIN on the 24th inst.	
	27.9.17		Received "Warning order" regarding the relief of the 40th Division by the 20th Division about 10th October.	
	29.9.17		Inspected 137 Field Ambulance.	

O. V. Buxton
Colonel
A.D.M.S. 40th Division.

SECRET.   COPY No. 18

MEDICAL ARRANGEMENTS 40TH. DIVISION.
No. 6.

Map Reference 57c S.E. 1/20.000.   5/9/1917.

1.   Three Brigades in the line.

   135th. Field Ambulance with Headquarters at FINS will be responsible for the evacuation of sick and wounded from the Left and Centre Brigades plus Left Battalion of Right Brigade

   137th. Field Ambulance with Headquarters at V.18.c. and Advanced Dressing Stations at HEUDECOURT and VILLERS GUISLAIN, will be responsible for the evacuation of sick and wounded from the Right Brigade less Left Battalion.

2.   LINES OF EVACUATION.

   (A) Left Brigade.

         R.A.P. Left Battalion.   ... R.13.a.1.8
         R.A.P. Right   "   ... R.13.a.8.2
         R.A.P. Support   "   ... R.19.a.5.4.
         R.A.P. Reserve   "   ... Q.27.d.8.1.

   From the two Battalions in th line cases are evacuated to Bearer Post at Q.30.b.6.2, passing through Bearer Post at R.19.central. Thence to Advanced Dressing Station at Q.29.d.2.9. From here to Loading Point at Q.27.a.9.3, and thence by Decauville Railway to Main Dressing Station at FINS.

   (B) Centre Brigade.

         R.A.P. Left Battalion.   ... R.20.a.2.9.
         R.A.P. Right   "   ... R.25.d.2.8.
         R.A.P. Support   "   ... R.31.c.0.9.
         R.A.P. Reserve   "   ... Q.30.d.8.8.
                    Battalion.

   From the left/evacuation is to Advanced Dressing Station Q.29.d.2.9. through Bearer Posts at R.19.central, and Q.30.b.6.2. From the right through Bearer Post at Q.30.b.6.2. and thence to Advanced Dressing Station.

   (C) Right Brigade.

         R.A.P. Left Battalion.   ... R.26.d.3.1.
         R.A.P. Right   "   ... X.3.d.5.3.
         R.A.P. Support   "   ... X.2.d.8.9.
         R.A.P. Reserve   "   ... X.13.c.1.3.

P.T.O.

Cases from the Left Battalion are evacuated to Advanced Dressing Station Q.29.d.2.9. through Bearer Post at Q.30.d.2.9. From the Right and Support Battalions to Advanced Dressing Station at X.9.a.2.2. Thence either to Loading Point at X.13.c.2.0. and on to Main Dressing Station by Motor Ambulance.
In case of necessity, cars can evacuate direct from Advanced Dressing Station, or the Decauville Railway can be used to convey cases direct from Advanced Dressing Station to Divisional Main Dressing Station.

3. From Headquarters of both Ambulances serious wounded cases are evacuated direct to nearest Casualty Clearing Station. Otherwise all cases pass through Divisional Main Dressing Station (137th.Field Ambulance) at V.18.c.

4. Acknowledge.

Divl.Headquarters.

Colonel.
A.D.M.S.40th.Division.

Distribution - Normal plus A.D.M.S. 35th.Division.

SECRET. COPY No. 17

MEDICAL ARRANGEMENTS 40TH. DIVISION.
No. 7.

Map Reference 57c. S.E. 1/20.000.   9/9/1917.

1.   Three Brigades in the line.

        135th. Field Ambulance with Headquarters at FINS, will be responsible for the evacuation of sick and wounded from the Left and Centre Brigades plus Left Battalion of Right Brigade.

        137th. Field Ambulance with Headquarters at V.18.c. and Advanced Dressing Stations at HEUDECOURT and VILLERS GUISLAIN, will be responsible for the evacuation of sick and wounded from the Right Brigade less Left Battalion.

        The following amended evacuation scheme will come into operation from 7.p.m. 10th. September.

2   LINES OF EVACUATION.
   (A)   Left Brigade.

            R.A.P. Left Battalion   ...   R.13.a.1.8.
            R.A.P. Right   "   ...   R.13.a.8.2.
            R.A.P. Support "   ...   R.19.a.5.4.
            R.A.P. Reserve "   ...   Q.27.d.8.1.

        From the two Battalions in the line, cases are evacuated to Bearer Post at R.25.c.4.8, passing through Bearer Post at R.19.b.1 05. Thence to New Advanced Dressing Station in GOUZEAUCOURT at Q.36.d.6.9. From here to Loading Point on Decauville Railway at Q.36.c.0.4. and thence to Main Dressing Station at FINS. At night, Motor and Horsed Ambulances can evacuate direct from Advanced Dressing Station to Main Dressing Station

   (B)   Centre Brigade.

            R.A.P. Left Battalion.   ...   R.20.a.2.9.
            R.A.P. Right   "   ...   R.25.d.2.8.
            R.A.P. Support "   ...   R.31.c.0.9.
            R.A.P. Reserve "   ...   Q.30.d.8.8.

        From the Left Battalion in the line, evacuation is to Advanced Dressing Station at Q.36.d.6.9. through Bearer Posts at R.19.b.1 05. and R.25.c.4.8. From the right, cases are evacuated direct to Advanced Dressing Station.

   (C)   Right Brigade.

            R.A.P. Left Battalion   ...   R.26.d.3.1
            R.A.P. Right   "   ...   X.3.d.5.3.
            R.A.P. Support "   ...   X.2.d.8.9.
            R.A.P. Reserve "   ...   X.13.c.1.3.

Cases from the Left Battalion in the line are evacuated direct to Advanced Dressing Station at Q.3C.d.6.9. From the Right and Support Battalions to Advanced Dressing Station at X.9.a.2.2. Thence to Loading Point at X.13.c.2.0., and on to Divisional Main Dressing Station at V.18.c. by Motor Ambulance. In case of necessity, cars can evacuate direct from Advanced Dressing Station, or the Decauville Railway can be used to convey cases direct from Advanced Dressing Station to Divisional Main Dressing Station.

3. From Headquarters of both Ambulances, serious wounded cases are evacuated direct to nearest Casualty Clearing Station. Otherwise, all cases pass through Divisional Main Dressing Station (137th. Field Ambulance) at V.18.c.

4. Acknowledge.

A. J. Luther.

Colonel.
A.D.M.S. 40th. Division.

Divl. Headquarters.

Distribution - Normal plus A.D.M.S. 35th. Division.

A.D.m.S. 40th Division

Oct 1917

No. 1491

COMMITTEE FOR THE
MEDICAL HISTORY OF THE WAR
Date -5 JAN.1918

VOL. XVII.

7

Secret **WAR DIARY** of A.D.M.S. 40th Division
or
~~INTELLIGENCE~~ **SUMMARY**.
Army Form C. 2118.

(Erase heading not required.)

Place	Date	Hour	Summary of Events and Information	Remarks and references to Appendices
SOREL-LE-GRAND	1-10-17		Received 40th Division Orders No. 93. The 40th Division, less Artillery, will be relieved by the 20th Division, less Artillery, between the 5th & 10th October and will move into VII Corps area, and become Third Army Reserve.	
			All moves will be carried out by Brigade Groups and for the purpose Field Ambulances will be grouped as follows — 135 F.A. with 120th Inf. Bde. 136 F.A. with 119 Inf. Bde. 137 F.A. with 121 Inf. Bde. and from the time when they will be respectively relieved by Field Ambulances of 20th Division, they will come strictly under orders of the G.O.C. Brigade concerned.	
	2-10-17		Issued Routine Order No. 33. Probable dates of relief of Field Ambulances are given, but it is not thought best that communication with D.D.M.S. 20th Division.	Routine order No. 33 attached
	3rd-10-17		A.D.M.S. 20th Division called. Relief of Field Ambulances arranged to begin with 135 F.A. on the 5th inst. and to be completed by the 9th inst. after 137 F.A. will hand over to 61st F.A. 20th Division — 62nd F.A. 20th Division will take over III Corps Rest Station for 136 Field Ambulance. 40th Division on the 8th inst. All attached personnel of this division will be relieved by corresponding personnel of the 20th Division, to be completed by 9th inst. Received 20th Div. D.M.S. Junction order No. 94.	
	4-10-17		135 F.A. will entrain at Peronne on 9th inst. and will be in their new billets that evening?	
			136 F.A. —	- 10th —
			137 F.A. —	- 11th —

VOL XVII.

Secret WAR DIARY of A.D.M.S. 40th Division
INTELLIGENCE SUMMARY
(Erase heading not required.)

Army Form C. 2118.

Instructions regarding War Diaries and Intelligence Summaries are contained in F. S. Regs., Part II. and the Staff Manual respectively. Title pages will be prepared in manuscript.

Place	Date	Hour	Summary of Events and Information	Remarks and references to Appendices
FOSSEAUX Map France 51c. F.10.d.9.9	5.10.17.		Office of A.D.M.S. will close at SOREL and open at FOSSEAUX (Map. 51c. F.10.) at 8AM 9th October. The Command of the present Divisional Front passes to G.O.C. 20th Division at 10AM on 10th inst.	
	9.10.17.	12.Noon	Office of A.D.M.S. opened at FOSSEAUX.	
	10.10.17.		D.D.M.S. VII corps called. Evacuations will be to 6 C.C.S. Duisans. 135 Field Ambulance then arrived at BERNEVILLE. and 136 Field Ambulance at GOUY-EN-ARTOIS.	
	12.10.17		137 F.A arrived at BARLY.	
	18.10.17.		Received 'warning order' regarding move of the Division to G.H.Q. Reserve in 3rd or 2nd army areas. about the 27th inst. Since the Troops arrived in the area there has been devoted to training, and every endeavour made to note at an exhibition Programme of Recreational Training in addition. Troops resisting markedly from the change from Trench life and sick wastage is very low. although many evacuations to C.C.S. have been done owing to lack of suitable accommodation in Field Ambulances.	
	22.10.17		Proceeded on 10 days leave to England today. Lt. Col. Rowan Robinson R.A.M.C. assumed duties of A/A.D.M.S.	
	27.10.17		Received 'Q' instructions regarding advance parties to proceed tonight to HAZEBROUCK.	

Vol. XVII.

Secret WAR DIARY of A.D.M.S. 40th Division

or

INTELLIGENCE SUMMARY.

Army Form C. 2118.

(Erase heading not required.)

Instructions regarding War Diaries and Intelligence Summaries are contained in F.S. Regs., Part II. and the Staff Manual respectively. Title pages will be prepared in manuscript.

Place	Date	Hour	Summary of Events and Information	Remarks and references to Appendices
	28.10.17		This was cancelled same night.	
			Received 40th Division Operation orders No. 95. The Division (less Artillery. HdQrs. R.E. 2 & Field Coys. and 12th Bn. Yorks Regt.) will march on the 29th inst. to LUCHEUX area.	Recce orde No 95
			Issued Recce order No. 34. Field Ambulances will remain in Lawe Brigade group.	Recce order No 34 attend
LUCHEUX (Inf. Brigade Sic. F.M.A. central)	29.10.17	10 A.M.	Office of A.D.M.S. opened at LUCHEUX at 10 AM. Field Ambulances are billeted in neighbouring villages. Received instructions from 'G' that until further orders the Division will come directly under Third Army administration	

H Portnant Portnower
Lt Col Paine.
A/A.D.M.S. 40th Division

SECRET.   COPY No. 18

40TH. DIVISION R.A.M.C. ORDER No. 33.

Map Reference 57c. S.E. 1/20.000.   2/10/17.

1.   The 40th. Division will be relieved by the 20th. Division between the 6th. and 11th. of October, and will move into the 7th. Corps area via PERONNE.

   The majority of the R.A.M.C. personnel will move by rail. The remainder and all transport will proceed by road. Further orders regarding this are being issued.

2.   Troops will move by the following routes:-

   20th. Division - BUS-YTRES-EQUANCOURT-FINS.
   40th. Division - FINS-NURLU-AIZECOURT.

3. **Brigade Groups.**

   135th. Field Ambulance will be grouped with 120th. Inf. Bde.
   136th.   "   "   "   "   "   "   119th. "   "
   137th.   "   "   "   "   "   "   121st. "   "

4.   Probable dates of handing over between Field Ambulances will be:-

   135th. Field Ambulance to a Field Ambulance of 20th. Division
                                                  6th. October.
   136th. Field Ambulance to a Field Ambulance of 20th. Division
                                                  9th. October.
   137th. Field Ambulance to a Field Ambulance of 20th. Division
                                                  10th. October.

   Exact dates will be notified later.
   On relief, Field Ambulances will join Brigade Groups, arrangements being made direct with Headquarters, concerned.

5.   Field Ambulances will accommodate incoming Field Ambulances pending completion of reliefs.

6.   Command of the Divisional Front will pass to G.O.C. 20th. Division, at 10.a.m. on the 11th. October.

7.   40th. Divisional Headquarters will close at SOREL at 10.a.m. on the 11th. October, and open in new area at the same hour.

8.   Acknowledge.

                                                    Capt.
                                                    Colonel.
Divl. Headquarters.   A.D.M.S. 40th. Division.

        Distribution - Normal plus A.D.M.S. 20th. Division.

SECRET.   Copy No. 19

Addendum to 40th., Division R.A.M.C., Order No 33.

                                                3/10/17.

Para 4.   The dates of handing over to Field Ambulances
of the 20th., Division will be:-

   135th., Field Ambulance - to be completed by 5 p.m. 5th.inst.
   136th.,   "   "   - "   "   "   "   " " 8th., "
   137th.,   "   "   - "   "   "   "   " " 9th., "

Details of relief to be arranged direct between Os/C.,
concerned.

Completion to be reported to this Office.

                                  A. J. Luther.
                                        Colonel,
                         A.D.M.S., 40th., Division.

Distribution:- To all recipients of above Order.

SECRET.   Copy No. 21

40th., Division R.A.M.C. Order No. 34.

Reference Map 51c 1/40000.
28/10/17.

1. The Division (less Artillery, H.Qrs.R.E., 2½ Field Coys,R.E., 12th.,Yorks Regt) accompanied by one Divisional Supply Column, will march on the 29th., October to the LUCHEUX AREA.

   March Table attached.

2. BRIGADE GROUPS. Field Ambulances will be grouped as for last move.

3. REFILLING POINTS.

   119th., Infantry Bde. Group............COULLEMONT.
   120th.,   "   "   "   ....FONDICOURT.
   121st.,   "   "   "   ....WARLUZEL.

4. The Office of the A.D.M.S., will close at FOSSEUX at 10 a.m. and open at LUCHEUX at the same hour.

5. Issued at 2 p.m.

                                          J. Gilatch
                                          Capt, R.A.M.C.,
                                    for Lieut-Colonel, R.A.M.C.,
28/10/17.   A/A.D.M.S., 40th., Division.

Distribution Normal, plus 62nd., Division.

MARCH TABLE ISSUED WITH 40TH: DIV./OPERATION ORDER NO. 34 dated 28/10/17.

R.A.I.C.

Serial No.	Unit.	From.	To.	Route.	Remarks.
1.	Div. H.Q.	FOSSEUX.	LUCHEUX.	SOMBRIN.	Not to be west of BARLY before 9 a.m.
2.	119th. Bde. Group.	GOUY-SIMENCOURT Area.	LUCHEUX - COUTURELLE Area.	Any.	Not to enter BAVINCOURT before 9 a.m. and to be west of the line BAVINCOURT -LAHERLIERE by 10.30 a.m.
3.	120th. Bde. Group.	BERNEVILLE - SIMENCOURT AREA.	* POMMERA - GRINCOURT Area.	Main ARRAS -DOULLENS Road.	Not to be west of LAHERLIERE before 10.30 a.m.
4.	121st. Bde. Group.	BARLY - BAVINCOURT Area.	* SUS ST.LEGER WARLUZEL - SOMBRIN Area.	Any.	BARLY and BAVINCOURT by 9 a.m.
5.	244 M.G.C.	LAHERLIERE	WARLINCOURT.	-	To clear L'HERLIERE by 8.30 a.m.

(a) Units not belonging to any Brigade Group will receive instructions direct from "Q".
(b) Billeting Areas will be notified by "Q" to representative of units.
(c) * Denotes Brigade Headquarters.
(d) Intervals of 200 yards will be maintained between all units and between companies.

CONFIDENTIAL.

MEDICAL SERVICES.

WAR DIARY

OF

A.D.M.S. 40TH DIVISION.

135TH. FIELD AMBULANCE.

136TH. " "

137TH. " "

FOR

MONTH OF

NOVEMBER 1917.

VOLUMES XVIII

COMMITTEE FOR THE MEDICAL HISTORY OF THE WAR
Date 17 JAN. 1918

Vol XVIII

Secret

Army Form C. 2118.

WAR DIARY of A.D.M.S. 40th Division

INTELLIGENCE SUMMARY

(Erase heading not required.)

Place	Date	Hour	Summary of Events and Information	Remarks and references to Appendices
LUCHEUX (Map France - 51c T.16.d Central)	1.11.17		From today - the 40th Division will cease to be administered by the III Corps.	
	14.11.17		From tomorrow the Division will be administered by the V Corps.	
	15.11.17		During the past fortnight the Division has been training, and the troops are in excellent condition. Regimental Medical Officers have each 32 trained Stretcher bearers. Received 40th Division order No. 96. The Division will move from LUCHEUX to the billets in FOSSEUX area tomorrow.	
			Issued R.A.M.C. order No. 35. Office of A.D.M.S. will close at LUCHEUX at 10am 16th inst & open at FOSSEUX at the same hour.	Routine Orders No. 35 attached
FOSSEUX	16.11.17 12 noon		Office of A.D.M.S. opened at FOSSEUX. Received 40th Division O.O. No. 97. The Division will move from FOSSEUX area to ACHIET area on the night November 17/18.	
ACHIET-LE-PETIT	18.11.17		Office of A.D.M.S. opened at ACHIET-LE-PETIT. Received 40th Div: O.O. No. 98. The Division will move to BARASTRE area on the night 19/20.	
HAPLINCOURT (1.34.c.3.5. N4)	19.11.17 11.30 pm		Office of A.D.M.S. opened at 1.34.c.3.5.	
France 57c 1/40,000	20.11.17		On receipt of operation order from G branch, issued R.A.M.C. operation order No. 37. The 40th Division will move to the BEAUMETZ - DOIGNIES area at one hour's notice. 137 Field Ambulance will be	Routine operation order No. 37 attached

Secret WAR DIARY of A.D.M.S. 40th Division

VOL. XVIII II

Army Form C. 2118.

INTELLIGENCE SUMMARY
(Erase heading not required.)

Place	Date	Hour	Summary of Events and Information	Remarks and references to Appendices
			supplemented at once by Bearer Division & horsed ambulance wagons of 136 F.A. and move behind	
			121 F.Amb. The remaining F.As will remain in their present situations until further orders - 135 F.A. at BEAULENCOURT and 136 F.A. at BARASTRE.	
			137 F.A. will be responsible for the evacuation of wounded for the Divisional front, & will evacuate to IV Corps Main Dressing Stations at BEUGNY and LEBUCQUIÈRE. 137 F.A. will move under orders from H.Q. 121 W. Bgd.	
	21.11.17.		The Division moved to BEAUMETZ, DOIGNIES area, 135 and 136 F.A. remaining in their present sites. Advanced D.H.Q. opened at BEAUMETZ at Rear D.H.Q. at YPRES.	Rawe. D.O. No 39 attached
	22.11.17		Rear D.H.Q. joined advanced D.H.Q. at BEAUMETZ. Issued Rawe D.O. No 39 dealing with evacuation routes for Right sector of IV corps front, which the 40th Division was now in. Received 40th Division operation order. The 40th Division will move from BEAUMETZ area to HAVRINCOURT, whence they will relieve 62nd Division in the line and attack BOURLON WOOD and VILLAGE. Issued Rawe operation order No 40. It was thought an advanced dressing station would be taken over from the 62nd Division in GRAINCOURT, and if not, one should be established there, being in a central position, although the state of the roads East and West of the CANAL DU NORD could not be ascertained, but it was	Rawe s.o. No 40 attached

Vol. XVIII
III
Army Form C. 2118.

WAR DIARY
or
INTELLIGENCE SUMMARY.
(Erase heading not required.)

Place	Date	Hour	Summary of Events and Information	Remarks and references to Appendices
	23.11.17.		Informed that an evacuation route could be established as in Para 2, of R.A.M.C. O.O. N° 39. Adv: D.H.Q. formed at HAVRINCOURT, and Rear D.M.Q. established at NEUVILLE. K.19.b. 137 F.A. established an A.D.S. at GRAINCOURT, and an evacuation route via K.9.b. K.14.b. K.19.b. to HERMIES, when the cars were taken over by M.A.C. for the A.D.S. of the 36th.	
HAVRINCOURT. Map Reference throughout 57 c. 1/40,000.	throughout		Division. This entailed a carry from GRAINCOURT to K.19.b. and owing to the condition of the roads &c. this took a bearer squad 3 hour to accomplish. The horsed vehicles were practically useless at this stage. The Division attached with two Brigades at 10-30 A.M. each Battalion led R.A.M.C. bearer attached to the Regimental M.O. at Battalion stretchers were carried by Battalions.	
	25.11.17.		Sector fighting continued throughout the 23rd and 24th abating a little on the 25th. The Division captured BOURLON WOOD, and at one time the village also, but was forced to hold the latter a Battalion of the 1st Cavalry Division operated under orders of G.O.C. 40th Division, and 20 personnel and 6 light Cavalry ambulance wagons were attached to O.C. 137 Field Ambulance. GRAINCOURT. During the 23rd all evacuation was carried out as arranged - via HERMIES, but owing to the length of carry &c. the A.D.S. GRAINCOURT 9th Corps composite, and so evacuation of lying cases were changed to FLESQUIÈRES, and it was now possible to use the horsed ambulances wagons for the first few and at daylight on the 25th inst. 5 Ford Motor Ambulances were added	

Vol. XVIII.

Army Form C. 2118.

Secret WAR DIARY of A.D.M.S. 40th Division

or

INTELLIGENCE SUMMARY.

(Erase heading not required.)

Place	Date	Hour	Summary of Events and Information	Remarks and references to Appendices
			to reach FLESQUIERES via GRAINCOURT. A number of Cars were who went to a small A.D.S. at HAVRINCOURT from there they were evacuated to 21 & 48 CCS.; YPRES, as were Cases for FLESQUIERES.	Name C.O. No 42 attached.
			Owing to some misunderstanding apparently, between O/c ADS. GRAINCOURT and OC MAC, a large number of Cars were held up at FLESQUIERES, and no Cars could be found there till the morning of the 25th inst.	
			at 5 pm on the 25th inst. 40th Div: O.O. was received and Names O. distinguished The 62" Division will relieve the 40th Division tonight, and on relief Field Ambulances will return to AdQrs of their units. On the 23rd inst. 135 and 136 Field Ambulances were moved up to TRESCAULT at all available personnel of both F.As. sent up to reinforce 137 F.A. in GRAINCOURT. On relief - Field Ambulances were located accordingly, as follows - 137 F.A. - HERMIES. 136 F.A. - TRESCAULT. 135 F.A. TRESCAULT.	
	26.11.17		relief of all posts was completed by 5 p.m. 26th inst, and all the previous afternoon and during the night 25/26 Capt. GAFFIKIN R.A.M.C. & Bearers of 136 F.A. had through search BOURLON WOOD and the area South of it, and were satisfied that no wounded were lying out, and on relief the only cases handed over were a very few of the 40th Division and about 50 of the 62" Division who had been wounded during	

Vol. XVIII

Secret WAR DIARY of A.D.M.S.
or
INTELLIGENCE SUMMARY.
(Erase heading not required.)

Army Form C. 2118.

Place	Date	Hour	Summary of Events and Information	Remarks and references to Appendices
			The relief was carried out to evacuation upon completion quickly.	Camp OO No 43 attached
			Issued Camp O.O. No. 43. Regarding move of Brigades into Trenches.	
	27.11.17		The Division moved today into different area of VI Corps, and come under the administration of that Corps.	
			Today, Divisional Hd Qrs opened at BASSEUX, and the Brigades are in neighbouring villages in huts and billets. There was much loss and destruction of Field Ambulance equipment during the operations between the 22nd and 25th inst, and recoupling is proceeding as rapidly as possible.	
			Casualties reported to date are as follows. At 1,500 wounded of this Division have been reported to CCS, and IV Corps Main dressing station. R.A.M.C. Casualties soon Officers killed one - wounded one - other ranks killed 4 four, wounded fifteen	
	28.11.17		Orders received for Colonel Luther A.M.S. A.D.M.S. 40th Division to proceed forthwith and take over duties of D.D.M.S. XV Corps.	
	29.11.17		Colonel Luther A.M.S. departed today. Lt Col Rowan Robinson R.a.M.C. assumed duties of A/A.D.M.S.	
	30.11.17		D.A.D.M.S. attended Conference at Divisional Hd Qrs. When arranged that in future each Brigade will have 40 other ranks in readiness for use as additional stretcher bearers, in the event of the Division being again engaged in operations on a large scale. Received orders to be ready known at two hours notice.	

J W Fletcher Capt R.A.M.C.
Lt Col Rowan R.A.M.C. A/A.D.M.S. 40 Division

SECRET.   Copy.No. 7

         40th. Division R.A.M.C. Operation Order No. 35.
                                                                   14/11/17.
                    Reference Map 51c 1:40.000

1.   The Division (less Artillery, H.Q., R.E., 2½ Field Coys.R.E.
and 12th. Yorks Regt.) will move from LUCHEUX Area to FOSSEUX Area
on November 16th.

2.   The Depot Battalion will not move.

3.   Strict March Discipline must be maintained, and clock hour
halts observed by all units.

4.   Completion of move of each Field Ambulance will be reported to
this office.

5.   Brigade Groups. Field Ambulances will be grouped as for last
move.

6.   Lorries for the carriage of blankets are being detailed by "Q".
Baggage wagons will report to units at 9 a.m. on 15th.Nov.

7.   Refilling Points on November 16th.

        119th. Bde. Group.   GOUY-EN-ARTOIS.
        120th. "   "   BERNEVILLE.
        121st. "   "   BARLY.

8.   All units will re-occupy original billets in FOSSEUX Area
with the exception of D.A.D.O.S. who will be located at LA HERLIERE.
        Billeting parties will be despatched under unit arrangements
on 15th. inst.

9.   The office of the A.D.M.S. will close at LUCHEUX at 10 a.m.
and open at FOSSEUX at the same hour.

10.   Acknowledge.

        Issued at 3 p.m.
                                        A. J. Luther
                                              Colonel,

                                        A.D.M.S. 40th. Division.

        Distribution.- Normal I -- D.D.D.S. V Corps.

SECRET. COPY No.

40TH. DIVISION R.A.M.C. OPERATION ORDER No 37.

Reference Map. 57c.1/40.000.

20/11/1917.

1. The 40th. Division will move at one hour's notice to BEAUMETZ - DOIGNIES Area, and will then advance in an easterly direction.

2. 137th. Field Ambulance (less Motor Transport) supplemented by one Officer and Bearer Division and Horsed Ambulance Wagons of 136th. Field Ambulance, will follow 121st. Infantry Brigade.
Officer Commanding 137th. Field Ambulance, will be responsible that close contact is kept with all Regimental Aid Posts.
Time of move will be ascertained direct from 121st. Infantry Brigade Headquarters.

3. 135th. Field Ambulance and 136th. Field Ambulance, less Bearer Division and Horsed Ambulance Wagons of 136th. Field Ambulance will remain parked in their present situation until further orders.

4. All Motor Transport of the three Field Ambulances will be parked this evening with 136th. Field Ambulance at BARASTRE, and after that time, they will come under orders of A.D.M.S. direct.

5. Headquarters 137th. Field Ambulance will move with First Line Transport of 121st. Infantry Brigade.

6. Casualties will be evacuated from the front line under Divisional arrangements.
During the first phase, all casualties will be sent to the Main Dressing Stations of the IVth. Corps situated at BEUGNY and LEBUCQUIERE, walking cases being directed down the CAMBRAI - BAPAUME Road to the Main Dressing Station, BEUGNY.
On the advance Northwards, Divisions will make their own arrangements for both Advanced and Main Dressing Stations, locations being notified to this Office as soon as possible.

7. Personnel and Horsed Ambulance Wagons of 136th. Field Ambulance should report at once to Officer Commanding 137th. Field Ambulance, ROCQUIGNY.

8. Acknowledge.

Issued at 1.30.p.m

Colonel.
A.D.M.S.40th.Division.

Distribution :- Normal plus D.D.M.S. IV Corps,
A.D.M.S.Guards Division.
and A.D.M.S. 59th."

SECRET.

40TH. DIVISION R.A.M.C. OPERATION ORDER No.40.

Reference Map 57c. 1/40,000.   22/11/1917.

1. The 40th.Division will attack BOURLON WOOD.

    119th.Infantry Brigade will lead followed by 121st. Infantry Bde.

    120th.Infantry Brigade will be in reserve.

    The 40th.Division will have the 36th.Division on its Left, and the 51st.Division on its Right.

2. 119th. and 121st.Infantry Brigades will move tonight, route being via DOIGNIES - HERMIES and HAVRINCOURT.

    137th.Field Ambulance will follow 119th.Infantry Brigade, and will be responsible for the evacuations of casualties from the Divisional front.

3. Headquarters of the two Brigades will be in GRAINCOURT and it is possible that an Advanced Dressing Station may be taken over here from the 62nd.Division; if not, one should be established.

4. As the advance North from HAVRINCOURT will bring the Division into the Left Sector, casualties will be evacuated accordingly.

5. Frequent reports will be rendered to the A.D.M.S. Advanced Headquarters, regarding the Medical situation, giving position and all changes in Advanced Dressing Stations, etc.

6. Advanced Headquarters will open at HAVRINCOURT CHATEAU at 8.p.m. tonight. Rear Headquarters will close at BEAUMETZ at 8.p.m. and open at NEUVILLE BOURJONVAL at the same hour

                                            A. J. Luther
                                            Colonel.
                                            A.D.M.S.40th.Division.

Distribution Normal plus A.D.M.S.36th.Division. and
                          A.D.M.S.51st.   "

Secret   Copy 21

40th Division R.A.M.C. Operation order. N° 42

reference sheet 57c 1/40,000.

1. The 40th Division (less artillery, 120th and M.G. Coys. and 12th Yorks Pioneers) will be Relieved by the 62nd Division tonight 25/26th instant.

2. On relief, units of 119, 120 & 121 Inf. Bgds will be withdrawn for the night into the trenches in K.13 - K.19.
   2. 120th Inf. Bgd. HQ. will remain where they now are.
   119th Inf. Bgd. will be at the Cemetery HAVRINCOURT
   121st Inf. Bgd will be in dugouts in K.16 c.3.7

3. When Relief by Field Ambulances of 62nd Division is complete, R.A.M.C. personnel will be withdrawn as follows:-
   135 F.A. to Field Ambulance HdQrs. TRESCAULT
   136 —   —   —   —   TRESCAULT
   137 —   —   —   —   HERMIES
   All vehicles, including horsed ambulance wagons, will proceed to HdQrs 136 Field Ambulance TRESCAULT

4. All equipment in excess of Mobilization Store Table, will be handed over to 62nd Division.

5. On Relief by detachments of Field Ambulances of 62nd Division, detached parties will rejoin HdQrs of whichever Field Ambulance is nearest their post.

6. Orders for a further move of the 40th Division will be issued later.

7. acknowledge.

25th November 1917
issued at 5 pm.

J. G. Latitia
Capt. R.A.M.C.
for Colonel
A.D.M.S. 40th Division

to OC 119 and CO's 130th
M.G, 57 & 1/40 Divs.   26-11-17

1. The 46th Div (less Artillery, 130th, and 137th M.G.Co, R.E,
and 12th Yorks Pioneers) will move from Nr. K17
area today 26/11/17)
119 Inf Bde will move to LECHELLE.
138 Inf Bde will be accommodated in TRESCAULT.
137 Inf Bde will move to BERTINCOURT.

2. Tr. Aubs. grouped as under, will join their
   Bdes with the least possible delay.
      125 M.   — 130 D.
      130 M.   — 119 Bde.
      137 M.   — 121 I.D.
   137 M should be clear of cross roads G.10.a.24
   by 10 A.M.

3. OC. 130 M will detail 2 horsed Aub wagons
   to march with 137 Inf Bde and on arrival at
   BERTINCOURT they will report to OC 137 M.
   119 I Bde be clear of Cross Roads G.10.a.2.c
   by 11 a.m.

4. DHQ will close at Havrincourt at 10 A.M. &
   will open at NEUVILLE at the same time.
5. Acknowledge
                              C.G. Liveson
                                  Colonel
                              A.A.& Q.M.G. 46th Division

Confidential

Medical Services

War Diaries

of

A.D.M.S. 40th Division.
O/c 135th Field Ambulance.
O/c 136th " "
O/c 137th " "

For Month of

December 1917.

Volume XIX.

COMMITTEE FOR THE
MEDICAL HISTORY OF THE WAR
Date 29 JAN. 1918

J. Humphry
Colonel
A.D.M.S. 40th Div.

Vol. XIX

Secret. WAR DIARY of A.D.M.S. 40th Division. I

INTELLIGENCE SUMMARY

(Erase heading not required.)

Army Form C. 2118.

Place	Date	Hour	Summary of Events and Information	Remarks and references to Appendices
BASSEUX	1.12.17		Received instructions that Relief of 16th Division in the line would commence at once, and that 121st Inf Bgd group would march at once to 16th Divisional reserve area, HAMELINCOURT, and relieve the reserve Bgd of 16th Division, and on the 2nd	R.A.M.C. O.O. No 44 attached
			without further delay in the line 137 Field Ambulance marched with this Bgd group. issued R.A.M.C. O.O. No 44 giving detail of relief of Field Ambulances of 16th Division by Field Ambulances of 40th Division. This was arranged in conjunction with A.D.M.S. 16th Division. The existing evacuation scheme for that Sector was also issued with the operation orders. 136 F.A. at HAMELINCOURT to responsible for the evacuation of the centre half of the sector, 135 & 137 F.As each having a small A.D.S. and Car stand, which clear cases from the right and left R.A.Ps respectively.	
BEHAGNIES	3.12.17	10am	Office of A.D.M.S. opened at BEHAGNIES. Relief of 16th Division Completed. 137 Field Ambulance will complete the construction of VI Corps Rest Station as soon as possible at ERVILLERS. D.D.M.S. Vth to inspected 137 F.A.	
			Colonel Humphry C.M.G. A.D.M.S. 40th Division arrived	F.P. Bowya Returned for Leave
	5.12.17		Issued Medical Arrangement No 8. dealing with disposal of sick requiring in the Divisional area, also instructions No 1 regarding medical arrangements in the forward area.	
	7.12.17		Issued addendum No 1. to Medical arrangements "Evacuation Scheme". 136 Field Ambulance with advanced Dressing Stations at CROISILLES, ST LEGER and HENIN POST will be responsible for the evacuation from the whole front with the exception of the right extraction of the right sector, which is cleared by 135 Field Ambulance with advanced dressing station at ECOUST and Main dressing station at SAPIGNIES.	Medical arrangement No 8 and addenda No 1 attached

WAR DIARY or INTELLIGENCE SUMMARY

Army Form C. 2118.
VOL XIX

Place	Date	Hour	Summary of Events and Information	Remarks and references to Appendices
			Inspected A.D.S. at CROISILLES & ST LEGER. The former has good accommodation for 30 lying cases & further construction of dressing rooms etc. is being carried out. Other than this is intended to prepare to give up ST LEGER except for a small holding party, and evacuate cases direct from CROISILLES Evacuation Case to be done direct from A.D.S. to C.C.S. BOISLEUX by Daimler, or by Ambulance Car either to C.C.S. or to Main Dressing Station of 136 Field Ambulance at HAMELINCOURT.	
	8.12.17		Attended D.D.M.S. VI Corps Conference. The question of further gradient units in a Reorganization of the back area of the Corps was discussed. It was decided that each Division should have two F.As. forward, and one in reserve. Sites were suggested.	
	12.12.17		D.H.Q. will move from ARRAS HOLAM to THONICOURT. Issued R.O.N.A. Order No. 45 to this effect	Reproduced No 44 appendix No 45 appendix No 46 appendix
	13.12.17		Issued R.O.N.A. Order No. 46 dealing with moves of Field Ambulances which will commence tomorrow. 135 F.A. will hand over the present post at MAPIGNIES to a F.A. of the 25th Div. on the 14th inst. and will open at BOIRY BECOURELLE, taking over a site from a F.A. of the 24th Division at from this 15th inst. they will take over the evacuation of casualties from the left subsector by reception night cases from 136 F.A. Site later will take over that of the right subsector in reverse of order. 135 F.A. Evacuation Posts hereafter altered in accordance with Scheme in reverse of Order No 46.	
			137 F.A. will hand over their site at the VI Corps Workers Column to a F.A. of the 3rd Div.	

Vol XIX

Secret

WAR DIARY of A.D.M.S. 46th Division III

or

INTELLIGENCE SUMMARY.

(Erase heading not required.)

Army Form C. 2118.

Place	Date	Hour	Summary of Events and Information	Remarks and references to Appendices
			on the 15th visit and will then go into billets at CLONMEL CAMP, HANELINCOURT at present located there. It will retain no Coen nuclear local sick.	
GOMIECOURT	14.12.17	12 nn	Office of A.D.M.S. found at GOMIECOURT. Dressings made wholly by Ambulance Decauville Trams will be available to that A.D.S. at S LEGER at HENIN when required. Evacuate wounded direct to CCS at ACHIET-LE-GRAND and BOISLEUX-AU-MONT respectively. As it is expected that an attack will be made on the Divisional Front, at an early date 136 F.A. has been supplemented by 20 Bearers early for 135 & 137 F.A. & the latter will also supply Bearers for Battalion of Brigade in reserve to reinforce them in the event of their moving into the line at short notice.	
	15.12.0		119 Inf Regt carried out a successful minor enterprise this evening. 36 wounded were evacuated via numb 3 An Ambulance Train soon sent for the injuries from S LEGER	
	16.12.17		The enemy has been making a Gradually raids of gas shells on the last few days. at from 6 am 13th to 6 pm 16th inst 6 officers and 94 O.R. were evacuated suffering from effects of hostile gas poisoning. 16 O.R. & R.A.M.C. attd Division awarded Military medal for services at Bourlon Wood	

VOL XIX

SECRET

Army Form C. 2118.

WAR DIARY of A.D.M.S. 40th Div
INTELLIGENCE SUMMARY
(Erase heading not required.)

Instructions regarding War Diaries and Intelligence Summaries are contained in F.S. Regs., Part II. and the Staff Manual respectively. Title pages will be prepared in manuscript.

Place	Date	Hour	Summary of Events and Information	Remarks and references to Appendices
COMIECOURT	21-12-17	6 pm	Captain F.C. THATCHER, DADMS proceeded on 14 days leave to ENGLAND. Capt. P. JACOB GAFFIKIN RAMC (SR) assumed temporary duty in his place. Visited site of ADS at ECOUST. ADS is in large cellars giving accommodation for 25 lying cases in addition to personnel.	
	23-12-17	6 am	Visited ADSs ST LEGER & CROISILLES & Factory & KNUCKLE Cross posts. Inspected Trench foot Treatment rooms at CROISILLES & Baths at ST. LEGER	
	24-12-17	6 pm	The company units of 135 FA relieve ADS of T. Rees at VAULX which will shortly be taken over. Ample accommodation & evacuation is carried out by Decauville Railway. Inspected site of proposed ADS at Sugar Factory of B24 & B8. The Supplies in & material & station were on the railway so that cases from ADS ECOUST can be cleared by Train.	
	26-12-17		Visited Baths at MORY & ERVILLERS which will serve the new divisional area. Baths at MORY are now much improved. Visited v. Corps Scabies Station which will be taken over by 137 FA.	
	27-12-17		Visited 49 CCS to complete dental arrangements. Officers at 49 CCS Sundays Sewerage Farm OR & a F.A. were early visited 741 136 FA. Division taken our portion of the front previously held by the Division. Part portion of	

SECRET

Vol XIX

WAR DIARY of A.D.M.S. 40th Div.
or
INTELLIGENCE SUMMARY.

Army Form C. 2118.

(Erase heading not required.)

Place	Date	Hour	Summary of Events and Information	Remarks and references to Appendices
GOMIECOURT	27-12-17	6 p.m.	of the front formerly held by 40th Div. as handed over to 94 Division. A.D.S. at CROISILLES taken over by 94 Div. A.D.S. at ECOUST to be handed over taken over from III Div by 135 F.A. 40 Div. Scheme of evacuation until the arrival of an ambulance	App. I Scheme of arrangt adopted
	29-12-17		Remainder of III Div front taken over by 40 Div. A.D.S. at VAULX and from III Div 3 motor stations taken over from F.A. by 135 F.A. III Div Posts 3 motor stations taken over by 137 Field Amb "U"	
	30-12-17		Scheme of evacuation from the whole front in operation. Work back at MORY. Improvements are being constructed by the R.E. Numbers MORY SOUTH CAMP, & MORY NORTH CAMP. SOUTH CAMP is south of Numer huts, F in a bare & comfortless state. No beds or stoves. North Camp of Adrian huts fitted with 9 Tier beds, throughout cooking arrangements	App. I Scheme of evacuation from
	31-12-17		Visited A.D.S. ECOUST and head qrs of F.Amb. in RAILWAY RESERVE.	

Thompson
Colonel
A.D.M.S. 40th Div.

SECRET.
*****

COPY No. 18

40TH. DIVISION R.A.M.C. ORDER No.44.

Reference Maps 51b.& 57c.

1/40.000.   1/12/1917.

1. The 40th.Division will relieve the 16th.Division in the line in accordance with attached table.
Field Ambulances will be grouped as for last move.

2. 137th.Field Ambulance will relieve 112th.Field Ambulance with Headquarters at ERVILLERS on the night of 1st.December.
136th.Field Ambulance will relieve 111st.Field Ambulance with Headquarters at HAMELINCOURT on the 2nd.December.
135th.Field Ambulance will relieve 113th.Field Ambulance, with Headquarters at SAPIGNIES on the 3rd.December.

3. Officer Commanding 136th.Field Ambulance will detail an advance party of 2 Officers and 20 Other Ranks to proceed to HAMELINCOURT, to arrive there by 9.a.m. on 2nd.inst.
Officer Commanding 135th.Field Ambulance will detail an advance party of 1 Officer and 10 Other Ranks to proceed to SAPIGNIES, to arrive there by 2.p.m. 2nd.inst.

4. Details of relief to be arranged between Officers Commanding concerned, and completion reported to this office.

5. Command of the Sector will pass to General Officer Commanding 40th.Division, at 10.a.m. December 3rd.

6. Office of A.D.M.S. will close at BASSEUX at 10.a.m. 3rd. December, and open at BEHAGNIES, at the same hour.

7. Acknowledge

Issued at 8.p.m.

J.G.Matthews
Captain,R.A.M.C.
for Lieut-Colonel,R.A.M.C.
A/A.D.M.S.40th.Division.

Distribution normal - plus A.D.M.S. 16th Division.

MARCH TABLE

Serial No.	Unit.	Date.	From	To	Remarks.
1	121st.Inf.Bde.	1st.Dec.	BAILLEULMONT area.	HAMELINCOURT (Reserve Bde area)	In relief of 48th.Inf. Brigade, 16th.Division.
2	"	2nd.Dec.	HAMELINCOURT area	Line. Left Section.	In relief of 49th.Inf. Brigade, 16th.Division.
3	119th.Inf.Bde. Group.	2nd.Dec	POMMIER area	Line. Right Section.	In relief of 47th.Inf. Brigade, 16th.Division. By lorries. Lorries carry 2 battalions at a time and return for remainder.
4	49th.Inf.Bde. 16th.Division	2nd.Dec	Line Left Section	HAMELINCOURT (Reserve Bde. area)	On relief by 121st.Bde.
5	120th.Bde. Group.	3rd.Dec	BLAIREVILLE area	HAMELINCOURT (Reserve Bde. area)	In relief of 49th.Inf. Brigade, 16th.Division. To arrive in Reserve Brigade area by 1.p.m.

Details regarding lorries are being arranged by "Q"

SECRET.
******

A.D.M.S. 40th. Division No. 85(M).

Medical Arrangements for evacuation of Sick and Wounded from the 40th. Division Sector of the line, which will come into operation on relieving 16th. Division.
Location of Medical Detachments and Units.

Map Sheet 51b except where otherwise stated.

Medical Detachments or Units.	Left Section.		Right Section.	
	Left Sub-section.	Right Sub-section.	Left Sub-Section.	Right Sub-section
Regimental Aid Posts	"Shaft 126" (in Shaft Trench) T.6.d.5.8.	"Quarry" T.18.b.9.4.	"Knuckle" U.19.b.6.4.	Railway Reserve U.25.b.7.2.
R.A.M.C. Bearer Relay Posts.	Shaft 126 T.6.d.5.8. "Red Cross Mebu" T.5.a.5.2.	Quarry T.18.b.9.4.	Knuckle U.19.b.6.4. Factory Post, CROISILLES. T.24.b.3.5	Railway Reserve U.25.b.7.2.
Advanced Dressing Stations and Ambulance Car Stands.	Henin Post T.2.b.7.7. (Car Stand only at present)	CROISILLES.West. T.23.d.3.9. ST.LEGER T.27.d.5.6. (A.D.S. and Car Stands)		ECOUST Sh.57c.C2.c.4.8 A.D.S.
Main Dressing Stations.	137 Field Ambulance, ERVILLERS 57c.B.13.d.2 7.	136 Field Ambulance HAMELINCOURT, S.29.d.9.6.		135 Field Ambulance, SAPIGNIES 57c.H.8.b.3.2.
Trench Tramways likely to be of use in evacuation.	From Fit Lane at T.6.d.2.6 to "Greystones" T.4.c.5.8.	From "Janet" and "Nelly" Trenches at U.7.c.4.9. and U.13.b.1.8.to "Royal" Dump at T.18.d.9.5.		From junction of "Tiger" and "Pelican" trenches at U.26.b.6.4. to "Guinness Dump" at 57c.C.2.a.7.8

NOTE.

The Left Sub-section of the Left Section is evacuated by 137th. Field Ambulance; the Right Sub-section of Left Section and the Left Sub-Section of Right Section by 136th. Field Ambulance and the Right Sub-section of the Right Section by 135th. Field Ambulance.

In addition to the Regimental Aid Posts above mentioned, there are also small Aid Posts in Support Lines at T.22.d.60.95. and T.22.a.7.5. for the Left Section, at U.25.a.3.9. for the Right Section.

[signature]
Captain, R.A.M.C.
for Lieut-Colonel, R.A.M.C.
A/A.D.M.S. 40th. Division.

D.H.Qrs.
1/12/17.

Distribution:- "G" 119th. 120th. 121st. Inf. Bdes. 12th. Yorks.
(P) Regt. 135th. 136th. 137th. Field Ambulances and all Regimental Medical Officers.

SECRET.
******

COPY NO.

40TH. DIVISION R.A.M.C. ORDER NO. 45.

12/12/17.

The Office of the A.D.M.S. will close at BEHAGNIES at 12 noon on 14th. December, and open at GOMIECOURT at the same hour.

Issued at 9.p.m.

Divl. Headquarters.

Colonel.
A.D.M.S. 40th. Division.

SECRET.
*****

COPY NO.

40TH. DIVISION R.A.M.C. ORDER NO. 46

Reference Maps 51b.S.W. & 57c.N.W.   13/12/1917.

1. In view of the temporary readjustment of the VIth. Corps Front, the following moves of Field Ambulances will take place:-

    (a) 135th. Field Ambulance will move from SAPIGNIES on 14th. December, and take over Field Ambulance site at BOIRY-BECQUERELLE from a Field Ambulance of 34th. Division.

    (b) 137th. Field Ambulance will hand over VIth. Corps Scabies Station to 7th. Field Ambulance, 3rd. Division, at a date to be notified later, and will then move into billets in ERVILLERS or HAMELINCOURT Area.

2. From the 15th. December, 135th. Field Ambulance will be responsible for the evacuation of casualties from the Left Sub-section, Left Section, and will take over all posts etc., from 136th. Field Ambulance; evacuations from A.D.S. HENIN POST being to Headquarters 136th. Field Ambulance, HAMELINCOURT.
   136th. Field Ambulance will take over the evacuation of casualties from the Right Sub-section, Right Section from 135th. Field Ambulance; the evacuation route being altered in accordance with attached scheme. A small holding party will be left at the Advanced Dressing Station, ECOUST.

3. Details of reliefs will be arranged between Os.C. concerned, completion being reported to this Office.

4. 137th. Field Ambulance will continue to supply bearers to Units of the Brigade in reserve when necessary, in accordance with this Office No.85(M) dated 12/12/1917.

5. Acknowledge

    Issued at 4 p.m.

                                            Humphry
                                            Colonel.
                                            A.D.M.S. 40th. Division.

Distribution normal - plus A.D.M.S. 3rd. Division &
                               "   34th   "

EVACUATION SCHEME.

Medical Units or Detachments	Left Section.		Right Section	
	Left Sub-section	Right Sub-section	Left Sub-section	Right Sub-section
R.A.P. and R.A.M.C. Bearer Post	T.6.d.5.8. ↓	T.18.b.9.4 ↓	U.19.b.6.4 ↓	U.25.b.7.2. ↓
R.A.M.C. Relay Posts	T.6.a.4.4. ↓ T.5.a.5.2. ↓	By hand trucks on Decauville. ↓	Factory T.24.b.3.8. ↓	U.25.a.6.5. ↓ Factory T.24.b.3.3. ↓
Advanced Dressing Station	HENIN POST. T.2.b.7.7.	CROISELLES T.23.d.3.9 and ST.LEGER T.27.d.5.6.	CROISELLES and ST.LEGER	CROISELLES and ST.LEGER
Main Dressing Station	HAMELINCOURT (S.29.d.9.6.) 136th.Field Ambulance.			

SECRET.

ADDENDUM No.1. TO 40TH. DIVISION R.A.M.C. ORDER No.46.

"EVACUATION SCHEME"

When necessary, Ambulance Trains will be sent up to Advanced Dressing Stations at CROISELLES, ST.LEGER and HENIN to evacuate wounded direct to C.C.S.

D.H.Qrs.
14/12/17

Colonel.
A.D.M.S. 40th. Division.

To all recipients of 40th. Division R.A.M.C. Order No.46.

SECRET.   Copy No........

40th. DIVISION R.A.M.C. ORDER NO. 47.

Reference Map 51b.S.W. & 57c.N.W.   24/12/17.

1. In view of the readjustment of the VI Corps Front, the following moves of Field Ambulances will take place.

   (a) On the 27th.inst. 135th. Field Ambulance will hand over the A.D.S. and Bearer Posts of the left sub-section, left section to a Field Ambulance of the 34th.Division.
   They will move from BOIRY-BECQUERELLE to Field Ambulance site at BEHAGNIES ; move to be completed by 2 p.m.

   (b) On the 27th.inst. 136th. Field Ambulance will hand over the A.D.S. at CROISELLES to a Field Ambulance of the 34th.Division.

2. 135th. Field Ambulance will take over from a Field Ambulance of the 3rd.Division the A.D.S. and Bearer Posts at ECOUST, and be responsible for the evacuation of cases from the present Left Section of the 3rd.Division which is being relieved by the 121st.Brigade.
   Move to be completed by 2 p.m.

3. On the 29th.inst. 137th. Field Ambulance will move from billets in CLONMEL CAMP and take over VI Corps Scabies Station at ERVILLERS from a Field Ambulance of the 3rd.Division.

4. On the 29th.inst. 135th. Field Ambulance will take over A.D.S. and Bearer Posts on the Right Section of the 3rd.Divisional Front which is being relieved by the 120th.Brigade.

5. Details of reliefs will be arranged by Os.C. concerned, completion being reported to this office.

6. Detached personnel, other ranks, with 136th.Field Ambulance will rejoin their respective units on the 26th.inst.

7. The Office of the A.D.M.S. will remain at GOMIECOURT.

8. Acknowledge.

   Issued at 8 p.m.

                                             Humphry
                                             Colonel,
                                          A.D.M.S. 40th. Division.

Distribution normal plus 3rd. and 34th.Divisions.

Ref Maps 57c N.W. & 51b S.W. EVACUATION SCHEME ISSUED WITH REFERENCE TO 40th.DIV.R.A.M.C.ORDER NO.47.   SECRET.

	LEFT SECTOR.		CENTRE SECTOR.		RIGHT SECTOR.
R.A.P. & Bearer Post.	KIRKCUDBRIGHT POST.U.19.b.6.4.	R.A.P. & Bearer Post.	Rt.Sub.Section U.27.b.9.2.(left) Lt.Sect. U.28.c.9.2.(right) RAILWAY RESERVE U.25.b.7.2. By wheeled stretcher and hand carry.	R.A.P. & Bearer Post.	Left. C.5.c.8.0. Right.C.11.c.7.1. Res. C.11.a.7.5. By wheeled stretcher and hand carry.
	By wheeled stretcher and hand carry.				
Relay Post.	FACTORY POST.T.24.b.5.0.	2nd.Relay Post.	U.27.d.2.4. By wheeled stretcher or hand carry.	3rd Relay Post.	Bell's Post.C.10.b.9.3. By wheeled stretcher or hand carry.
	By wheeled stretcher or hand carry.				
			By wheeled stretcher or hand carry.	Bearer Collecting Post.	C.10.c.7.7. By hand carry or wheeled stretcher.
Car Loading Point	CROISELLES. T.20.d.2.9.	1st.Relay Post.	C.2.d.7.7. By wheeled stretcher or hand carry.	2nd.Relay Post.	C.10.c.9.7. By hand carry or wheeled stretcher.
	By Ambulance Car.			1st.Relay Post.	C.15.a.9.8. By wheeled stretcher or hand carry.
A.D.S.	ST.LEGER. T.27.d.5.6.	A.D.S.	ECOUST. C.2.c.4.8.	A.D.S.	C.20.d.2.8.
	To H.Q.,136th.F.A., ERVILLERS by ambulance car, or direct to C.C.S. by car or BEAUVILLE Rly.		By Ambulance Car to H.Q. 137th.F.A., ERVILLERS, H.Q. 138th.F.A. HAMELINCOURT or direct to C.C.S., or by ambulance car to Railway loading Point B.24.b.8.0. thence by ambce Train to Rly.unloading point, B.28. a.1.8. and thence by Amb. Car to H.Q., 136/7 F.As or direct to C.C.S. by train.		By Ambulance Train or by car to H.Q. 136 & 137th. F.As.or direct to C.C.S. as from CENTRE SECTOR.

29th.December, 1917.

[signature]
Colonel,
A.D.M.S. 40th.Division.

Confidential

Medical Services

War Diaries

of

A.D.M.S. 40th Division.
o/c 135th Field Ambulance.
o/c 136th " "
o/c 137th " "

For Month of
January 1918.

Volumes XX

COMMITTEE FOR THE
MEDICAL HISTORY OF THE WAR
Date 4 MAR. 1918

J. Glalihu Capt
+ R. A. Nauci
A/ADMS. 40 Division

SECRET

VOL XX

T

WAR DIARY of A.D.M.S. 40th Division

or

INTELLIGENCE SUMMARY.

(Erase heading not required.) MAP REF. trench S¹O S.W. Y 57c N.W.

Army Form C. 2118.

Place	Date	Hour	Summary of Events and Information	Remarks and references to Appendices
GONNECOURT	1/1/18	6 p.m.	Visited HQ 135 F.A. BEHAGNIES	
	2/1/18		Visited ADS VAULX. Heavy frosts on right sector, & Right forward & night support R.A.P.	
			Right forward R.A.P. be being rebuilt & fitted for 12 lying cases. Visited A.D.S. ECOUST, in	
			inspected ambulance BUCQUOIE Trevin arranged Trevin to run at fixed hours, in	
			order to show loads A.D.S. VAULX & ECOUST by Trevin.	
	3/1/18		Visited A.D.M.S. 25th Div & arranged joint occupation and that Division of A.D.S. at VAULX	
	4/1/18		Visited ADS ST LEGER, & R.A.P. KNUCKLE POST. Arranged sites for new R.A.P. in STRAY SUPPORT	
			Visited 229 Coy R.E. to arrange the evacuation of the new R.A.P. Visited baths ST. LEGER.	
	5/1/18		Visited A.D.S. ECOUST & R.A.P.s & bearer posts in centre sector. 170½ aft B¹ᵗʰ centre	
			sector, wished to Bomm R.A.P. at U.27.6.8.2 to withdrawn & put at Vaux & try. The	
			was approved.	
	8/1/18		Captain I.R. Huddleston R.A.M.C. appointed to command of 136 Field Ambulance and to be supp. Lt Colonel	
	11/1/18		Arrangements made with D.D.M.S.VI corps regarding the establishing of a Gas Centre at ERVILLERS.	
			Here all gassed cases from the Divisional front will be collected and receive initial treatment	
			When the Serve cases will be evacuated and slight Cases retained.	
			Inspected the Cooker of Battalions in Brigade at MORY, and arranged for examination of all kinds	

Secret

VOL XX

Army Form C. 2118.

WAR DIARY A.D.M.S. 40 Division
OR
INTELLIGENCE SUMMARY.
(Erase heading not required.)

Instructions regarding War Diaries and Intelligence Summaries are contained in F. S. Regs., Part II. and the Staff Manual respectively. Title pages will be prepared in manuscript.

Place	Date	Hour	Summary of Events and Information	Remarks and references to Appendices
			Must refer regard to March. Carlo at all auxiliary y AD.M.S.	
	12.1.18		During the past week there has been great minor operations. Casualties on the 10th sp 9.21 prisoners, our casualties have been very slight. With the exception of two days there has been very hard frost, except for one of hand frost for four days. Arch. linensfull cantern peron by field ambulance, accin los at ERVILLERS, MORY, ST LEGER ECOUST and are being constructed at NOREUIL. MWR	
	13.1.18		Lt. Col. Dunderdale D.S.O. OC 132 Field Ambulance was admitted to hospital off the strength of the Division. MWR	
	14.1.18		Captn M°Culloch N.C.D.S.O. R.A.M.C.(S.R.) appointed to command of 132 Field Ambulance. Attended Divisional Conference at 11 [?] HQ & addressed him of large influx of Adm. on the lines necessarily for very precaution to be taken against trench fit etc. MWR	
	18.1.18		Very severe weather during this week y frosts are all well over the house in most. conditions of the lines very bad - not in inhabited for the men. Adv. day y many of the Adv. temp Trench Shelters have available frozen fast in becoming one frequent on that great precaution. MWR	
	20.1.18		Inspected Corps of Pioneer are afraid them slightly improved, but still much with the same inefficiencies according KDRMS VI Corps. Good indeed considerably encouraging not noted on the Hy S. Weather has frequently changed R.W.O. Frail just so am. They arranged for the 19th inst. MWR	

A6945 Wt. W14221/M1160 350,000 12/16 D. D. & L. Forms/C/2118/14.

Vol. XX

WAR DIARY of A.D.M.S. 40 Division
or
INTELLIGENCE SUMMARY.
(Erase heading not required.)

Army Form C. 2118.

Place	Date	Hour	Summary of Events and Information	Remarks and references to Appendices
	21.1.18		Troops are now doing 48 hrs in front line, rest 4 days, then 6 in the forward area altogether 10 days in sector	
			but doing one night on working party out of the line.	
			Inspected the huts held by the Centre Hospital. Sewers in very bad condition. D.I.O. advance today	
			that the Klein huts for 10 days were available replacement to the units fortieth occupation.	
			Also issued scale of personnel in case of active operation. The closure of the line from RA13	
			to A.D.S's inclusive to attacks to O.C. 135 F.A. that of A.D.S's similarly appended to O.C. 137 F.A. All wounded	Scheme for action to be issued
			left entirely to 5th Corps. Sick both in and throughout to O.C. 136 F.A. will be evacuated to C.C.Ss ACHIET LE GRAND & Acheville Railway	
	25.1.18		D.M.S. Third Army inspects 136 and 137 Field Ambulances.	
			Sick rate is assuming low, and cases of trench feet have dropped to average of two or three	
			a day.	
	26.1.18		Assumed duties of A/D.D.M.S. V Corps at 6pm. Lt Col Hunt D.S.O. O.C. 135 Field Ambulance in addition	
			duties of A/A.D.M.S. 40 Division.	
	30.1.18		On nights 28 and 29 and 30 much enemy shelling of FRUNIERS MORY etc. artro. Rose Cunard etc our	
			1 O.R. killed and 2 O.R. wounded. Field Ambulance batols at no Frobault all finish and	

Vol. XX

War Diary of ADMS 40 Divsn

INTELLIGENCE SUMMARY.

Army Form C. 2118.

IV

Place	Date	Hour	Summary of Events and Information	Remarks and references to Appendices
	31.1.18		Tent hosp hospital round the huts.	
			Received 40th Division order No.116 regarding the relief of the 3rd Divisional artillery on the night of 1st/2nd Feb. Adv Divisional HQ on the night of 2nd to 3rd Feb.	
			Rendered report to Third army labor officer estimating the numbers of Cases of Trench Feet and the amount of dubbing returned to base — no correlation exists.	

J M Kent
Lt. Col. I.M.S.
A/ADMS 40 Division

Confidential

Medical Services

War Diary

of

A.D.M.S. 40th Division

O.C. 135th Field Ambulance

O.C. 136th " "

O.C. 137th " "

For Month of

February

1918.

Vols. XXI.

T. G. Mathew
Capt. R.A.M.C.
for Lt-Col R.A.M.C.
A/A.D.M.S. 40th Div.

Secret

vol. XXI

WAR DIARY
or
INTELLIGENCE SUMMARY. Not inferior to
(Erase heading not required.)

Army Form C. 2118.

of A.D.M.S. 40 Division

France - 57c.N.W. & 51.C.S.W.

Place	Date	Hour	Summary of Events and Information	Remarks and references to Appendices
BEHAGNIES	2.2.18		Evacuation scheme drawn up from the point of view of the Division being the right of a Corps Divisional Front, and that the line had been withdrawn to 2nd Battle System, which is a line running roughly just in front of ECOUST and NOREUIL. The present advanced dressing stations would be abandoned and others established at B.24.G.8.2. and at MORY. Evacuation from the latter being direct to C.C.Ss. by Dicceville, or if necessary to D.H.D.S. ERVILLERS for adopt cases on large numbers in horsed wagons, walking etc.	
	5.2.18		Received 40th Division order No. 117. The 40th Division (less Artillery & Pioneers) will be relieved on the line by the 59th Division (less artillery) on the 10th, 11th & 12th inst, and after relief will be in Corps Reserve, with D.H.Q. at GOMIECOURT for the 13th February inclusive. Relief of Field Ambulances to be arranged direct with A.D.M.S. 59th Division.	Received order No. 49 attached
	7.2.18		Colonel Humphry C.M.G. returned from temp. duty as D.D.M.S. VI Corps. Issued Warning order - R.A.M.C. ord. No. 48, states R.A.M.C. ords No. 49, 135 Field Ambulance will be relieved by the 2/1 North Midland Field Ambulance on the 11th inst. & will then taken over the VI Corps Main Station Gout. and approximate station BARLY 136 v 137 Field Ambulances will be with Brigades at BLAIRVILLE and MERCATEL respectively. Offices Nelson & C.N. 1/2 and 2/3 North Midland Field Ambulances Offices of A.D.M.S. will open at BEHAGNIES and open at GOMIECOURT on the 13th inst.	

Vol. XXI.

Army Form C. 2118.

WAR DIARY of A.D.M.S. 40 Division
or
INTELLIGENCE SUMMARY

(Erase heading not required.)

Instructions regarding War Diaries and Intelligence Summaries are contained in F.S. Regs., Part II. and the Staff Manual respectively. Title pages will be prepared in manuscript.

Place	Date	Hour	Summary of Events and Information	Remarks and references to Appendices
	9.2.18		Received Reinf. order No. 39 of 57th Division regarding relief of this Division.	
			Received Reinforcement order No. 68 of 6th Division regarding the relief of the 25th Division on the present night of the Division. M.	
	10.2.18		Relief of 46th Division commenced today. M.	
	12.2.18		A.D.M.S. inspected 3 Camps on Divisional Area & M.R.R. found them all in a most unsatisfactory condition. Report rendered to D.R. Relief of Division completed. M.	
GONNECOURT	13.2.18	10 AM	Office of A.D.M.S. opened M.	
	22.2.18		Majority of time has been occupied in inspecting sites of Field Ambulances, Troops having been training and much interest has been shown in Camp + improving Sanitation etc.	
	23.2.18		Issued Medical Arrangements for defence scheme in Yver sphere in Corps sector of present VI Corps front. This scheme is based on arrangements for the defence of the line being withdrawn some 5 miles from present line. M.	
	24.2.18		Received 46th Division Order who Division is in VI Corps reserve – dated 24-2-18. Also 46th Division Orders 122-126 dealing with detail of moves of troops & other matters as required of Defence Scheme.	Issued at 9.30 am
			Issued Medical Arrangements to all Admin. orders No. 50 in connection with the above.	Defence Scheme attached

A6945 Wt. W14422/M1160 350,000 12/16 D. D. & L. Forms/C/2118/14.

Vol XXI.

Secret WAR DIARY of A.D.M.S. 40 Division III
or
INTELLIGENCE SUMMARY.
(Erase heading not required.)

Army Form C. 2118.

Place	Date	Hour	Summary of Events and Information	Remarks and references to Appendices
			Have dealt with the movements & disposition of any including the possibility of the Division being required to assist either the XVII or IV Corps on our left & right Corps flanks respectively. M	
	26.2.18		Received 40th Division warning order No. 127 dated 26-2-18. The 34th Division will relieve Lieut: section of G.H.Q. left front and the 40th Division will move into G.H.Q. reserve in the BASSEUX area. Issued R.A.M.C. warning order No. 51. M	
	27.2.18		Received 40th Division order No. 126 beginning about the 3rd inst: the above will take place on the 28th February. Issued R.A.M.C. order No. 52 - 135 and 136 F.A. will not move, but will collect sick of Brigades. 137 Field Ambulance will move to BAILLEULMONT with 121 Inf: Bgd: on the 28th inst. M	R.A.M.C. order No. 52 attached
BASSEUX	28.2.18	10am	Office of A.D.M.S. opened. Col. Hunter C.M.G. A.D.M.S. 40 Division proceeded on 14 days leave to U.K. Lt Col. Hunt D.S.O. assumed duties of A/A.D.M.S. M	

J Hunt Lt Col
Clerk
A.D.M.S. 40 Division

SECRET.

COPY No.

40TH. DIVISION R.A.M.C. ORDER NO. 49.

7/2/18.

1. The 40th. Division (less Artillery and Pioneers) will be relieved in the line by the 59th. Division (less Artillery) on the 10th. 11th. and 12th. February.

2. 135th. Field Ambulance will be relieved by the 2/1 North Midland Field Ambulance on the 11th. inst., and on completion will move to YORK CAMP, MERCATEL, for the night 11/12th. February

    136th. Field Ambulance will be relieved by the 2/2 North Midland Field Ambulance on the 12th. February, and will move to BLAIRVILLE, and take over Field Ambulance site from a Field Ambulance of the 59th. Division.

    137th. Field Ambulance will be relieved by the 2/3 North Mid. Field Ambulance on the 12th. February, and will move to DURHAM CAMP No.1 MERCATEL.

3. On the 12th. inst., 135th. Field Ambulance will move from MERCATEL TO GOUY-EN-ARTIOS, and will take over the VIth. Corps Rest Station, GOUY, and the Officers' Rest Station BARLY, from a Field Ambulance of the 34th. Division.

    An advance party of 1 Officer and 50 Other Ranks will be detailed to proceed to GOUY on the 8th. inst.

    On arrival in MERCATEL, O.C. 137th. Field Ambulance will establish a Main Dressing Station for the sick of 119th. Infantry Brigade.

    136th. Field Ambulance, BLAIRVILLE, will act as Main Dressing Station for 120th. and 121st. Infantry Brigades, and will collect sick from the Brigades accordingly. The Advanced Collecting Post, ERVILLERS, will also be taken over from a Field Ambulance of the 59th. Division.

4. Details of relief to be arranged between Officers Commanding concerned, and completion to be reported to this Office.

5. Office of A.D.M.S. will close at BEHAGNIES at 10.a.m. 13th. February, and open at GOMIECOURT at the same hour.

6. Acknowledge.

    Issued at 4.p.m.

    Humphrey
    Colonel.
    A.D.M.S. 40th. Division.

Distribution normal plus A.D.M.S. 34th. Division.
A.D.M.S. 59th. Division.

SECRET.   COPY NO.

40TH. DIVISION R.A.M.C. ORDER NO. 50.
24/2/18.

TO BE ACTED UPON OF RECEIPT OF TELEGRAPHIC ORDERS.

Reference Maps.
LENS.11. 1:100,000.
51b   1:40,000.
----

1. With reference to 40th Division Defence Scheme, Medical Arrangements No.85(M) dated 24/2/18, the 40th. Division will move into the Line at a time and date to be notified by telegram

2. The relief of Brigades in the Line and move of units in the back areas will be in accordance with the attached Table.

3. All details of relief not mentioned in this Order will be made between Officers Commanding units concerned direct.

4. All Trench stores, Maps, Aeroplane photographs, Schemes of work etc., will be taken over from units relieved and receipts given.

5. Units moving out of hutments, camps and horselines will obtain certificates of cleanliness from Area Commandant.

6. Arrangements for additional transport and for accommodation of Transport in the new area will be notified later.

7. Brigadiers Commanding Infantry Brigades will assume command of their sub-sector on completion of reliefs
   The hour at which the command of the sector passes to the G.O.C. 40th. Division will be notified later.

Colonel.
A.D M.S. 40th. Division.

Table to accompany 40th.Division R.A.M.C. Order No.50

Serial No.	Formation & Units	From	To	Relieving	Route	Remarks
1.	MERCATEL Bde.	MERCATEL Area.	Right Bde. Area. 3rd.Division.	'A' Brigade 3rd.Division.	Any except that if the MAISON ROUGE FARM Road is used HAMELINCOURT Bde. should be arranged with.	
2.	HAMELINCOURT Brigade.	HAMELIN-COURT Area.	Left Brigade Area 59th.Division.	'A' Brigade 59th.Division.	Any, but if MAISON ROUGE FARM Rd. is used it should be arranged with MERCATEL Brigade.	
3	BLAIRVILLE Bde.	BLAIRVILLE Area.	HAMELINCOURT Area.	HAMELINCOURT Brigade	Any	Bus: to occupy ENNISKILLEN BELFAST, CLONMEL Camps.
4.	136th.Fd.Amb.	BLAIRVILLE	HAMELINCOURT	A Field Ambce. 59th Division	Any	Taking over Field Amb.site
5.	137th.Fd.Amb.	DURHAM Camp	BOIRY BECQUERELLE.	A Field Ambce. 3rd.Division.		Pending completion of relief will remain in DURHAM Camp.
6.	135th.Fd.Amb.				Move will be notified later.	

A.D.M.S.40th.Div.No.85(M).   SECRET.   COPY No.. 19.

APPENDIX NO. 1
to
40th. DIVISION DEFENCE SCHEME.

MEDICAL ARRANGEMENTS

dated 24th. February 1918.   Reference Maps :-
                                  LENS 1:100,000.
                                  51b. 1:40,000

Reference para 3(a) & 4(a). Field Ambulances will move under orders of Headquarters MERCATEL and BLAIRVILLE Brigades respectively.

                                        [signature]
                                           Colonel,
25th February, 1918.   A.D.M.S. 40th. Division.

SECRET.

No. 85(M)

COPY NO. 19

40TH. DIVISION
DEFENCE SCHEME
MEDICAL ARRANGEMENTS
WHEN
DIVISION IS IN VIth. CORPS RESERVE

Reference Maps.
LENS.   1:100,000
51b.   1:40,000.

1. In the event of a warning being received of an impending attack when the VIth. Corps front is held by two Divisions in the line, the 40th. Division will take over the Centre Sector of VIth. Corps Front.
   (a) The Brigade in the HAMELINCOURT area will take over the front of the Left Brigade 59th. Division.
   (b) The Brigade in the MERCATEL area will take over the Right Brigade front of the 3rd. Division
   (c) The Brigade in BLAIRVILLE area will move into the HAMELINCOURT area.
   (d) O.C. 137th. Field Ambulance will be responsible for the evacuation of casualties from the Divisional Front, and two Bearer sub-divisions of 136th. Field Ambulance will be placed at his disposal in addition to his own personnel.
   O.C. 136th. Field Ambulance will establish a Divisional Main Dressing Station at HAMELINCOURT, leaving a small party at BLAIRVILLE pending further instructions.

2. In the event of an attack taking place when the 40th. Division is out of the line.
   (a) The Brigades will be prepared to move to any of the rendezvous shown on Special Map (issued to Field Ambulances only).
   From the rendezvous the Brigades may be ordered to
   (i) Occupy a portion of the 3rd. system on the threatened front
   (ii) To carry out an immediate local attack to regain any portion of the 2nd. system in which the enemy may have gained a footing.
   (b) Pending the arrival of 136th. Field Ambulance from BLAIRVILLE, 137th. Field Ambulance will supply additional bearers to the Field Ambulances of the Divisions in whose sectors the Brigades of the 40th. Division are operating.
   On the arrival of 136th. Field Ambulance, the latter will supplement the Bearers in the sectors of 119th. and 121st. Inf. Bdes.
   137th. Field Ambulance those in the sector of 120th. Inf. Bde.

*Divisional Headquarters FAVREUIL.

3.   If the enemy attack is delivered on the IVth. Corps front, the Division will move via the MONUMENT (H.15.c.5.6) as follows
 (a) *HAMELINCOURT Brigade   )
      MERCATEL Brigade   ) Eastern outskirts of BEUGNATRE.
      137th. Field Ambulance)

      BLAIRVILLE Brigade   )
      156th. Field Ambulance) Eastern outskirts of FAVREUIL.

 (b) The Infantry Brigades will be prepared to move from the above rendezvous to occupy the 3rd. system in the Left Sector of the IVth. Corps area from I.8.a.0.8. northward to boundary between IVth. and VIth. Corps.
 (c) From the 3rd. system the Division may be required to counter-attack to regain the spurs immediately South and North of LAGNICOURT.
 (d) 137th. Field Ambulance will supplement the Bearers in the sectors occupied by the HAMELINCOURT and MERCATEL Brigades, 156th. Field Ambulance those in the sector occupied by the BLAIRVILLE Brigade.

4.   If the enemy attack is delivered on XVIIth. Corps Front, the Division will move as follows:-
 (a) Divisional Headquarters   York Lines (M.22.b.9.0.)
      MERCATEL Brigade   )
      137th. Field Ambulance)   to rendezvous "H" (N.13.b.)
      (less Transport)   )

      HAMELINCOURT Brigade   to rendezvous "G" (N 20.d.)

      BLAIRVILLE Brigade   )
      156th. Field Ambulance)   to MERCATEL area.

      In the event of Infantry Brigades moving to any of the rendezvous other than "G" and "H", 137th. Field Ambulance will continue to move with the MERCATEL Brigade, but 156th Field Ambulance will move to HAMELINCOURT area with the BLAIRVILLE Brigade.

 (b) The Infantry Brigades of the Division will be prepared to move from the above rendezvous to occupy the 3rd. system from the River SCARPE Southwards to XVIIth. and VIth. Corps boundary.
 (c) From the 3rd. system the Division may be required to counter-attack to regain the 2nd. system South of MONCHY-LE-PREUX.
 (d) 137th. Field Ambulance will supplement the Bearers in the sectors occupied by the HAMELINCOURT and MERCATEL Brigades, 156th. Field Ambulance those in the sector occupied by the BLAIRVILLE Brigade.

5. Os.C. Field Ambulances concerned will arrange for the carrying out of reconnaissance of the areas which they are detailed to take over. This is to be done at once with regard to Para 1. and all details arranged between Os.C. concerned, so that relief can be carried out without delay

6. Acknowledge.

[signature]
Colonel.
A.D.M.S. 40th Division.

24th. February 1918

Distribution normal plus A.Ds.M.S. 3rd. & 59th. Divisions.

140/2726

A.D.M.S. 40th Div.

COMMITTEE ~~~~
MEDICAL HISTORY
Date -6 JUN.1918

Vol. XXII.

Army Form C. 2118.

WAR DIARY of A.D.M.S. 49 Division
Reference Map LENS II. 1/100,000

INTELLIGENCE SUMMARY
(Erase heading not required.)

Vol 22

Place	Date	Hour	Summary of Events and Information	Remarks and references to Appendices
BASSEUX	1.3.18		49th Div. were it will be prepared to return according to the Standard order of Entrainment of trains on Division on G.H.Q. reserve. Entraining stations will be GOUY-en-ARTOIS, SMARTY and BEAUMETZ-LES-LOGES. Field Ambulances will be grouped for the move as follows:—	Pamphlet No 53 attached
			119 Fd Amb. — 135 F.A.	
			120 Fd Amb. — 137 F.A.	
			121 Fd Amb. — 136 F.A.	
	4.3.18		Received 40th Division order No 129. During the use the Division is on G.H.Q. Reserve it will be prepared to move by Rail at 24 hrs notice. Entraining may take place at PUISIEUX, SAVY, TINQUES, or ST POL, PETIT HOUVIN and FREVENT, necessitating staging at HERMAVILLE or LE CAUROY area. As 135 Field Ambulance yesterday handed over the IV Corps Rest station and moved to BENNIERS with 120th Fd Amb group the units for the move are allotted as follows:—	
			119th Fd Amb — 136 F.A.	
			120th Fd Amb — 135 F.A.	
			121st Fd Amb — 137 F.A.	

VOL. XXII

Secret

WAR DIARY of A.D.M.S. 40 Division
INTELLIGENCE SUMMARY.
(Erase heading not required.)

Army Form C. 2118.

Place	Date	Hour	Summary of Events and Information	Remarks and references to Appendices
	7.1.18.		Whilst in this area the Division has been doing considerable training. All ranks to & from the trenches.	
			BARRUELS, which is being built as a Corps Rest Station but which is not yet completed.	
			The Fld Ambulances only collect ad transport sick & ad not in training. It has now been arranged per day to have in hand in preparation to evacuate the larger number for temporarily.	
	8.1.18.		Received 40th Division Instruction N°.1, dealing with the disposition of the Division in the event of an enemy attack. It is as follows. following units (1) an attack on Li corps front, on the Right Division XVII corps or on Left Division IV corps. For this the 137th Div were to be placed at disposal of G.O.C. VI corps. (2) attack limited to IV corps will attack limited to XVII corps front. Should 40th Division move orders N°53 dealing with medical arrangements on any of the contingencies. Fld Ambulances have and to attached to each Brigade as well as utilized to Supplement the other divisions in whose area they are working 136 & 137 Field Ambulances will move to assembly places, but 135 Field Ambce will move in with the Infantry to the Places of Deployment. More casualties are laid down in the order.	Name Ward Set 2 Trucks

Vol. XXII.

Army Form C. 2118.

Scarf **WAR DIARY** of A.D.M.S. 40 Division

or

INTELLIGENCE SUMMARY.

(Erase heading not required.)

Place	Date	Hour	Summary of Events and Information	Remarks and references to Appendices
	11.3.18.		Received 40th Division order No.130. From information received it appears probable that the enemy will launch an attack on the VI corps front on morning of 13th march. The Division will accordingly move from KRASSEUX area on 12th march, to the SOISSONS area — from where they came into the present area. Board R.M.F.C. order No.33 156 Field Ambulance will Remain at BLAIRVILLE and alternate that act as a Main dressing Station in the event of active operations. The movements and the rearrangement of brigade groups as follows:— 120th Inf. Bgd. — 135 F.A. 121st Inf. Bgd. — 136 F.A. 119th Inf. Bgd. — 137 F.A. only the Bearer Division of 136 F.A. will accompany 121st Bgd. of the next forward for BLAIRVILLE. On the position which the Division may be required to take up in unknown, Field Ambulance Commanders have been instructed to hold ourselves of Regimental M.Os. and thoroughly explain all the possibilities regarding evacuation etc. 120 R. will be attached to each R.M.O. and 1 H.D. to each Bgd. H.Q. He latter will be responsible for the evacuation of the lines of communication his sector attendant on the position of the Rear of the Division holding the line.	R.M.F.C. order No.33 attached.

VOL. XXII.

WAR DIARY of A.D.M.S. 40 Division
INTELLIGENCE SUMMARY.

Army Form C. 2118.

Secret

(Erase heading not required.)

Instructions regarding War Diaries and Intelligence Summaries are contained in F.S. Regs., Part II, and the Staff Manual respectively. Title pages will be prepared in manuscript.

Place	Date	Hour	Summary of Events and Information	Remarks and references to Appendices
	12.3.18		The Brigades moved up to the war areas at dusk this evening. Field Ambulances being accommodated as follows: 135 F.A. Remaining at ALBERT. 136 F.A. also at MILLENCOURT. 137 F.A. HDrs BRESLEUX STAMPS. HDrs & 2 O.R. have been left at CARNOY. K tuts of the details of 121st & 9. on that area of HDrs of 120 & 2 Bgd at BAIZIEUX area. W/	
	13.3.18		No enemy action throughout this morning. Eight remain in BRESLEUX area in the meantime. W/ Instructions received from D.D.M.S. V corps that 136 F.A. will open as V corps acates station at Meault. Cars being transferred today from Corps Collecting Station at ERILLERS. W/	
	17.3.18		Received addendum No 1 to 40 Div Instruction No 1. Issued an amendment to 40th Div. Mary. Order No 54. This is necessary owing to the Brigades being kept in the former area – so changing the positions of assembly – also the Field Ambulances have to be regrouped, as 136 F.A. does not move with 119 Inf Bgd. and so now exchanges groups with 137 F.A. W/	amended pencil onto WD.54 attached
	20.3.18		Received 40th Division Order No 132. Should the situation remain as at present, the	

VOL. XXII

Secret

WAR DIARY of A.D.M.S. 40 Division
INTELLIGENCE SUMMARY

Army Form C. 2118.

Place	Date	Hour	Summary of Events and Information	Remarks and references to Appendices
			40th Division will relieve the 3rd Division on the left sector of V Corps front between the 22nd and 24th inst.	Tracing notes No 358 attached
			Issued Reconnaissance order No 58. 136 and 137 Field Ambulances will be responsible for the evacuation of casualties for the Divisional Front relief commencing on 22nd inst. 135 F.A. will take over the Divisional Main Dressing Station, which is also the gas station. Centre for the northern ⅔ of Corps front. The Corps scabies station will be handled over to No 8 F.A. 3rd Division on the 23rd inst.	
21.3.18			at 5 A.M. this morning the enemy put down a barrage on Corps front from FONTAINE South. 40 D.H.Q. standing to.	
		1 pm	advanced HdQrs opened at HAMELINCOURT. One Brigade of 2nd [?] Division moved into 3rd Line of defence in each of their divisions of the Corps. 121st Infantry Brigade in the centre, in a line west of ECOUST – NOREUIL – VAUX VRAUCOURT the latter in advancing in a line west of CROISILLES and just East of CROISILLES.	
			Field Ambulances not opened with Brigades – HdQrs Field Ambulances remained at HAMEVILLE, MERCATEL and HAMELINCOURT. Heavy Divisions were with their respective Bgdes.	
	22.3.18	12 m.d.	all three Brigades met in third line system in front of HAMELINCOURT, ERVILLERS, KEKAGNIES	

MAPS 1B.
57C.

VOL XXII

Secret

WAR DIARY of A.D.M.S. 40 Division

INTELLIGENCE SUMMARY

(Erase heading not required.)

Army Form C. 2118

VI

Place	Date	Hour	Summary of Events and Information	Remarks and references to Appendices
	22.3.18.	8 A.M.	Orders issued to 137 Field Ambulance to meet HAMELINCOURT from MERCATEL.	
		12 Noon	Orders issued to 135 F.A. to move from HAMELINCOURT and establish a D.M.D.S. at AYETTE, in rd. of Nation hutted which is a good winter hutted camp. But the line evacuation granules from 40 Div. had been on the lines of the Division in whose sector the Division was operating. Orders had already been detailed to the C.C.S. Receiving, namely, Band 29 GREVILLERS + 45 at 49 ACHIET LE GRAND	
		3 P.M.	Report Rece᠁ orders᠁ to᠁ ᠁ to advance D.H.Q. closed at HAMELINCOURT and opened at BUCQUOY. HdQn. of 137 F.A. ordered to proceed to AYETTE at jcuk no. 135 F.A.	
		8 P.M.	Rec᠁ orders for 136 F.A. to land over F.A. site at BLAIRVILLE and join the other F.A. at AYETTE. O.C. 137 F.A. when all teams of the Division passed at his disposal and will be responsible for the evacuation of casualties from the Divisional Front. OC 135 will run the D.M.D.S. AYETTE, which all casualties on occurred. C.C.S. Receiving No 43 BAC DU SUD, those others have been sent. Persons CCS had been closed, although no orders to the effect had been received by me. The Divisional Front now held was roughly from front in front of ERVILLERS up to and widening MORY.	
	23.3.18.	8 A.M.	Reports received during the night to the effect that all RATS were clear, that an A.D.S. had been established at HAMELINCOURT and that the M.D.S. AYETTE was receiving & evacuating casualties satisfactorily.	
		8.30 A.M.	Heavy enemy attack on MORY commenced — D.A.D.M.S. sent to 135 F.A. & got in touch with 137 F.A.	
		2 P.M.	136. F.A. arrived at AYETTE.	
		2.35 P.M.	Line now held in roughly from B16, 6,00, to 1 yd south of MORY copse.	
		4.30 P.M.	Satisfactory evacuation reports received from D.M.D.S. & O.C. Bearers. 4 horses were asked for for Lt cops. & chas waters cars, arrived.	
		7.30 P.M.	D.M.D.S. reports nursery establ᠁ Cases awaiting evacuation — It is in communication with 30 H.A.C. evacuation from HAMELINCOURT arrived, owing to southern side slip of Divisional Front. HAMELINCOURT being very heavily shelled. Good evacuation routes established via ERVILLERS — GOMIECOURT — COURCELLES — AYETTE	

MAPS 51B 57D. VOL. XXII.
57C.

Secret

WAR DIARY of A.D.M.S. 40 Div.

or

INTELLIGENCE SUMMARY

Army Form C. 2118

VII

(Erase heading not required.)

Place	Date	Hour	Summary of Events and Information	Remarks and references to Appendices
	24.3.18	9.30pm	Reports from M.D.S. & O.C. Bearers satisfactory.	
		8 AM	Quiet night, evacuation satisfactory. 137, 136 F.As. ordered to move to BUCQUOY. Sent O.C. Bearers to satisfy myself that clearing of casualties for Divisional Front was satisfactory. Visited M.D.S.	
		3.30pm	Orders for relief of Division by 42nd Division received.	
		9 pm	Enemy reported to have broken through Division on our right. 137 & 136 F.A. ordered to MONCHY au BOIS. The latter to establish an A.D.M.S. order issued to 135 F.A. to hang on as long as possible at AYETTE, and in case of a retirement to close and act as an A.D.S. with M.D.S. at MONCHY.	
	25.3.18.	2 AM	136 F.A. report that an M.D.S. has been established at MONCHY in huts - satisfactory report from O.C. Bearers. Division was not relieved owing to military situation.	
		8 AM	Right of Division slightly withdrawn during the night. Line now about 200 yards east of ERVILLERS - BEHAGNIES Road.	
		11 AM	Command of Division passed to G.O.C. 42 Division, orders issued to 135 F.A. to hand over to F.A. 42 Div: N. moves to MONCHY. O.C. Bearers ordered to remain in as long as Brigade 40 Div: was in the line. 136 F.A. to remain open at MONCHY for the present.	
		6 pm	Div: Hd. Qrs. moved to MONCHY au BOIS. Brigade relieved in the Line - O.C. Bearers Hd.Qrs. at COURCELLES. all three F.As. in MONCHY area.	
		9 pm	Orders issued to F.A.s to move to POMMIER at 8 A.M. on the 26th inst. 136 F.A. to hand over to F.A. 42 Division. During afternoon & evening large numbers of casualties arrived at 136 F.M. from other Divisions chiefly 41st Div:	
	26.3.18.	8 AM	Brigade relieved during the night and ordered to concentrate near ADINFER WOOD F.As. camped with Bgde. Worked to detail 1 M.O. & O.R. & Bgde. as liaison personnel.	

MAB. 51 A
57 c 1 D.

Vol XXII

Secret

WAR DIARY of A.D.M.S. 40 DIV.
or
INTELLIGENCE SUMMARY
(Erase heading not required.)

Army Form C. 2118

Instructions regarding War Diaries and Intelligence Summaries are contained in F.S. Regs., Part II. and the Staff Manual respectively. Title Pages will be prepared in manuscript.

Place	Date	Hour	Summary of Events and Information	Remarks and references to Appendices
	Nepr.	10 p.m.	Divl. Hd Qrs. moved to BAILLEULMONT, but found no accommodation so proceeded to HABARCQ. Brigades retant there also.	
	27.3.18.	12 noon	Brigade Dunster to WARLUZEL area. accompanied by Field Ambulances. Divisional Hd Qm. moved to WARLUZEL.	
LUCHEUX	28.3.18	9 p.m.	Divisional Hd Qm. moved to LUCHEUX. Brigade groups remain in WARLUZEL area.	
CHELERS.	30.3.18.		Divisional Hd Qm moved to CHELERS and came into XIII Corps. Brigade moved to same area as 40th Division order N°. 142 received. The Division will be transferred to XV Corps, and will relieve the 57th Division in the line, moving to MERVILLE area commencing today.	
MERVILLE	31.3.18		Divisional Hd Qm. opened at MERVILLE. Found N° 63, Relief of 57th Division Ambs, N°. 135 Field Ambulance will to hospital for the completed by Night of 1st April. 137 Field Ambulance will be in the meanwhile. 135 Field Ambulance will receive wounded and clearing the United Divisional Front in the meanwhile. 136 Field Ambulance will receive wounded and receive all sick of the Division at to in RUSNOY.	N°s 1065 W°963

Colonel
A.D.M.S. 40 Division

SECRET
******

COPY NO. 17

40TH. DIVISION R.A.M.C. ORDER NO.53.

Reference Map
LENS. 1:100,000

2/3/1918

1. 135th. Field Ambulance will hand over the VIth. Corps Rest Station GOUY, and the Officers' Rest Station BARLY to a Field Ambulance of 34th Division on March 4th., and will move to Field Ambulance site BIENVILLERS.

2. Details of relief to be arranged between Officers Commanding concerned.

3. From the 5th March inclusive, 135th. Field Ambulance, will collect sick of 120th Infantry Brigade, and will transfer them to 136th. Field Ambulance BLAIRVILLE, for treatment

4. 135th. Field Ambulance to acknowledge

Captain, R.A.M.C.
for Lieut-Colonel, R.A.M.C.
A/A.D.M.S. 40th Division.

Distribution normal plus A.D.M.S. 34th. Division.

SECRET.　　　　　　　　　　　　　　　　　　　　　　　　　　　　　COPY NO. 20

ADDENDUM NO. I. TO 40TH. DIVISION R.A.M.C. ORDER NO.54, DATED 8/3/18.

Reference Maps.
LENS. II. 1:100,000.
Sheet. 51b. 1:40,000.　　　　　　　　　　　　　　　　　　　　　18/3/1918.
Sheet. 57c. 1:40,000.

1　　　With the exception of Divisional H.Qrs., the moves referred to in Para. 2 have been completed.

2　　　The attached amended Tables A A(i), A(ii) and A(iii) are substituted for those issued with R.A.M.C. Order No.54.

3.　　　Para. 7(B)(i) should be amended to read -

　　　Divisional H.Qrs.　　　　　　to　　YORK LINES. M.22.b.9 0.
　　　119th. Inf. Bde.
　　　Bearer Divn 137th. Fd. Ambce　－　Deployment Position "H"
　　　　　　　　　　　　　　　　　　　　　　M.13.b.& c.
　　　137th. Fd. Ambce less
　　　Bearer Divn.　　　　　　　　　－　Remains in MERCATEL area.
　　　120th. Inf. Bde. Group.　　　　－　Deployment Position "G"
　　　121st. Inf. Bde. Group.　　　　－　MERCATEL area.

4.　　　Field Ambulances are grouped for the purpose of moves as follows:-

　　　119th. Inf. Bde. Group................ 137th. Field Ambulance.
　　　120th.　"　　"　　"　　.............. 135th.　"　　　"
　　　121st.　"　　"　　"　　.............. 136th.　"　　　"

5.　　　Acknowledge

　　　　　　　　　　　　　　　　　　　　　　　　　　　　Humphrey
　　　　　　　　　　　　　　　　　　　　　　　　　　　　Colonel.
　　　　　　　　　　　　　　　　　　　　　　　　　A.D.M.S. 40th. Division.

Issued to all recipients of the above quoted Order.

Table 'A'.

Table to accompany Addendum No.1 to 40th.Division R.A.M.C. Order No.54.

Serial No.	Unit.or Formation.	From	To	Route.	H.Qrs. located at.	Remarks.
1	119th.Inf.Bde. Bearer Division 137th.Fd.Ambce.	BOISLEUX ST.MARC. and MERCATEL.	"H" Deployment Position(H.13.b & d).	H.23 - H.28.	N.19.c.2.8.	
2.	137th.Fd.Ambce. less Bearer Divn.		Remain at BOISLEUX ST.MARC.			
3.	120th.Inf.Bde. Bearer Division 135th.Fd.Ambce.	ERVILLERS HAMELINCOURT area.	Deployment Position "G" N.20.d.	BAPAUME- ARRAS Road.	N.19.c.2.8.	
4.	135th.Fd.Ambce. less Bearer Divn.	HAMELINCOURT area.	BOISLEUX ST.MARC.	BOISLEUX- AU-MONT.	BOISLEUX ST.MARC.	Not to interfere with march of troops Eastwards.
5.	121st.Inf.Bde. Bearer Division, 136th.Fd.Ambce.	BLAIRVILLE.	MERCATEL area.	FICHEUX.	M.38.c.8.0.	
6.	136th.Fd.Ambce. less Bearer Divn.	BLAIRVILLE.	BOISLEUX ST.MARC.	BOISLEUX- AU-MONT.	BOISLEUX ST.MARC.	Marching under Orders of O.C. 12th.Yorks.(P).

Table to accompany Addendum No.1 to 40th.Division R.A.M.C. Order No.54.   Table 'A'(1)

Serial No.	Unit or Formation.	From.	To.	Route.	H.Qrs. located at.	Remarks.
7	119th.Inf.Bde. Bearer Division 137th.Fd.Ambce.	MERCATEL area.	Deployment Position "F" T.1.c.& d.	BAPAUME-ARRAS Rd.	Remains at M.36.c.6.0.	
8	137th.Fd.Ambce. less Bearer Divn.		Does not move.			
9	120th.Inf.Bde. Bearer Division, 135th.Fd.Ambce.	HAMELINCOURT ERVILLERS area	Deployment Position "E" T.7.d.	BAPAUME-ARRAS Rd.	R.F.C. Directing Station, BOIRY BECQUERELLE.	
10	135th.Fd.Ambce. less Bearer Divn.	HAMELINCOURT area.	BOISLEUX ST.MARC.	via BOISLEUX-AU-MONT.	BOISLEUX ST.MARC.	
11	121st.Inf.Bde.	BLAIRVILLE.	MERCATEL area.	FICHEUX.	M.36.c.8.0.	
12	136th.Fd.Ambce.	BLAIRVILLE.	BOISLEUX-AU-MONT. DURHAM "B" LINES.	via BOISLEUX-AU-MONT.	BOISLEUX-AU-MONT.	
13	H.Q.40th.Division.	BASSEUX	DURHAM "B" Camp.	Ary	Battle H.Qrs. with 3rd.Division H.Qrs. BOISLEUX-AU-MONT.	

Table to accompany Addendum No.1 to 40th.Division R.A.M.C. Order No.54.

Serial No.	Unit or Formation.	From.	To.	Route.	H.Qrs. located at.
14	119th.Inf.Bde. Bearer Division, 137th.Fd.Ambce.	MERCATEL.	Deployment Position "D" T.20. & 26	ARRAS-Bapaume Rd.	Corps Report Centre T.19.a.3.4.
15	137th.Fd.Ambce. less Bearer Divn.	MERCATEL.	ERVILLERS area.	ARRAS-BAPAUME Road.	ERVILLERS
16	120th.Inf.Bde. Bearer Division, 135th.Fd.Ambce.	HAMELINCOURT area.	Deployment Position "C" B.3.c.	via ERVILLERS.	YORK EXCHANGE B.2.b.8.4.
17	135th.Fd.Ambce. less Bearer Divn.	HAMELINCOURT area.	ERVILLERS.		ERVILLERS.
18	121st.Inf.Bde Group.	BLAIRVILLE.	HAMELINCOURT.	via BOIRY ST. MARTIN.	HAMELINCOURT.
19	H.Qrs.40th.Division.	BASSEUX.	BELFAST LINES.	Any.	Battle H.Qrs GOMIECOURT.

Table 'A' (114)

Table to accompany Addendum No.1. to 40th.Division R.A.M.C Order No.54.

Serial No	Unit or Formation.	From.	To.	Route.	H.Qrs.located at.	Remarks.
20	120th.Inf.Bde. Bearer Division. 135th.Fd.Ambce.	HAMELINCOURT area.	Deployment Position "A" E.24.	via MORY & B.22. & B.23	Bde.H.Qrs. C.19-c.5 3.	
21	135th.Fd.Ambce. less Bearer Divn.	Does not move.				
22	119th.Inf.Bde. Bearer Division, 137th.Fd.Ambce.	MERCATEL area.	Deployment Position "B" B 16.d. & B.22. b.	ARRAS-BAPAULE Rd. B.27.b.7.7. -MORY.		
23	137th.Fd.Ambce. less Bearer Divn	MERCATEL area.	ERVILLERS.	ARRAS-BAPAUME Rd. ERVILLERS.		
24	121st.Inf.Bde.Group.	BLAIRVILLE.	ERVILLERS.	BOIRY ST.MARTIN-HAMELINCOURT.	BELFAST LINES.	
25.	H.Qrs.40th.Division.	BASSEUX.	BELFAST LINES.	Any.	Divl.Battle H.Qrs. BEHAGNIES.	

Herewith 40th.Division R.A.M.C. Order No.54
dated 8/3/18.

Please acknowledge.

[signature]

Lieut-Colonel,R.A.M.C.
A/A.D.M.S.40th Division

9th.March,1918.

Distribution:-

1.	D.D.M.S. VIth.Corps	12.	O.C. 137th.Field Ambce.
2.	"G" 40th.Division.	13.	O.C. 40th.Divl.Train.
3.	"Q" " "	14	A.P.M. 40th.Division.
4.	H.Qrs.40th.Divl.R.Arty.	15.	S.C.F.(C. of E)
5.	C.R.S.40th.Division.	16	A.D.M.S.3rd.Division.
6.	H.Qrs 119th.Inf.Bde.	17.	A.D.M.S.34th. "
7.	H.Qrs. 120th " "	18	A.D.M.S.59th. "
8.	H.Qrs. 121st. " "	19	A.D.M.S. Left Div.IVth.Corps.
9.	O.C.12th.Yorks.Regt.	20	A.D.M.S. Right " XVIIth."
10.	O.C. 135th.Field Ambce	21	O.C.40th.Divl.M.G.Battn.
11.	O.C. 136th. " "	22	Diary.
12.	O.C. 137th " "	23	"
		24	Office.

SECRET.   40TH. DIVISION R.A.M.C. ORDER NO.54.   COPY.NO. 24

Reference Maps.
LENS.II 1:100,000
Sheet 51b. 1:40,000
"   57c. 1:40,000

8/3/1918

1.   In the event of an attack taking place on the front of the VIth. Corps or of the Left Division IVth. Corps or Right Division XVIIth. Corps, the Division would be placed at the disposal of G.O.C. VIth. Corps.

2.   The Division will be prepared to move forward to the following:-

Positions of Assembly.
Division Battle H.Qrs.   GOMIECOURT or BOISLEUX-AU-MONT.
Division H.Qrs.   BELFAST or DURHAM "B" LINES.
120th. Inf. Bde. Group.   ERVILLERS.
121st.   "   "   "   HAMELINCOURT.
119th.   "   "   "   BOISLEUX ST. MARC. & MERCATEL.
Divisional Artillery.   HAMELINCOURT & MOYENNEVILLE.

3.   From these positions of assembly, the Division may be ordered forward to any of the

Places of Deployment shewn on Special Map in accordance with attached Tables "A"

4.   From these places of Deployment the Division may be ordered
    (a) to occupy a portion of Third System on the threatened front,
    (b) to carry out an immediate counter attack (i.e. within 24 hours of the original attack) to regain any portion of the Second System in which the enemy may have gained a footing. For this purpose the Division will carry out reconnaisance so as to be able to counter attack to regain and hold
    (i) The front line of the Second System between NOREUIL and LONGATTE (both inclusive)
   (ii) The front line of the Second System between ECOUST and CROISELLES (both inclusive)
  (iii) The front line of the Second System immediately North of CROISELLES.
   (iv) HENIN HILL
    (v) AFCOURT TOWER RIDGE.
   (vi) The front line of the Second System North of the River COJEUL, probably in co-operation with the Reserve Division XVIIth. Corps.

5.   The Division will also be prepared in combination with one or more Divisions to carry out a deliberate counter attack (i.e. after the lapse of 24 hours), to regain any larger portion of the Battle Zone which may have been lost.
     The arrangements for this attack would be in greater detail.

6.   On the Infantry Brigades moving forward to any of the places of Deployment, they will be accompanied by the Bearer Divisions of their respective Field Ambulances and in the event of any of the operations mentioned in Para 4 being undertaken, the Bearers will be used to supplement those of the Division in whose Sector the Brigade may be operating.
     The transport will remain parked in the areas shown in Tables "A" and Officers Commanding will be prepared to move the transport and Tent Division personnel necessary to establish new advanced dressing stations if required.
     Location of Dressing Stations etc., in VIth. Corps front, are shown in Table "B". Those of the Left Division IVth. Corps and Right Division XVIIth. Corps, will be forwarded later.

7. In the event of an attack limited to the front of a flank Corps, the 40th. Division will be prepared to move from present location as follows:-

(A) Attack limited to the IVth. Corps Front.

(i) D.H.Qrs. to the MONUMENT.
119th. Inf. Bde. Group H.18.a & c. near LEUGNATRE.
120th " " " H.12 a & c. " "
121st. " " " H.10.d.

(ii) The Infantry Brigades will be prepared to move from the above rendezvous to occupy the Third System in the Left Sector of the IVth. Corps Area (from I.6.a.0.8. 400 yards North of MORCHIES, Northwards to the boundary between IVth. & VIth. Corps).

(iii) From the Third System to counter attack to regain the spurs immediately South & North of LAGNICOURT.

(iv) R.A.M.C. personnel will be employed as in Para.6. H.Qrs. Transport and Tent Divisions remaining at above rendezvous pending further instructions

(B) Attack limited to the XVIIth. Corps. Front.

(i) D.H.Qrs. to YORK LINES (M.22.b.9 0.)
119th. Inf. Bde Group "H" Deployment Position (N 20 d.)
121st. " " " "G" Deployment Position (N.20.d.)
120th " " " MERCATEL AREA

(ii) The Infantry Brigades will be prepared to move from these rendezvous to occupy the Third Trench System from the River SCARPE Southwards to the boundary between VIth. & XVIIth. Corps.

(iii) From the Third System the Division may be required to counter attack to regain the Second System South of MONCHY-LE-PREUX

(iv) As in Para 7(a)

8. Officers Commanding Field Ambulances will carry out all necessary reconnaisances, and make themselves thoroughly conversant with all existing lines of evacuations, position of Aid Posts, Dressing Stations etc

9. For all moves, Field Ambulances will be grouped as heretofore, and 136th Field Ambulance will be prepared to hand over the Field Ambulance site at BLAIRVILLE at two hours notice.

B N Hunt
Lieut-Colonel, R.A.M.C.
A/A.D.M.S. 40th Division.

TABLE "A"

To accompany 40th Division M.A.M.C. ORDER NO.54.

Serial No	Unit or Formation	From	To	Route	H.Qrs to be established at
1	119th Inf.Bde. Bearer Division. 135th.Fd.Ambce.	BOISLEUX ST.MARC. and MERCATEL	"H" Deployment Position (H.13.b & d)	BAPAUME-ARRAS Rd. thence as shown on Special Map	N.19.c.2.8.
2	136th.Fd.Ambce. less Bearer Divn.		BOISLEUX ST.MARC.		BOISLEUX ST.MARC.
3	121st.Inf.Bde. Bearer Divn. 137th.Fd.Ambce.	HAMELINCOURT.	"G" Deployment Position (N.20.d.)	BOISLEUX-M.38- M.25-N.20.	N.9.c.2.8.
4	137th.Fd.Ambce. less Bearer Divn.	HAMELINCOURT.	BOISLEUX ST.MARC.	via BOISLEUX.	BOISLEUX ST.MARC.
5	120th.Inf.Bde. Bearer Divi 135th.Fd.Ambce.	ERVILLERS Area	MERCATEL Area.	BAPAUME-ARRAS Rd.	M.36.c.8.9
6	135th.Fd.Ambce. less Bearer Div	ERVILLERS Area	BOISLEUX ST.MARC.	BAPAUME-ARRAS Rd	BOISLEUX ST.MARC.

TABLE "A"(i).

To accompany 40th.Division R.A.M.C. Order No.54

Serial No.	Unit or Formation.	From.	To	Route	H.Q.to be established at
7	119th.Inf.Bde.Group	Remain in MERCATEL Area.			
8	120th Inf.Bde. Bearer Div'n 135th.Fd.Ambce.	ERVILLERS Area	"A" Deployment Position (T.M.e.8.d)	BAPAUME-ARRAS Rd.	M.36.c.8 O.
9	135th.Fd.Ambce. less Bearer Div	ERVILLERS Area.	BOISLEUX ST.MARC.	HAMELINCOURT - BOISLEUX-AU-MONT Road, but not to interfere with march of 121st. Inf.Bde. when passing through HAMELINCOURT	BOISLEUX-AU-MONT
10	121st.Inf.Bde. Bearer Divn 137th.Fd.Ambce.	HAMELINCOURT.	"B" Deployment Position (T.7.d.)	via BOYELLES.	R.F.C Directing station BOIRY BECQUERELLE.
11	137th.Fd.Ambce less Bearer Div.	HAMELINCOURT	BOISLEUX ST.MARC.	via BOISLEUX-AU-MONT.	BOISLEUX ST.MARC.

To accompany 40th.Division R.A.M.C. Order No.54.

TABLE "A" (ii)

Serial No	Unit or Formation.	From	To	Route.	H.Q. to be established at.
12	119th.Inf.Bde. Bearer Divn 136th.Fd.Ambce.	BOISLEUX ST.MARC. and MERCATEL Area.	"D" Deployment Position (T.20 c 26)	via BOVELLES & T.25 b.	Corps Report Centre T.19.a.2.4.
13	136th.Fd.Ambce. less Bearer Divn	- do -	ERVILLERS Area.	ARRAS-BAPAUME ROAD	ERVILLERS.
14	120th.Inf.Bde. Bearer Divn. 135th.Fd.Ambce.	ERVILLERS Area	"C" Deployment Position (D.3.c.)	B.8.a. & B.2.c. YORK EXCHANGE B.2.b.8.4.	
15	135th.Fd.Ambce. less Bearer Divn.		Remains in ERVILLERS Area.		ERVILLERS.
16	121st.Inf.Bde. Group.		Remains in HAMELINCOURT Area		

TABLE "A" (iii).

To accompany 40th.Division R.A.M.C. Order No.54.

Serial No.	Unit or Formation.	From.	To	Route.	H.Q. to be established at
17	120th.Inf.Bde. bearer Divn. 135th.Fd.Ambce.	ERVILLERS Area.	"A" Deployment Position (B.24)	Via MORY & B.23 & 23.	Bde.H.Q.rs at C.19.c.5.3.
18.	135th.Fd.Ambce. less bearer Divn.	Remains at ERVILLERS.			ERVILLERS.
19	121st.Inf.Bde. bearer Divn. 137th.Fd.Ambce.	HAMELINCOURT Area.	"B" Deployment Position. B.16.d. & B.22.b.	ERVILLERS & MORY.	B.27.b.7.7.
20	137th.Fd.Ambce. less bearer Divn.	HAMELINCOURT Area.	ERVILLERS.	HAMELINCOURT-ERVILLERS Rd.	ERVILLERS.
21	119th.Bde. Group.	MERCATEL & BOISLEUX ST.MARC.	ERVILLERS.	ARRAS-BAPAUME Rd.	BELFAST LINES.

To accompany 40th. Division R.A.M.C. Order No.54   TABLE "B"

Position of Medical Units in VI(th). Corps in the event of the evacuation of First System and defence of Second System being taken up.

Division.	Advanced Dressing Station.	Walking Wounded Collecting Posts.	Main Dressing Station.
LEFT.	NEUVILLE VITASSE. HENIN. T.9.b.3.6	T.T.cent. N.24.cent.	"BRICKFIELDS" (S.2.b.7.4) For all cases.
CENTRE.	ST.LEGER (T.27.d.5.6 BOIRY BECQUERELLE (S.12.d.8.9)	ERVILLERS (B.14.c.5.1) BOIRY BECQUERELLE	ERVILLERS. (For W.W.only) Stretcher cases direct from A.D. to C.C.S.
RIGHT.	MORY. (H.22.a.9.6)	MORY.	As for centre division.

SECRET.
8 copies

Reference Para 8. 40th.Division R.A.M.C.Order No.54. dated
8/3/18.

Position of Medical Units.

Left Sector of XVIIth.Corps Front.

1. (A) "A" Field Ambulance.
    H.Qrs. of M.D.S.   FAVREUIL.   H.18.d.9.0
    Advanced Dressing Station.   VAULX.   C.20.d.1.0.
    R.A.M.C. Relay Posts   C.17.d.7.5.
                                                            C.17.b.9.7.
                                                            C.16.b.8.1.
                                                            C.16.a.4.3.

   (B) "A" Field Ambulance collects from the Left Brigade in the
        line clearing the following R.A.Ps.

            C.17.d.7.2.
            C.23.b.3.9.

   (C) The Advanced Dressing Station at VAULX is not in the direct
        line of evacuation and so only deals with local casualties.
        Therefore cases from the front are evacuated to a Loading
        Post at C.23.c.6.5. and thence direct to M.D.S. FAVREUIL.

2. (A) "B" Field Ambulance.
    H.Qrs. & M.D.S.   FAVREUIL.   H.18.d.95.40.
    Advanced Dressing Station.   LAGNICOURT.   C.29.a.6.0.
    R.A.M.C. Relay Posts   D.25.d.7.5.
                                                            C.24.d.95.50.
                                                            C.30.a.5.0.

   (B) "B" Field Ambulance collects from the Centre and Right
        Brigades in the line clearing the following R.A.Ps.
            D.25.d.9.5.(combined).
            C.24.d.95.50.
            C.30.a.5.0

Right Sector of XVIIth.Corps Front.

	Right Brigade.	Left Brigade.
R.A.Ps.	H.30.d.2.5. (2)	H.24.b.5.7
	H.36.c.1.9.	H.24.a.5.7. (2)(Triple Arch)
Relay Posts.	H.29.c.8.4.	H.24.a.5.7.
	H.24.c.2.8.	H.18.d.2.5. (Single Arch)
A.D.S.	FAMPOUX LOCK (H.23.a.9.5.)	
	FEUCHY. (H.21.c.9.5)	
Divisional Walking Wounded Collecting Post.	ATHIES LOCK (H.21.a.9.6.)	
Corps Walking Wounded Collecting Post.	ST.NICHOLAS.	
	TILLOY.	
C.M.D.S.	ECOLE NORMALE.	

H.Qrs.   Lieut-Colonel, R.A.M.C.
13/3/18.   A/A.D.M.S.40th.Division.

A.D.M.S.
40th DIVISION.
No. 156(m)
Date 13-3-18

SECRET.   COPY NO. 23

40TH. DIVISION R.A.M.C. ORDER NO. 55.

Reference Maps.
LENS.II.   1:100.000.
Sheet 51b. 1:40.000.
Sheet 57c. 1:40.000.   11/3/1918.

1.   From information received it appears probable that the enemy will launch an attack on the VIth.Corps front on morning of 13th.March

2.   The 40th.Division will move from the BASSEUX AREA to the BOISLEUX AREA on the 12th. March in accordance with attached March Table.

3.   Pending the above move, the Division is still to be held in readiness to march at 12 hours notice, and the instructions regarding movements other than by rail, contained in 40th.Division R.A.M.C. Order No.54 dated 7/3/18 remain in force until 3.p.m. 12th.March
        Divisional Order No.129 dated 4/3/18, may be brought into force at any time even after the march to BOISLEUX AREA has been completed.

4.   Any instructions and Tables contained in 40th.Division R.A.M.C. Order No.54 not cancelled or amended by this Order, will remain in force.

5.   For the purpose of the move and for accommodation in the BOISLEUX AREA, Field Ambulances will be brigaded as follows:-

        135th.Field Ambulance............120th Infantry Bde. Group.
        136th. "   "   ....121st.   "   "   "
        137th. "   "   ....119th.   "   "   "

6.   In the event of the Brigades moving forward from the BOISLEUX AREA Bearer Divisions 135th. & 137th. Field Ambulances will be prepared to operate as laid down in 40th.Division R.A.M.C. Order No.54. The Tent Sub-divisions of 135th. & 137th Field Ambulances will be prepared to assist at Main Dressing Stations at FICHEUX (S.2.0.7.4.) and ERVILLERS if required. 136th.Field Ambulance will remain at BLAIRVILLE and continue to administer that Field Ambulance site, as laid down in VIth.Corps Medical Defence Scheme. The Bearer Division of 136th.Field Ambulance will be held in reserve and prepared to move forward at one hour's notice.

7.   Advanced parties will be sent forward on 12th.March.

8.   Care must be taken that no extra lights or fires which might be seen by the enemy are lit by troops arriving in the new area.

9.   135th. & 137th.Field Ambulances will dump surplus kits, equipment etc., in accordance with this Office No.156(M) dated 10/3/18.

10.   Greatcoats will be taken on the man.
        One blanket per man will be conveyed by lorries to the new area.

11.   Office of A.D.M.S. will remain at BASSEUX for the present.

12.   Acknowledge.

                                        [signature]
                                        Lieut-Colonel,R.A.M.C.
                                        A/A.D.M.S.40th.Division.

Distribution normal,- plus A.D.M.S. 3rd. 34th. & 59th.Divisions
                            A.D.M.S.Left Divn.IVth.Corps
                            A.D.M.S.Right   "   XVIIth.Corps.

Table to accompany 40th.Division R.A.M.C. Order No.55. dated 11th.March,1918.

Serial No	Unit.	From	To	Route.	Remarks.
1.	119th.Inf.Bde.	BLAIRVILLE Area.	MERCATEL & BOISLEUX Areas.	Any.	Bde.H.Qrs S.5.b.5.9.
2.	137th.Fd Ambce	BAILLEUMONT Area.	MERCATEL or BOISLEUX Area.	BELLACOURT-BRETENCOURT-BLAIRVILLE.	To accompany 121st.Inf.Bde. as far as BLAIRVILLE.
3.	120th.Inf.Bde. 135th.Fd.Ambce	POMMIER Area	HAMELINCOURT & ERVILLERS Area.	MONCHY-ADINFER-AYETTE-MOYENNEVILLE-or COURCELLES.	Bde.H.Qrs. A 5.b.5.2.
4.	121st.Inf.Bde.	BAILLEUMONT Area.	BLAIRVILLE.	BELLACOURT-BRETENCOURT.	Bde.H.Qrs. BLAIRVILLE.
5.	136th.Fd.Ambce		Remains at BLAIRVILLE.		

SECRET   COPY NO. 20

40TH. DIVISION R.A.M.C. ORDER NO. 56

Reference Map.   20/3/18.
51b.1:40,000.

1.   Should the situation remain as at present, the 40th.Division will relieve the 3rd.Division in the Left Sector of the VIth.Corps front, in accordance with attached table.

2.   The Infantry reliefs will be completed by 6.a.m. 24th.March.

3.   Details at present in the BASSEUX Area will rejoin their units on afternoon 21st.March

4.   137th.Field Ambulance will take over the Left Sub-Sector, with Advanced Dressing Station at MARLIERE (N.17.d.2.5) and H.Qrs.at BOISLEUX-AU-MONT (S.10.central) from No.7th.Field Ambulance on the evening of the 22nd.March.
        136th.Field Ambulance will take over the Right Sub-Sector, with Advanced Dressing Station at HENIN (N.32.d.2.0) and H.Qrs. at BOISLEUX-AU-MONT (S.10.central) from No.8th.Field Ambulance on the evening of 23rd.March.
        The evacuation of cases from the Centre Sub-Sector will be carried out by 137th.Field Ambulance, unless it is found more advisable for 136th.Field Ambulance to take over the Right of that Sector.
        135th.Field Ambulance will take over the Divisional Main Dressing Station at FICHEUX (S.2.b.7.4) from 142nd.Field Ambulance on the 24th.March.

5.   136th.Field Ambulance will hand over the VIth.Corps Scabies Station to No.8 Field Ambulance on the 23rd.March.

6.   Advanced parties will proceed as follows:-

137th.Field Ambce. 1.Off. 20.O.Rs. to MARLIERE on 21st.inst.to take over line
136th.   "   "   "   "   HENIN   "   "   "   "   "   "
135th.   "   "   "   "   FICHEUX   " 23rd.   "   "   "   " DMDS
 5th.   "   "   12.O.Rs. " BLAIRVILLE " 22nd.   "   "   "   " CSS

7   All details to be arranged between Os.C. concerned, and completion of reliefs reported to this Office

8.   All hutments, Camps and horse lines will be handed over in a perfectly clean condition, and certificates of cleanliness obtained.

9.   The G.O.C. 40th.Division will assume command of the Left Sector of the VIth.Corps Front at 10.a.m. 24th.March.

10.   Office of A.D.M.S. will close at BASSEUX at 10.a.m. 24th.March and open at BOISLEUX-AU-MONT, at the same hour

11.   Acknowledge.

                                                    Colonel.
                                              A.D.M.S 40th Division.

        Distribution normal plus A.Ds.M.S. 3rd & 34th.Divisions.
                  A.D.M.S. Right Division XVIIth.Corps.

Table to accompany 40th.Division R.A.&.C. Order No.56 dated 20/3/18.

Serial No.	Date	Unit or Formation	From	To.	Route.	Remarks.
1.	Night 22/23rd.Mar.	119th.Inf.Bde. 229th.Field Coy.R.E.	ERCATEL Area.	Line,Left Sub-Sector.	Any.	Relieving 76th.Inf.Bde.
2.	Night 22/23rd.Mar.	120th.Inf.Bde. 231st.Field Coy.R.E.	HABLINCOURT Area	Line,Right Sub-Sector.	Bus.	Relieving 9th.Inf.Bde.
3.	Night 23/24th Mar.	121st.Inf.Bde. 224th.Field Coy.R.E.	BLAINVILLE Area.	Line, Centre Sub-Sector Bus.		Relieving 8th.Inf.Bde.
4.	23rd March.	12th York Regt.(Pnr)	BLAINVILLE.	ERCATEL (YORK LINES).	Any.	
5.	Night 24/25th.Mar.	40th.Div.Artillery. 2 Sections per Batty.	Wagon Lines OISNEVILLE & BOIRY ST RICTRUDE	Line.	Any.	In relief of corresponding sections of 3rd.Div.Arty.
6.	Night 25/26th Mar.	40th.Div.Artillery 1 Section per Batty.	... do ...	Line.	Any.	To complete relief of 3rd. Div.Artillery.
7.	26th March	40th.Div Artillery Wagon Lines.	... do ...	FICHEUX.	Any.	

SECRET.   COPY NO. 16

40th. Division R.A.M.C. Order No. 63.

Reference Map.   31/3/18.
  36 & 36A.
  1/40.000.

1.   The 40th. Division will relieve the 57th. Division in the line between the 31st. March and 2nd. April.

2.   120th. Infantry Brigade relieves 172nd. Infantry Brigade in the Right Sector on night 31st. March - 1st. April.
        121st. Infantry Brigade relieves 171 Infantry Brigade in the Left Sector on night 1/2nd. April.
        119th. Infantry Brigade moves into SAILLY-SUR-LYS MONDE area on April 2nd., and remains there in Divisional Reserve.

3(a)   O.C. 137th. Field Ambulance will relieve the 3/2 West Lancs. Field Ambulance in the Right Sector of the Line on April 1st., relief to be completed by 12 noon. He will relieve the 2/3 Wessex Field Ambulance in the Left Sector on April 1st., relief to be completed by 4.p.m. O.C. 137th. Field Ambulance will established his Headquarters at FORT ROMPU (H.7.d.6.3) and will be responsible for the evacuation of casualties from the Divisional Front.
 (B)   O.C. 136th. Field Ambulance will take over from O.C. 137th. Field Ambulance on April 2nd., the Main Dressing Station at SAILLY (G.17.a.7.3) and will receive all wounded from the Divisional Front, and transfer them to C.C.S.
 (C)   O.C. 135th. Field Ambulance will take over on April 1st. the Main Dressing Station at DOULIEU (H.25.d.4.4.) from O.C. 2/2 Wessex Field Ambulance, and will receive all sick from the Division.

4.   Details of reliefs to be arranged between Officers Commanding concerned, and completion reported to this Office.

5.   Office of A.D.M.S. will close at MERVILLE at 10.a.m. April 2nd. and open at CROIX-DU-BAC at the same hour.

6.   Acknowledge.

                                                (sd) F.G. THATCHER, Capt.
                                                       for Colonel.
                                                   A.D.M.S. 40th. Division.

Distribution normal - plus A.D.M.S. 57th. Division.

Confidential.
Medical Services.
War Diaries
of
A.D.M.S. 48th Division.
O.C. 135th Field Ambulance.
O.C. 136th " "
O.C. 137th " "
For Month of
April, 1918.
Vols. XXIII.

Humphrey
Colonel
A.D.M.S. 48th Division

Reference Maps
France & Belgium 36 & 36A Secret
HAZEBROUCK 5A
sht 27)

VOL XXIII

WAR DIARY of A.D.M.S. 40 Div.
or
INTELLIGENCE SUMMARY
(Erase heading not required.)

Army Form C.2118

Place	Date	Hour	Summary of Events and Information	Remarks and references to Appendices
CROIX DU BAC	2.4.18	10 AM	Officer of A.D.M.S. found at CROIX DU BAC. Relief of 57th Division complete. Units of Medical units as follows:- 135 F.A. at DOULIEU. Removing Main dressing station for sick. 137 Field Ambulance at FORT ROMPU, and clearing the line. 136 Field Ambulance at SAILLY, receiving wounded and gassed cases, and evacuating direct to C.C.S.	
	5.4.18		Bearer Divisions clearing the line of their respective Infantry Brigades. At present 137 F.A. clearing the left sector and 136 F.A. the right.	
	9.4.18		Position of medical units at midnight 8/9th April was as follows:- 137 F.A. with H.d.Qrs. and Tent Division at FORT ROMPU, advanced dressing station at AUX TROIS TOULETTES (H.22.6.61) and Bearer and Car posts connecting with Battalions in the line. 136 Field Ambulance with H.d.Qrs. and Main Dressing Station at SAILLY (G.11.d.6.4) and advanced dressing station for Right Bgd. at LA CROIX LES CORNET and Bearer and Car posts connecting with Battalions in the line. 135 Field Ambulance with H.d.Qrs. and present Main dressing station at DOULIEU (A.25. d.4.4) within a short time. At 4-15 A.M. on the 9th inst enemy bombardment opened on whole Divisional Front, & casualties began to come down. All Bearer Posts were at once reinforced. Cases were evacuated to 136 F.A. SAILLY and thence to C.C.S. until 8 A.M. when the SAILLY - BAC ST MAUR Road became impassable for lateral evacuation; accordingly FORT ROMPU and SAILLY became advanced dressing stations, and evacuation was carried out over the River to DOULIEU which now became the D.M.D.S. The 136 F.A. A.D.S. at LA CROIX LES CORNET apparently became isolated, and the whole medical personnel are missing. Rest on the Right Sector on SAILLY about 8 A.M. At 10-15 A.M. 136 F.A. was ordered to leave sufficient personnel at SAILLY to run an A.D.S. and to withdraw Remainder of Tent Division to DOULIEU and form a walking wounded collecting Post at a set already prepared near 135 F.A. Owing to destruction of bridges over River LYS this Field Ambulance had to abandon a considerable part of one sections transport at SAILLY. At the same time 137 F.A. was ordered to withdraw all transport to Bleu Horse Lines	

Vol. XXIII.

Secret WAR DIARY of A.D.M.S. 40 Division

INTELLIGENCE SUMMARY

(Erase heading not required.)

Army Form C. 2118

Place	Date	Hour	Summary of Events and Information	Remarks and references to Appendices
			at CROIX DU BAC. Remaining open at FORT ROMPU as an A.D.S. at 9 a.m. 135 F.A. was ordered to send forward their Bearer Division and Report to 120th Inf. Bgde. which was still in Reserve at this hut – This was done, and the Brigade becoming engaged, an A.D.S. was opened at G.8.d.8.6 at 11 a.m. Up to this time contact and evacuation was maintained until 11.9th & 120th Inf. Bgdes; but owing to the A.D.S. at AUX TROIS TOULETTES being captured, touch was temporarily lost with 121 Inf. Bgde. Owing to continuous heavy shellfire, about 2 p.m. the advanced dressing stations at SAILLY and FORT ROMPU were moved north by the main and car posts established as near the river as possible, evacuation being still to M.D.S. DOULIEU. The latter was visited by A.D.M.S. at 4 p.m. and owing to large number of cases awaiting evacuation, D.D.M.S. XV Corps was asked for extra cars, which arrived about 6 p.m. After this, evacuation was satisfactory. At 4 p.m. Divisional H.Q.M. moved to VIEUX BERQUIN. 137 Field Ambulance was ordered to meet H.Q.M. to VIEUX BERQUIN and open an emergency M.D.S. – This was ready at 9 p.m. On account of the number of casualties having diminished and on evacuation from 135 F.A. was satisfactory, 136 F.A. was ordered to close as a Walking Wounded Post at DOULIEU & move to VIEUX BERQUIN and await further orders.	
VIEUX BERQUIN.			135 F.A. .... CUL DU SAC FARM. 136 .... LE PETIT MORTIER 137 .... G.5.6. Central	
	10.4.18.	8 a.m.	at 8.30 a.m. 135 F.A. advanced dressing station moved back to DOULIEU bis Conforming with retirement of the Infantry, and took over site of M.D.S. N.Qm 135 F.A. moving to VIEUX BERQUIN – 136 F.A. advanced dressing station moved back behind 119 F.A.M. to CROSS ROADS 1 Klo. west of STEENWERCK, where they were soon afterwards joined by A.D.S. of 137 Field Ambulance. Evacuation was now via DOULIEU to M.D.S. VIEUX BERQUIN	
	at midnight 9/10th April.			

Vol. XXIII.

Secret WAR DIARY of A.D.M.S. 40 DIV:
or
INTELLIGENCE SUMMARY
(Erase heading not required.)

Army Form C. 2118

Instructions regarding War Diaries and Intelligence Summaries are contained in F.S. Regs., Part II. and the Staff Manual respectively. Title Pages will be prepared in manuscript.

Place	Date	Hour	Summary of Events and Information	Remarks and references to Appendices
	11.4.18		1 Chinese & C.C.Ss North of HAZEBROUCK: at 1 p.m. 136 F.A. was ordered to move back and then an emergency M.D.S. in the School STRAZEELE. They were followed later in the evening by HdQrs. 135 F.A. at 6 p.m. all advanced dressing stations were continued at DOULIEU. Requisites and posts being cleared chiefly by motor ambulance cars. These positions were maintained during the night. Evacuation to VIEUX BERQUIN Remaining satisfactory. JM at 9.30.a.m. combined A.D.S. was moved back to PRINCE FARM L.4.a. — wounded being cleared by cars from R.A.P.s in DOULIEU at 1 p.m. owing to a further retirement a new A.D.S. was formed by 135 F.A. and 136 F.A. at F.21.a. Caestre, Prince Farm being held by 137 Field Ambulance until 6 p.m. at 1.30 p.m. orders were received from Corps that C.C.Ss. were closing temporarily and that all cases were to be retained in M.D.Ss. until further orders. For this reason, VIEUX BERQUIN was reopened as a walking wounded post only, and STRAZEELE became the D.M.D.S. at 4 p.m. verbal orders were received that the Division would be withdrawn — orders were accordingly issued to O.C. Divisional Bearers (O.C. 137 F.A.) to withdraw his bearers with the Infantry Brigades. Divisional HdQrs. moved to LA MOTTE.	
LA MOTTE			at 4.30 p.m. 137 Field Ambulance closed at VIEUX BERQUIN and moved to PRADELLES. 136 F.A. handed over M.D.S. STRAZEELE to 31st Division and moved to BORRÉ. 135 F.A. Remaining at STRAZEELE. JM	
	12.4.18		In the course of night 11/12 April. Bearer Divisions rejoined their Field Ambulances. During the period midnight 9/10 — midnight 11/12 April, a total of 2267 casualties are recorded as having passed through Field Ambulances. Of which 1002 belong to the 40th Division. Total R.A.M.C. Casualties in above operations 5 Officers, 770 R. Killed, wounded and missing.	

1875 Wt. W593/826 1,000,000 4/15 J.B.C. & A. A.D.S.S./Forms/C. 2118.

Vol. XXIII.

WAR DIARY of A.D.M.S. 40th Division

INTELLIGENCE SUMMARY

Army Form C. 2118.

Place	Date	Hour	Summary of Events and Information	Remarks and references to Appendices
AU SOUVERAIN	12.4.18	8pm	Divisional H.Q. moved to AU SOUVERAIN.	
	13.4.18		Field Ambulances collecting at their Transport lines. Field Ambulances moved to HONDEGHEM. Two Composite Bgds under G.O.C. 119 & 121 Inf Bgds ordered to take up a position approximately along HAZEBROUCK - STRAZEELE Road, most of the troops being disposed to cover STRAZEELE. 136 F.A. found M.D.S. at HONDEGHEM in case of emergency & Bearers were disposed under orders of Divisional Bearer Officer.	
		5pm	D.H.Q. moved to RENESCURE.	
RENESCURE	14.4.18	1.45am	Found Name ord. No. 65. The Division will march today to area near ST OMER. Field Ambulances will accompany their Brigades.	
		2pm	D.H.Q. moved to LONGUENESSE. Division arrived in area. Field Ambulances being located as follows - 135 F.A. - ST OMER. 136 F.A. TILQUES. 137 F.A. ST MARTIN au LAERT.	
WIZERNES	15.4.18		D.H.Q. moved to WIZERNES.	
	16.4.18		135 Field Ambulance joins 16 Bgd. Group at LONGUENESSE.	
	17.4.18		Orders received that a Composite Brigade will be formed under G.O.C. 121 Inf. Bgd. from 3 complete Battalions from other Brigade. 137 F.A. to be made up to strength from the F.A's	

Vol. XXIII.

WAR DIARY of A.D.M.S. 40 Division
or INTELLIGENCE SUMMARY.

Army Form C. 2118.

(Erase heading not required.)

Place	Date	Hour	Summary of Events and Information	Remarks and references to Appendices
	18.4.18		and to join this Brigade. 137 Field Ambulance equipped & reinforced as far as possible, no wheeled stretcher carriage available in the Division. These the only outstanding deficiencies. Remaining 2 137 F.A.	W/
	20.4.18.		Received "A" Division order N°155. The complete Brigade will move to an area west of CASSEL tomorrow. The remainder of the Division (less J.H.Q. & Divisional artillery (attached to VI corps.)) will move tomorrow to the BOISDINGHEM area, west of QUELMES.	W/
	23.4.18.		Complete Brigade moved to area east of CASSEL under orders direct from VIII corps. Received 40th Division warning order N°157. Reposition has been received that the whole personnel of the Division, less Divisional Brigade and Battalion Hd.Qrs., at a small staff of instructors are to be sent to the Base. Pending further instructions it is intended to utilize the troops for digging the HAZEBROUCK – LE BREARD line – Less the establishment (provisional) for a training Division was received. This leaves Field Ambulances at disposal of D.G.M.S.	W/
	24.4.18		Attended Conference at office of D.M.S. Second army. In all probability the Division will be employed in training our American Division. Four Field Ambulances, less personnel, would be handed over to such a Division on completion of training. For training purposes one additional Field Ambulance will be posted to the Division, and the personnel of the four Field Ambulances	

Reference No/o.

Vol. XXIII.

Scott WAR DIARY of A.D.M.S. 40th Division V¹ Army Form C. 2118.

or

INTELLIGENCE SUMMARY.

(Erase heading not required.)

Place	Date	Hour	Summary of Events and Information	Remarks and references to Appendices
	26.4.18		Reported to the C.O. Quatremois. Lt. Major at about 200.R. Further instructions will however be received.	M
			Received 40th Division order N° 158. Orders have been received from Second army that Divl. Hd Qrs. and two composite Brigades from the 40th Division are placed at disposal of VIIIth Corps.	
			For this purpose a second Composite Brigade is formed, with 136 Field Ambulance attached.	
			Issued R.A.M.C. orders N° 65. 136 Field Ambulance will be made up to strength from 135 Field Ambulance — leaving the halls with only 2 officers. Command Hd Qrs. & N° 2 Composite Brigade to be prepared to move to STAPLE arts by 2 p.m. 27th inst.	M
	29.4.18.	10 A.M.	Orders received that all troops of 40th Division in the TILQUES area will be moved out of LUMBRES area. Division having information received that N° 1 Composite Bgde. has been moved to the PROVEN area.	M
		7.15 p.m.	40th Division order N° 160 received. N° 2 Composite Bgd. will march to the camp vacated by N° 1 Composite Bgd. at R WELD, march being completed in two stages. First being to MOMELIN area north east of ST OMER, Commencing 7 a.m. 30th inst. at the second being to R WELD, Commencing 8 A.M. 1st May. Issued R.A.M.C. orders N° 66 to this effect. Bogs not included in the two Composite Bgds. or D.H.Q. will move to the LUMBRES area tomorrow.	M
ST OMER	30.4.18. 11 a.m.		Divisional Hd Qrs. moved to ST OMER. N° 2 Composite Bgd. Commenced its march. 135 Field Ambulance moved back to SENINGHEM.	M

P.T.O.

Murray Fry
Colonel
A.D.M.S. 40th Division

Addendum to WAR DIARY of
ADMS. 40th Division.

28.4.18. Instructions received from D.D.M.S. VIII corps for a detachment of a Field Ambulance 40th Division to take over a dressing station at GODEWAERSVELDE, from personnel of 33rd Division.

O.C. 137 Field Ambulance instructed to detail 1 M.O. and 18 O.R. with 2 ambulance cars for this duty.

J. M. Malcolm Capt.

160/973

COMMITTEE FOR THE
MEDICAL HISTORY OF THE WAR
Date 9 JUL 1918

D.D.M.S. L. of C.

Vol. XXIV.

Reference Maps
HAZEBROUK 5A
F.S. Regs. 27, II Sec. 27.

Scott WAR DIARY of A.D.M.S. 40 DIV:
or
INTELLIGENCE SUMMARY.

Army Form C. 2118.

Vol I 214

Place	Date	Hour	Summary of Events and Information	Remarks and references to Appendices
ST OMER	3.5.18		Received instructions that the reduction of the Division to the Training Establishment could be proceeded with at once. Twice table of departure of surplus personnel to Base issued. Received instructions from D.M.S. 2nd army that Field Ambulances will be reduced to the establishment of Training Cadre with the addition of the two action commanders, who will remain with their unit until it actually commences training. The training cadre will be as follows: Commanding Officer, Quartermaster, Sgt. Major, two Staff Sgts., 3 Senior Sgts. 15 Other Ranks. The Complete transport will be retained.	
	4.5.18		Received order to dispatch the ambulance cars of one Field Ambulance to report to S.M.T.O. IX Corps, also issued 10 officers 40th Division. The Infantry Brigades have been withdrawn from forward area, and the Division is assembled aplits in an area just north of ST OMER. Dispatch graphical personnel 6 Base Details Commenced to-morrow. 6 officers sent to 29th Division and 3 to 33rd Division.	
	5.5.18		Orders received to dispose of an additional 7 officers to other Divisions.	
	7.5.18		All officers except the C.O. and Adm. Commander, and one reinforcement officer have now reported to other Divisions – no instructions received regarding the other Ranks.	
	8.5.18		Received administrative instructions regarding the "WINNIZEELE" line which is	

VOL. XXIV.

Secret **WAR DIARY** of A.D.M.S. 40th Division

or

INTELLIGENCE SUMMARY.

(Erase heading not required.)

Army Form C. 2118.

Place	Date	Hour	Summary of Events and Information	Remarks and references to Appendices
			being drawn up by Liaison group, would be submitted by H.Q.rs. 40th Division. Send R.A.M.C. warning order No. 68 regarding medical arrangements. Each Field Ambulance will establish a dressing station in their respective sectors, and receive sick from M.O's. of the Labour Groups, and warrants U/c 6 C.C.S. This line is divided into four Corps sectors, and a complete defence scheme is required for each sector. M	R.A.M.C. warning order No. 68 attached
	19.5.18		Sent R.A.M.C. order No. 69 and medical arrangements No. 13. The detachments detailed in order No. 68 will proceed tomorrow and establish dressing stations in their respective areas. All Infantry Transport of the Division, except that laid down for "a Training Division", ordered to proceed to ETAPLES - no further instructions regarding disposal of Field Ambulance personnel or transport received. M	R.A.M.C. order No. 69 and Medical arrangements No. 13 attached
	20.5.18		The Division has been engaged on the organization of the defences of the WINNIPEG Line and medical arrangements are being made out. Sites for R.A.P.s - A.D.S.s - relay posts and Main dressing stations are being selected, no work will be done on them etc., all quarters are farm buildings. M	
	25.5.18		Medical arrangements completed, and copies sent to Hd.Qrs. Division, VII Corps and Second Army. M	

VOL. XXIV.

Secret WAR DIARY of A.D.M.S. 40th Division III.

or

INTELLIGENCE SUMMARY.

(Erase heading not required.)

Army Form C. 2118.

Place	Date	Hour	Summary of Events and Information	Remarks and references to Appendices
	26.5.18		Orders received from 'A' that the Training Cadres of 135 and 136 Field Ambulances will proceed on 28th May, with complete Horse and Motor Transport, and report to H.Qrs. 4th American Division SAMER.	
			Orders received for 'Q' regarding staging etc - No instructions received regarding disposal of surplus personnel.	
	27.5.18		Issued Routine order No. 70. The Training Cadres will proceed forward work tomorrow 28/29 & completing march on 29.	Routine order No 70 attached
			Staging at BAYENGHEM-LES-SENINGHEM a night 28/29 & completing march on 29.	
			All surplus personnel will be moved to KINDERBECK and come under orders of O.C. 137 Field Ambulance - Surplus Officers will remain with the Division on the strength of the 137 Field Ambulance, and will carry on with the Dressing Station at present established in the forward area.	
	28.5.18		135 and 136 Field Ambulances departed today.	
	29.5.18		Instructions received that surplus personnel of 135 and 136 Field Ambulances will rejoin their units forthwith. Issued Routine order No.71. The personnel will proceed by train under one officer from BOUTREAU, where transport will meet them - They will then proceed by march route to JAMES. Application made to 'A' that those Officers Commanding surplus to establishment may be returned for the present within the Division.	Routine order No 71 attached

Vol. XXIV
Secret WAR DIARY of A.D.M.S. 40 DIV
or
INTELLIGENCE SUMMARY
Army Form C. 2118.

Place	Date	Hour	Summary of Events and Information	Remarks and references to Appendices
ST.OMER	30-5-18		Capt. J.G. THATCHER, R.A.M.C. D.A.D.M.S. severely wounded by bomb & sent to No 9. B.R.C. Hospital. Surplus personnel of 135 & 136 FA. less three officers entrained today to rejoin their respective units. MK	
	31-5-18.		Nil. MK	

Humphreys
Col a.D.M.S.
40 Div

SECRET.   COPY NO.

40TH.DIVISION R.A.M.C. ORDER NO.69.

Reference Maps.
HAZEBROUCK 1/100,000.   9/5/1918.
Sheets. 27 & 36A.

1.   In continuation of 40th.Division R.A.M.C. Order
          No.68 dated 8/5/18, the detachments mentioned in para.2
          of that Order will move tomorrow morning to the following sites:-

                135th.Field Ambulance.......To.........C.30.b.4.7.
                136th.   "   "   ...."..........P.31.a.3.2.
                137th.   "   "   ...."..........J.16.central.

2.   Officers Commanding Field Ambulances will arrange
with Headquarters Infantry Brigade concerned for the Medical and
Sanitary care of the Troops of the 40th.Division, and with the
Medical Officers of the 31st. and 75th. Labour Groups for the
reception and evacuation of sick from these units.

3.   Headquarters of Field Ambulances will remain in
          their present location in the meantime

4.   Acknowledge.

          Issued at 10.p.m.

                                              J.G.Shalkhu Capt
                                    p
                                                  Colonel.
                                        A.D.M.S.40th.Division.

          Distribution Normal - plus 31st. & 75th.Labour Groups.

SECRET.   COPY NO. 20

40TH. DIVISION R.A.M.C. ORDER NO. 70.

Reference H. Qrs. 40th. Division No.818(A) dated 25th. May, and 40th. Division No.818(Q) dated 26th. May, 1918.

1. The Training Cadres of 135th. and 136th. Field Ambulances, with complete Horse and Motor Transport, full A.S.C. H.T. and M.T. and attached "P.B" personnel, will proceed by march route at 9.a.m 28th. May, 1918, and report to Headquarters Fourth American Infantry Division at SAMER, on 29th. May.

2. Both Field Ambulances will march under orders of O.C. 135th. Field Ambulance who will report departure to this Office.

3. The Personnel laid down for a Training Cadre will not be exceeded, and no additional men will be taken to act as Wagon Orderlies etc.

4. Full detail of strength proceeding to Fourth American Division, and detail of surplus personnel remaining will be notified to this Office this evening.

5. Surplus personnel of 135th. and 136th. Field Ambulances, will come under orders of 137th. Field Ambulance from evening of 27th May, and will be accommodated in tents at KINDERBELCK, pending disposal. Instructions regarding drawing of tents will be issued later.

6. Officers i/c Dressing Stations of 135th and 136th. Field Ambulances will carry on for the present, under orders of O.C. 137th. Field Ambulance.

7. On return from leave of Lieut-Colonel I.R.HUDLESTON, R.A.M.C. O.C. 136th. Field Ambulance, Major H.W.BRUCE, R.A.M.C. will report to O.C. 137th. Field Ambulance, for duty.

8. Issued at 11.a.m.

9. Acknowledge.

Colonel.
A.D.M.S. 40th. Division.

27th. May, 1918.

Distribution:- Normal plus O.C. 40th. Divl M.T. Coy.
              H.Qrs. Fourth American Infantry Divn.

SECRET.

COPY NO. 18

40TH. DIVISION R.A.M.C. ORDER NO. 71.

1. The surplus personnel of 135th. & 136th. Field Ambulances, less 3 Officers, will rejoin their respective units on the 30th. May 1918.

2. Personnel will proceed by train to OUTREAU Siding ontraining at WATTEN at 1.30.p.m. May 30th. An N.C.O. will report to R.T.O. WATTEN, with the ontraining state, at 12.30 p.m
The party will be met at OUTREAU Siding by transport of their respective units, to carry rations and baggage to SAMER, the personnel proceeding by march route.

3. Rations for 31st. May, will be carried

4. Major A.J. BEVERIDGE, M.C. R.A.M.C. will proceed in charge of the party, and will remain with his unit on arrival at SAMER.

5. A marching out state will be forwarded to this Office and departure of the personnel notified.

6. Acknowledge.

Colonel.
A.D.M.S. 40th. Division.

29/5/18.

Distribution - Normal plus A.D.M.S. 16th. Division.

140/3073.

A.D.M.S. 40th Div.

June 1918

COMMITTEE FOR THE
MEDICAL HISTORY OF THE WAR
Date 7 AUG 1918

WAR DIARY of A.D.M.S. 40th DIV.

Army Form C. 2118.

WD 25

Instructions regarding War Diaries and Intelligence Summaries are contained in F.S. Regs., Part II. and the Staff Manual respectively. Title pages will be prepared in manuscript.

(Erase heading not required.)

Place	Date	Hour	Summary of Events and Information	Remarks and references to Appendices
ST OMER	1918 June 1st		NIL. Capt. Thatcher S.A.D.M.S. died of wounds	
	2nd		Section Commanders of 135 & 136 F. Ambulances left to report their respective units attached over to the 16th Div. Then leaves the O.C. & Men either Commanders the only M.O's in the Division	
	3rd		D.H.Q. arrived to LEDERZEELE	
LEDERZEELE	4th		NIL	
	5th		NIL	
	6th		NIL	
	7th		Capt. A.C. Jeans arrives today to take up appointment of D.A.D.M.S.	
	8th		A.D.M.S. interviewed O.C. 71 Smn. Section re adoption of the Prussian disinfecting pit in this area	
	9th		DADMS granted temp. rank of Major while holding his appointment	
	10th		NIL	
	11th		6 Garrison battalions formed from B. men arrived today for 120 Inf. Bde. M.O's for these battalions being sent up by G.H.Q. meanwhile the two A.D.S. have been withdrawn to Hd. Qrs. of 137 F. Amb. for duty with these battalions	

Alaston Thomson White
A/Lieut. Colonel
A.D.M.S. 40th Div.

Army Form C. 2118.

WAR DIARY
or
INTELLIGENCE SUMMARY.
(Erase heading not required.)

A.D.M.S. 40. Division.

Instructions regarding War Diaries and Intelligence Summaries are contained in F.S. Regs., Part II. and the Staff Manual respectively. Title pages will be prepared in manuscript.

Place	Date	Hour	Summary of Events and Information	Remarks and references to Appendices
LEDERZEELE.	12/9/17		NIL	
	13.		NIL	
	14.		NIL	
	15.		Capt GILCHRIST, J.S. and Lieut J.E. CARTER RAMC report from Base for duty. 40 Div O.O. 167 received and provisional RAMC orders issued as history of Divn. M.O. H2ERIEUER. 40. Divn 'G' have promised 300 labour men as stretcher bearers, trench 100 in N, Centre, & S. Sectors along with 30. D.R. RAMC to each Sector.	Appendix No 1
	16.		1st Lieut E.P. NORWOOD MORC U.S.A. reported here on today commendation as No.11 5th Labour Group. HQ Capt M. Macculloch RAMC	
	17.		Main 121. Bde HQ moved to St MARTIN AU LAERT. 18th Bn WELSH. 10/11 H.L.I., 20 MIDDLESEX, 14 A.&S.H. & 12 SUFFOLK training Staffs proceed to England etc.	
	18.		RAMC's went to HQ 119 Inf. Bde. and the MO's 12 N. STAFFS. (Capt J. GILCHRIST) and 13. R. Innis. Fus. (Lieut PARKER.) A.D.M.S. VIII Corps called and others & Capts called and D Dress	ae J

WAR DIARY or INTELLIGENCE SUMMARY

Army Form C. 2118.

A.D.M.S. 40. Division.

Place	Date	Hour	Summary of Events and Information	Remarks and references to Appendices
LEDERZEELE	19/8		A.D.M.S. visited the Camps of 10. Gas. Batn. K.O.S.B. interviewed the Medical Officer Lieut J.M.H. CALDWELL and visited 11. G. Bn. CAMERONS r 15. G. Bn. K.O.Y.L.I. The 11. CAMERONS were inspected today by D.A.S. for Q.M.G.	
	20/8		A.D.M.S. visited H.Q.rs & discussed general situation. M.O. 15.K.O.Y.L.I. and 13. E. LANCS. visited A.D.M.S. A.D.M.S. visited the newly arrived Battns of 121.Bde. 2.3.d G. Bn. CHESHIRES and 2.d G.Bn R.I.R. at TILQUES. and 17th G.B.n WORCESTERS at SMEERWICK and 23. G.Bn. Lanc Fus. at LONGUENESSE. and interviewed the M.Os. &c.	
	21/8		A.D.M.S. visited 137 F.Ambce and inspected the Russian disinfestation chamber. 40 Div. Warning Order 172. of 20 Td received re move to HAZEBROUCK WEST area.	
	22.		40 Div. Order No 174 of 22 Td received in consequence of Div Form VII & XV Corps & move in 23 rd unit to RENESCURE area. A.D.M.S. VII Corps visited A.D.M.S. & arranged medical details XV Corps re medical situation & arrangements.	
RENESCURE 27/T 20 or 8.6	23.		D.H.Q. moved to RENESCURE today. 137 F. Ambce moving by march route	a.f.

WAR DIARY
or
INTELLIGENCE SUMMARY
(Erase heading not required)

Army Form C. 2118.

A.D.M.S. 40 Div.

Place	Date	Hour	Summary of Events and Information	Remarks and references to Appendices
RENESCURE. 27/T.20 d 2.6	23/1/18		to SERCUS area. A.D.M.S called on D.D.M.S. XV Corps. Personnel of Divsn H.Q.-F. Ambce. were moved by bus. Many fell out during the short march to & from entraining and detraining points	
	24.		D.D.M.S. visited the proposed site of A.D.S. - Prev: inspects of drafts from G.H.Q arrived to-day & was accompanied by A.D.M.S. to inspect the battalions of 119 Bde. - Dr 49 Sani. Sectn. visited A.D.M.L. arrangements were made for equipping the camps in the L/O Bde area with sanitary appliances of standard pattern. D.D.M.S. XV Corps visited A.D.M.S. etc	
	25.		M.I. of drafts & D.A.D.M.S. continued the inspection of 120 Inf Bde and a section of 121/1 Bde. 136. F. Ambce arrived in camp near RENESCURE (27/T.22.a.3.6.) 136. F. Ambce arrived at late site of 2.C.C.S. EBLINGHEM (27/T.18.A.3.7.) V.A.D.M.S. held med. inspl. of board on no. officer & 2 OR today. A.D.M.S. met D.Drs XV Corps & arranged site of 136 F. Ambce near EBLINGHEM.	
	26.		Medical Inspects of drafts completed. Inspection of 121 Bde today & returned to G.H.Q. Rep.	

WAR DIARY or INTELLIGENCE SUMMARY

Army Form C. 2118.

A.D.M.S. 40. Divn.

Place	Date	Hour	Summary of Events and Information	Remarks and references to Appendices
RENESCURE.	27/6/18		ADMS visited 2 Amsterdam & 49 San Section to arrange supply of sanitary appliances for 119 & 120 Bdes. ADMS & OIASand reconnoitred a site for M.D.S. for S. Bde Sector of West HAZEBROUCK line - selected site at 20.M/B. I.P.C. a.o.o. Divn roads stores XV Corps sanction to new J-thros site. "CAPT. TROUNCE R.A.M.C. from 4th Divn and CAPT. PELLIER R.A.M.C. from 33 Divn reported for duty today. ADMS 40 Divn & 12/76 visited to all concerning ADMs Divn. 2	
	28/6/18		Arrangement made with N.2 Sanitary Section for supply of sanitary appliances for 121 F Bde. Conference of Medical Officers of the Division at 126 F Amb. 137 F Ambce moved to Sets of X.V.C. W.W.GS at 27/7.22.a.3.4. and 135 moved from there to 20.M/B.18.c.o.o to establish an M.D.S. for W. HAZEBROUCK line. A.D.M.S. attended conference at D.H.Q.	
	29/6/18		Capt. J.M. RYAN R.A.M.C. reported for duty from XV Corps Sups Park and posted to 15. G. Bn. K.O.Y.L.I. vice Capt. CARROLL. M.C. R.A.M.C. to XV Corps S. Pk.	
	30/6/18		Asst. Director visited 135 F. Ambce at at B.18.c.o.o/20.d to arrange for increase in the accommodation.	Also Dir T.C. M.C. acting Dir of Divn

A6945 Wt. W.1422/M.1160 350,000 12/16 D.D.&L. Forms/C/2118/14.

Appendix 1.

Secret.
Reference Maps:-
Sheet 27 & 36A.

40th. Division R.A.M.C. Operation Order No.74.

1. In the event of an enemy attack on the Second Army front, the 40th. Division and attached Troops will man the West Hazebrouck Line from D.25.c. in the South to V.C.d. in the North, a distance of about 13000 yards.

2. The Divisional Sector is divided into three Brigade Sections as shown on attached map. (Inf. Bdes only).

3. The Sections will be held by the following troops:-

   <u>Southern Section.</u>
   120th., Infantry Brigade.
   236th., A.T.Company, R.E.
   94th., Labour Company.
   12th., " "

   <u>Centre Section</u>
   121st., Infantry Brigade.
   224th., Field Coy.R.E.
   224th. " " "
   55th. Labour Coy.
   13th. " "
   93rd. " "
   67th. " "
   178th. " "

   <u>Northern Section</u>
   119th. Infantry Brigade
   231st. Field Coy. R.E.
   184th. Labour Coy.
   188th. " "
   111th. " "
   132nd " "
   61st. " "
   133rd " "
   147th. " "

   See L.O. O.E. No. 176

4. Full use must be made of A.D.Ss. and M.D.Ss. of other units which may come into the line

5. 300 Stretcher Bearers are being provided by 40th.Division 'G'. 100 of these will report to M.C. d/c 31st. Labour Group (Capt.W.L.JOHNSTON, R.A.M.C.) in charge Southern Sector at 36A/ C.2.c.3.9., who will establish an A.D.S. there.
   100 will report to M.C. i/c 5th. Labour Group (Lieut. E.G.P. *NORWOOD* McCULLOUGH, R.A.M.C.) in charge Centre Sector at 27/ U.16.b.8.4., who will establish an A.D.S. there.
   100 will report to M.C. i/c 75th. Labour Group (Capt.G.E. ELKINGTON R.A.M.C.) in charge Northern Sector, at 27/ V.1.c.7.2., who will open an A.D.S. there.
   These Bearers will be rationed by 137th. Field Ambulance.

6. O.C. 137th. Field Ambulance will provide 30 Other Ranks R.A.M.C., per Sector, to assist in the Bearer work and to staff the A.D.Ss. They will bring the necessary medical equipment etc.

7. Medical Officers i/c Labour Groups will take the Ambulance Cars at present with them to the A.D.Ss. More cars will be detailed by O.C. 137th.Field Ambulance, to report as under :-

 2 to report to M.O.i/c Southern Sector at 36A/ C.2.c.3.9.
 2 " " " " Centre Sector " 27/ U.16.b.8.4.
 1 " " " " Northern Sector " 27/ V.1.c.7.2

These will be supplemented by 3 Motor Lorries for each Sector, under arrangements to be made by this Office.

8. 137th.Field Ambulance will move to RENESCURE Area.

9. Major J.V.LINNELL, M.C. R.A.M.C. will be in charge of the ~~A.D.Ss., and will forward evacuation arrangements with Hqrs~~ forward evacuation arrangements, with Headquarters at 27/ U.16.b.8.4. He will render 4 hourly reports to this Office.

10. Evacuation to C.C.Ss. will be notified later.

11. "A.& D" Books will be kept as far as possible at A.D.Ss. A.T.S. will also be given there.

12. There is a dump of stretchers and blankets at old site of 13.C.C.S. at ARNEKE.
50 Stretchers and 100 Blankets per Sector will be drawn forthwith by O.C. 137th.Field Ambulance, and will be sent up with the 30 Other Ranks R.A.M.C. to the A.D.Ss.

13. Divisional Headquarters will move to RENESCURE.

14. These orders will come into force on the receipt of telegraphic instructions from this Office.

15. Issued at 10.15 p.m

Acknowledge.(F.A. R.M.Os. and Labour Group M.Os. only.)

/ Humphrey

D.H.Qrs.
15/6/18.
          Colonel.
          A.D.M.S.40th.Division.

Distribution - Normal plus OsC 5th. 31st. & 75th.Labour Groups.
      M.Os.i/c " " " " "
      D.M.S. Second Army. D.D.M.S.VIIth.Corps
      Labour Commandant VIIth.Corps.

SECRET
****

AMENDMENT NO.1 TO 40TH.DIVISION R.A.M.C. ORDER NO 74 DATED 15/6/18.

19/6/1918.

Reference Maps.
Sheets 27 & 36A.

1.   Delete para.3.

2   Delete para.5 and substitute

"300 Stretcher Bearers are being provided from 5, 31 and 64 Labour Groups, and will report as under:-
    100 men from 64th.Labour Group for Southern Section will report to Capt.W.L.JOHNSTON, R.A.M.C. at A.D.S. 36A/ B.18.c.5.6.
    100 men from 31st. Labour Group for Centre Section will report to 1st.Lieut.E.P.NORWOOD, M.O.R.C. U.S.A. at A.D.S. 27/ U.16.b.8.4.
    100 men from 5th.Labour Group for Northern Section will report to Capt.G.E.ELKINGTON, R.A.M.C. at A.D.S. at 27/ V.1.c.7.2".

3.   Acknowledge.(F.Amb. R.M.Os. and Labour Group M.Os.only.)

        Distribution as before - plus O.C.64th.Labour Group
                                (and copy of O.O.74.)

                    J.Humphkly
                        Colonel.
                    A.D.M.S.40th.Division.

SECRET.

Reference Maps.
Sheets 27 & 36A.

40TH. DIVISION R.A.M.C. ORDER NO. 75.

With reference to 40th. Division Order No.173 dated 21/6/18.

1. 137th. Field Ambulance will move on 23rd. inst. to SERCUS, (36A/ C.9.)

2. An Officer will report in advance to Area Commandant ELARINGHEM, to arrange billetting accommodation.

3. Patients for evacuation will be sent to C.C.S. at BLENDECQUES.

4. A.D.M.S. Office will close at 10.a.m. 23rd.inst., at LEDERZEELE, and open at the same hour at RENESCURE, (27/ T.21.c.3.5)

5. Acknowledge. (Field Ambce. only.)

                                                        Colonel.
22nd. June, 1918.   A.D.M.S. 40th. Division.

Distribution - Normal.

SECRET.   COPY NO.
******   **********

40TH. DIVISION R.A.M.C. ORDER NO. 76.

Reference Maps
Sheets 27 & 36A.   27/6/18.

1. 40th. Division R.A.M.C. Order No. 74 and Amendment are cancelled.

2. In the event of an enemy attack on the Second Army Front, the 40th. Division and attached troops will man the West HARBROUCK Line from 36A/D.25.c.80 27/V.6.central, a distance of about 13,000 yards.
    Divisional Headquarters is at RENESCURE 27/T.21.a.1.0.

3. The Divisional Sector is divided into Brigade Sections as follows:-
    Southern Section....120th. Inf. Bde. with H.Qrs. at 36A/C.21.d.0.3.
    Centre Section......121st.   "   "   "   "   " 36A/C.3.c.5.3.
    Northern Section....119th.   "   "   "   "   " 27/P.31.d.5.7.

4. The boundaries of Brigade Sections are as follows:-
    Southern Section. S.Boundary. A line drawn from D.26.c.4.3-D.25.d.3.5-C.29.d.5.8-to C.26.a.5.7.
        North Boundary. C.6.d.8.2-C.6.c.0.6-C.5.d.0.3-C.4.d.5.2-C.3.d.2.0-C.2.d.0.7.
    Centre Section.   S.Boundary. N.Boundary of Southern Section.
        North Boundary. V.21.b.9.0-V.15.c.5.7-V.14.b.6.0-U.17.a.0.0-U.13.a.0.0.
    Northern Section. S.Boundary. N.Boundary of Centre Section.
        North Boundary W.7.b.3.7-V.12.b.50.99-V.6.c.0.5-V.5.central-P.34.c.8.5-P.32.b.99.60-O.31.a.9.6.

5. O.C. 135th. Field Ambulance will be responsible for the evacuation of all casualties from the Southern Section.
    O.C. 137th. Field Ambulance will be responsible for the evacuation of all casualties from the Centre Section.
    O.C. 136th. Field Ambulance will be responsible for the evacuation of all casualties from the Northern Section.

6. A.D.Ss. will be established at the following points :-
        Southern Section 36A/C.14.a.1.0.
        Centre Section   27/ U.20.b.9.4.
        Northern Section 27/ V.1.d.9.5.

7. Car Posts will be established in front of the A.D.Ss. at the discretion of Os.C. Field Ambulances.

8. 136th. Field Ambulance will establish a M.D.S. for Stretcher cases at 27/T.18.c.8.7. for the Northern and Centre Sections.
    135th. Field Ambulance will establish a M.D.S. for Stretcher cases at 36A/B.18.c.0.0. for the Southern Section.
    137th. Field Ambulance will form the Corps Walking Wounded Collecting Station at 27/T.22.a.3.4. for all Sections.

9. "A & D" Books will be kept and A.T.S. given at the M.D.Ss. and C.W.W.C.S.

10. Each Field Ambulance will set aside special accommodation for the treatment of 'Gassed' cases.

11. The M.Ds.i/c Labour Groups will proceed with their attached Ambulance Cars and report for ~~duty~~ temporary duty to Os.C. Field Ambulances, and be at their disposal, as under:-
   M.Os.i/c 5 & 31 Labour Groups to 136th.Field Amb.27/T.18.c.8.7.
   M.O. i/c 26 Labour Group to 137th.Field Amb.27/T.22.a.3.4.
   M.O. i/c 64 Labour Group to 135th.Field Amb.36A/B.18.c.0.0.

12. 300 Stretcher Bearers are being provided from 5, 31 & 64 Labour Groups and will report as under:-
   100 men from 64 Labour Group will report to 135th. Field Ambulance at 36A/B.18.c.0.0.
   100 men from 5 Labour Group will report to 137th. Field Ambulance at 27/T.22.a.3.4.
   100 men from 31 Labour Group will report to 136th. Field Ambulance at 27/T.18.c 8.7.
   These men will be rationed by the respective Field Ambulances and by whom they will be supplied with stretchers.

13. A Dump of 150 stretchers and 250 blankets will be formed at C.W.W.C.S. at 27/T.22.a.3.4.

14. Evacuations from A.D.Ss. to M.D.Ss. and C.W.W.C.S., will be by Divisional Ambulance Cars.
   Evacuations from M.D.Ss. to C.C.Ss at BLENDECQUES, will be by M.A.C.Cars., and evacuations from C.W.W.C.S. by T.A.T. from EBBLINGHEM, or lorries, to No.4. Stationary Hospital, ARQUES, and 18 C.C.S. MALASSESE.

15. Os.C. Field Ambulances will furnish brief reports 4 hourly, on the situation, giving numbers evacuated etc., to this Office.

16. Os C. Field Ambulances will submit evacuation schemes showing Car Posts etc., to this Office as soon as possible.

17. Attention is directed to Q.M.G.Memo.82(Q A.1.) of 18/4/18, forwarded under this Office No.137(M) dated 29/4/18, (Field Ambulances only) regarding the use of Ambulance Cars in forward areas.

18. Acknowledge.(F.As. R.M.Os. and Lab.Groups M.Os.only)

Issued 9.p.m.

J Humphry
Colonel.
A.D.M.S.40th.Division.

D.H.Qrs.
Distribution normal plus:-
D.M.S. Second Army.
D.D.M.S.VIIth.Corps.
D.D.M.S.XVth.Corps.
A.D.M.S.9th.Division.
A.D.M.S.29th.Division.
A.D.M.S.31st.Division.
A.D.M.S.1st.Aus Division.
O.C.14.M.A.C.
Labour Commandant ST.OMER Defences.
Labour Commandant VIIth.Corps.

O.C.5.Labour Group.
O.C.26 Labour Group.
O.C.31 Labour Group.
O.C.64 Labour Group.
M.O.5 Labour Group.
M.O.26 Labour Group.
M.O.31 Labour Group.
M.O.64 Labour Group.

146/3123.

A.D.M.S. 40ᵗʰ Div.

July 1918.

Army Form C. 2118.

Vol XXVI

WAR DIARY
or
INTELLIGENCE SUMMARY

A.D.M.S. 40 Division

(Erase heading not required.)

Vol 26

Place	Date	Hour	Summary of Events and Information	Remarks and references to Appendices
RENESCURE	1/7/18		A.D.M.S. held a conference of O's C. F. Ambces & discussed instrs P.S. 27/18 of 20/6/18 re distribution of an F. Amb per Division & withdrawal of 1 Field Amb in the III Corps area. Agreed that the distribution of 1 Ambce per Division for F. Ambces is the lesser evil. Personnel can be brought up rapidly when required & that F. Ambce Officers are not attached to duty at C.C.S. Equipment of 1 Section can be spared except tent sub-divns. In addition no transport is not approved as F. Ambces have to carry into attacks & establish dispensary stns & there is no allowance made for men's kit.	
27/T.20.d.9.6			2nd Lieut 108/G of 20/6/18 received. From July 8 1 batt & each Bde will man the East H.Q.E. Broke Line for 4 days for instruction in their duties and to complete the construction of the line. A certain number of Officers, W.O., N.C.O., Rank & File in rotation on the am will be attached.	
	2/7/18		A.D.M.S. attended a conference at D.D.M.S. XV Corps regarding the proposed redistribution & number & size of Field Ambulances	

Army Form C. 2118.

WAR DIARY
or
INTELLIGENCE SUMMARY.
(Erase heading not required.)

A.D.M.S.
40. Div.

Place	Date	Hour	Summary of Events and Information	Remarks and references to Appendices
RENESCURE	2/7/18		Suggested that Equipment less tents be handed in. Div orders P.H. helmets, pyjamas suits &c (not blankets) authorized by G.R.O's should be retired and 1 Wagon G.S. and 1 Limber G.S. be retained in the F. Ambces. An alternative scheme suggested was all transport to be given in & a 3c. cwt lorry be sent to replace it. The Senior ADMS wagon should be retained. Started visit to the sta P.AMB &c in the North Sector in the W. Hazebrouck Area. Influenza cases shown an increase.	
	3/7/18		13 R. Innis Fus. 10 K.O.S.B. 23 Lan. Fus. moved forward tonight. This comprised the East HAZEBROUCK line to instruction in tines & clothing and to complete took in this line. Reference Order No. 77 of 3/7/17. Warned 15 R. KOYLI to arrange the clean clothing tour of 120 +121 Bdes and the A.D.M.S. inspected the Clean clothing & quarantine precautions arising for influenza epidemic. The Div HQ and 120 Bde HQ crews in the rear and the quarantine arranged for. SPANS west the HQs AID P3s & the three Battns in the E. HAZEBROUCK line. Due to Increase sickness in chargework — 35 cases at Dublin + 6 Australia 3 ".	Appendix 1.

WAR DIARY
or
INTELLIGENCE SUMMARY.   A.D.M.S. 40. Div.
(Erase heading not required.)

Army Form C. 2118.

Place	Date	Hour	Summary of Events and Information	Remarks and references to Appendices
REMESCURE 27/T.20.d.8.6	3/7/18		Major Gen: F. PONSONBY. C.B. C.M.G. D.S.O. handed over command of this division today to Major Gen Sir W. PEYTON C.M.G.	
	4/7/18		A.D.M.S. inspected 137 & 136 F. Amb'ces today. Sickness amongst Aux. 121. Bde H.Q. this evening. There are 100 cases of 'flue' in 12nd (G.Bn) R. Innis. Regt. Until this message received this unit of Division had been very few. A medical officer from 10 S. Stationary Hospital has been sent to 136 F. Amb. to continue services for a period. He commenced his duties today. Capt T. J. BUCKLEY. R.A.M.C. reported for duty on 3/7/18 was posted to 136 F. Amb.	
	5/7/18		A.D.M.S. inspected further "unfits" of 13 (G.Bn) K.O.Y.L.I. & sent 1 Officer and 2 O.R. 6/Bn under B/g. 4 + 5/1 of 119 /i/s. He visited 13" G.B. & 2 LANCS. and 12 G.Bn. N. Staffs. and 2 G. Bn. R.I. Regt. Inv 121. Regt. have nearly 100 cases of influenza in camp. Measures arranged for their prevention + treatment. Influenza in K.O.Y.L.I is assuming aspects rest of division is clear.	A.P.

WAR DIARY
~~INTELLIGENCE~~ SUMMARY. — A.D.M.S.
40 Division.

(Erase heading not required.)

Army Form C. 2118.

Place	Date	Hour	Summary of Events and Information	Remarks and references to Appendices
BERESCURE 27/7.20.81.86.	6/10		ADMS inspected men on board in the 13 (G.B) EAST LANCS, 23rd (G.Bn) CHESHIRES, 12 (G.Bn.) N. STAFFS, and a certain number of Off. & O.R. were ordered to the Tent & Barr for reclassification under DRO. 4457/1 of 16/1/17. The influenza epidemic is abating. The ADMS yesterday arranged for the 2 (G.Bn) to be also quarantined. Total admissions to the wards for influenza were 265.	
"	7/10		Influenza epidemic gradually decreasing. 2 field cars in R.I. Regt. and 8 in K.O.Y.L.I. Baths in East HAZE BROOK Lines are being tonight. These Mess to up to construction.	
"	8/10		ADMS visited 137 F Ambce and inspected units at 17. G.B. WORCESTER Regt. and 10th K.O.S.B. and organised 1 Offr of 12 (G. Bn.) N. STAFFS under DRO 4457/1 of 19/1/17. Influenza epidemic has diminished considerably. 9. M.O. arrived this evening & have been attached at 136 F Ambce for the night.	
"	9/10		ADMS visited 12. N STAFFS to enquire into their such wastage as it has been reported that many men are on light duty daily	A.J.

WAR DIARY
or
INTELLIGENCE SUMMARY

A.D.M.S. 40 Division

Place	Date	Hour	Summary of Events and Information	Remarks and references to Appendices
REMESCURE 27/T.20.d.8.6	9/7/18		A.D.M.S. visits 13. Bn. R. Berks: Fusiliers and inspected unfits at 2nd (6 Bn.) R.9. Regt. 9. Officers reinforcements, all M.O.R.C. U.S.A. reported last night for duty. They were interviewed by A.D.M.S. & are now 3 were posted to each Field Ambulance.	
			Lt. PARKER R.A.M.C. reported NoT. 13. E. LANCS. reported as unfit to hospital & nk to Hazeap. Officer from 138. F. Amla sent for temp duty.	
	10/7/18		Under orders from D.D.M.S XV Corps, 3 P. American M.O. who reported yesterday, have been posted in, one to 2/9 Bn and one to 31 (err?) R. Dety. A practice scheme of evacn: scheme of West HAZEBROUCK line was held today by 12.D. Bde & attached Return to R.B. units. The Stretcher bearer & Old Catrn. Groups reported to 135. F. Amle. for instruction in their duties. One 2 Sind impressed them. They were mostly unfit to do any stretcher carrying. The Russ'd instruct'd S.B.R of 2/21 Entrn Grenp then were sent to Tarau S. Bon. Reopn; & they will be expected to Base R/T'd inst'd the New Zealand Sanitain Section re appliances disinfesting Chambers visited the S.A. Field Ambce. G. Dns & see a Russian Disinfesting Chamber at work.	
	11/7/18		A.D.M.S inspected "unfits" of 13. G.B. R. Irish Fusiliers totn, and held a medl. cd board on 2 Officers of R.I. Regt. and 4 O.R. of 147. Nums by	

WAR DIARY or INTELLIGENCE SUMMARY

A.D.M.S. 40. Division

Army Form C. 2118.

Place	Date	Hour	Summary of Events and Information	Remarks and references to Appendices
RENESCURE 27/T.20.d.8.6	12/7/18		121 Bde collected Labour & Rft units held a practice manning of Amb Sectn of WEST HAZEBROUCK line. Stretcher bearer parties of 1/137 F. Amb. for instruction & instructed. 137 F Amb Stretcher bearers (2 Amb) arrived from & their billets ADSM re. orders re 137 F.Amb. seen. the Labour Corps Stretcher-bearers. They were 1. A mixed lot re type than normally. 1 case of CSM from 13 (SR) R. Irish Fus reported died at SP.CLS re 10¼ P. Oct. 136 F. Amb. They took were sent the patient was enemies informed & take necessary precautions. Teaching re CSM & t.R.I Amb Fus: Found that contacts who had been in same hut as patient taken by Bacteriologist. Sam. Sistem, re investigation outbreaks the 12th M STAFFS, 12th R.I. Regt. in the EAST HAZEBROUCK line. Influenza admission very few now - 2 trenchfoot. Reinforcement arrived etc. 30 B.R & 137 F. Amb. 10 OR & 135 F. Amb. some other duty 6 a Division to hospital.	
	13/7/18		ADMS inspected 'imports' of 11. G.B. Camerons & sent 13 to base under D/Thed coat 11 of 11/5/117. there was only 6 a Division to hospital yesterday including 1 influenza.	
	14/7/18		ADMS attended a conference at D.H.Q. at noon re further training of the Division in the Line: DA Dirt wired (7 Gen) WORCESTERs who have about 25 cases Influenza & arrange for most of them to be sent to hospital & suspects pulmonary measures are to be taken. A. Second suspected case of CSM in Transport SM. R.Irish Fusiliers reported by MO le - F.Amb and of Serums & Hut - OSM. Patient evacuated G W. 21 St Hospital. Transport isolated in 9 remountes, retood with 136 137 F Ambres ???	

WAR DIARY
INTELLIGENCE SUMMARY

A.D.M.S. 40. Division

Place	Date	Hour	Summary of Events and Information	Remarks and references to Appendices
RENESCURE 27/T.20.d.8.6.	15-7/8	—	A.D.M.S. visited 23rd Lanc. Fusiliers. The Regiment moves tonight to further Trench instructions in EAST HAZEBROUCK Line, preparing a Epidemic of P.U.O. came in WORCESTER. Regt.	
	16 7/8	—	A.D.M.S. inspected 'unfits' in 23rd Bn. L.anc. Fus. and sent 2 Officers and 10 O.Ranks to Base under S.M.S. Reg.S/I. 4/16 1/7. A.D.M.S. visited R.A.P.s of 1st Australian Division to make mutual arrangement re M.O.s for the 119 I. Bde. moving under the Relief of 1st Aust. Divn. on 17/7/8 in. the area. G.O.C. 40 Div. inspects the 137 and 135 Field Ambulances today. A.D.M.S. invites R.D.M.S. 2nd Div. to arrange to medical attendance on 119 Bde 1st Aust. Divn. in ROCQUINHEM area, R.D.M.S. 2nd Div. agrees to continue to look after them whilst his division was in the present Schedule, Arrangements were arranged A.D.M.T.F. verysuccessful-recovery time.	
	17/7/8		Operations Order (Route) No 78 and amendment issued regarding collection of sick & wounded of 119 Infantry Brigade, who are being transferred, attached Appendix 2. to 1 Aust. Divn. Medical Arrangement No 16 issued.	Appendix 2.
	18 7/8		A.D.M.S. visited D.D.M.S. II Corps and with him proceeded to visit the proposed A.D.S.s for the WEST HAZEBROUCK Line, and the Corps W.C.Sn at 27/V.19.a.7.0 (9th Divn Personnel) and 137 / Ambulance. Afterwards the G.O.C. on return 136 Field Ambulance the Report was bet attendance.	

Army Form C. 2118.

WAR DIARY
or
INTELLIGENCE SUMMARY.
(Erase heading not required.)

A.D.M.S.
40 Division

Instructions regarding War Diaries and Intelligence Summaries are contained in F. S. Regs., Part II. and the Staff Manual respectively. Title pages will be prepared in manuscript.

Place	Date	Hour	Summary of Events and Information	Remarks and references to Appendices
RENESCURE (T.20.d.8.6.)	18/7/18	-	Eliminating trials for the 1st Anzac Team to take on the Rifling near the 40 Div. P.S. shots at 2/7/18 mid-day team today & won by 13 F. Ambce. Range 0.1079 (mid-day) bright to all concerned.	Apppdx 3.
	19/7/18	-	A.D.M.S. visits 2nd Army Dental centre & mountain hostlery it would be before the first of the G.8 mir. Something supply & attention would secure attention. — A matter of about two months. RAMC's then visits the 2nd Army to bring the matter forth his notice & to have it occupied if possible.	
	20/7/18	-	A.D.M.S. VII Corps called on A.D.M.S. as to arrangement for taking over by VII Corps which will be attached to them soon in thanking the W. HAZEBROUCK line.	
	21/7/18	-	A Divisional Church Parade (C.G.E.) was held today. Divisional P.E. shots are held today. Ammunt. 101 & Rifle Op. 1079 mid Apppdx. 4.	
	22/7/18	-	R.A.M.C. instructs "reps" at WORCESTER Rifle went a few to Base. Preliminary meeting at 137 F. Ambce Evans to remove steps at an early date.	
	23/7/18	-	R.D.M.S. held several Medical Boards in the Office this morning. Appointment for 40 Div. men to attend 2nd Army Dental Centre have commenced & some at the rate of 20 a day. Commanding 2) not instruction inform units concerned arrange for the transport.	Apj

Army Form C. 2118.

WAR DIARY
or
INTELLIGENCE SUMMARY.

A.D.M.S. 40 Div.

(Erase heading not required.)

Instructions regarding War Diaries and Intelligence Summaries are contained in F. S. Regs., Part II. and the Staff Manual respectively. Title pages will be prepared in manuscript.

Place	Date	Hour	Summary of Events and Information	Remarks and references to Appendices
RENESCURE 27/T.20.a.86.	24/7/18	—	D.M.D.M.S. visits 2 by Trains & Bertin & 120 Inf Bde in Renescure and medical arrangements. Conversant in memo of D.M.S. wants that men who have had ten's extinct recently & while awaiting the supply of chlorine should not be sent into the line by day that there are about 120 cases in 121 Bde plans "D say" that there are about 120 cases in 121 Bde men have not all been under dental treatment referred arrangements for the D.D.M.D. Gas Officer to visit the units concerned tomorrow.	
	25/7/18	—	D.D.M.S. inspected men of D.T.L.I. Regt. (61.) 23rd L.A.F.C. FUS (9) and 22nd CHESHIRES. (14) who were considered unfit for work of 2 Bn and sent a number of the men under by Crucket 24. Arrived visited the M.O.i 9 Bn units & enquired into the sanitary & general condition.	
	26/7/18	—	R.A.M.S. inspects army 40 "unfits" of K.O.S.B. today — arrange for a number to be sent to Bax under Sy. Circular 24.	
	27/7/18	—	Two Officers auxiliaries reported arrived today – Lt. PHIPPS & Lt. H—. A.D.M.S. inspects "unfits" of 23rd L.A.M.C. FUS.; and sent — 2 Offns and R. OR to the Base under SyNds Circ. No 24.	
	28/7/18	—	A.D.M.S. inspected the camps of 137 & 136 Field Ambulances.	
	29/7/18	—	Routine Order No 80 issued re 121 Inf Bde coming under orders of 1st Australian Div inc. 119 Inf Bde — to be relieved re 21 Div. 31/7/18.	Appendix 5

Army Form C. 2118.

WAR DIARY
or
INTELLIGENCE SUMMARY.

A.D.M.S. 40. Div.

(Erase heading not required.)

Place	Date	Hour	Summary of Events and Information	Remarks and references to Appendices
RENESCURE T.20.d.8.6/27	30/10	—	Orders issued that 135th Field Ambulance (– Sec.) 2 Off. + 1 Lieut. Subdivision to take over sick at QUIESTEDE (26ª/A 30a) of Junior Corps Sick Depot.	
	31/10	—	ADMS visited 10th I.C.C.S. and will arrange to relieve the M.O. & Personnel work. CALDALE. q.s. 62 Am. Personnel work. MAJOR McKNIGHT Capt TROUNCE & 1 Sub Subdivision took over F. Hunter site at QUIESTEDE today for 61 Division. L't Col W. McK. H. McCullagh D.S.O. M.C. 137th Amb. proceeded at 14 Fayse Cap to U.K. The general health this month has been good; the influenza epidemic caused about 6 to 20 admissions per day for the first week but rapidly decreased thereafter. During this month there has been great improvement in the general hygiene and morale. 12 Officers & 200 O. Ranks were sent to their Own Depots as they had not improved with the treatment. Recreational training is greatly appreciated by all ranks. A. 18 aux 119. Inf. Bde were attached to the 1st Australian Division and took over a portion of the Front Line System. Medical arrangements were carried on by the 1st Australian F Ambulance. 135 F Amber. carries out the evacuation of an Australian Inf. Bde in MACQUINGHEN area.	

Austin Majr RAMC
for ADMS
40 Div.

SECRET. COPY NO. 20

40TH. DIVISION R.A.M.C. ORDER NO. 77.

Reference Maps.
Sheets 27 & 36A.   3rd. July, 1918.

1.   Field Ambulances will arrange to evacuate all casualties of Battalions from their affiliated Brigade, while in occupation of the EAST HAZEBROUCK LINE.

2.   A suitable stand for an Ambulance Car will be found in close proximity to the R.A.Ps.

3.   Evacuation of Sick will be as at present.
        Any casualties of a severe nature will be evacuated to the nearest M.D.S. These are located as under :-

        Left Division.   V.4.c.2.6.
        Centre Division.   V.9.b.1.5.
        Right Division.   C.5.a.6.9.

                                            J Humphrey
                                            Colonel.
                                            A.D.M.S. 40th. Division.

Distribution - Normal plus A.Ds.M.S. 9th., 31st. & 1st. Aus.
                                                    Divisions.

SECRET.   COPY NO.
******   ***********

40TH. DIVISION R.A.M.C. ORDER NO.78

Reference Maps
Sheets 27 & 36A.   17/7/18.

1. 119th. Infantry Brigade on moving into the line, on night of 17/18th. inst., will come under the orders of 1st. Australian Division.

2. By arrangement with A.D.M.S. 1st. Australian Division, all evacuations will be carried out by the 1st. Australian Division.

3. Location of Medical Posts.

   Right Brigade.
   R.A.P.   E.4.d.3.1.
   A.D.S.   BORRE. (Brasserie)
   M.D.S.   V.9.b.1.5.
   D.R.S.   U.5.a.9.3.

4. (a) All wounded of 40th. Division will be shown on "A.& D" Books of 1st. Australian Division.
   (b) No Sick cases of 40th. Division will be entered in "A.& D" Books of 1st. Australian Division.
   Such cases will be sent to Australian D.R.Sn. at U.5.a.9.3.

5. O.C. 136th. Field Ambulance will arrange to collect those cases daily from the 1st. Australian D.R.S. They will be sent with their 'Sick Reports'.

6. In cases of sick of 40th. Division who require immediate evacuation to C.C.S., A.F.W.3210 will be made out by the 1st. Australian Division, and sent to O.C.136th. Field Ambulance for entry in their "A.& D" Books.

7. Acknowledge.

   Issued at 11.30.a.m.

                                         J Humphrey
                                         Colonel.
                                         A.D.M.S. 40th. Division.

Distribution:-   D.M.S. Second Army.
                 D.D.M.S. XVth. Corps.
                 A.D.M.S. 1st. Australian Division.
                 "G" 40th. Division.
                 "Q" 40th. Division.
                 H.Qrs. 119th. Infantry Brigade.
                 136th. Field Ambulance.
                 M.O.i/c 13th. R.Innis.Fus.
                    "   13th. East Lancs.
                    "   12th. N. Staffs.
                 War Diary.
                 Office.

AMENDMENT NO.1 TO R.A.M.C. ORDER NO.78.
****

1. Para.4.(b) After "1st.Australian Division", add (except as specified in para.6.).

2. Cancel para.6 and substitute :-

Cases of Sick of the 40th.Division who require immediate evacuation to C.C.S., will be entered in the "A.& D" Books of the Australian Field Ambulance concerned, and a copy of the entry will be sent on A.F.W.3210 to O.C. 136th.Field Ambulance, for his information and transmission to this Office.

D.H.Qrs.
17/7/18.

Colonel.
A.D.M.S. 40th.Division.

SECRET.

COPY NO 47

40TH. DIVISION R.A.M.C. ORDER No. 79.

Reference Maps.
Sheets 27 & 36A.

18/7/18.

1. 40th. Division R.A.M.C. Order No.76 dated 27/6/18, is cancelled.

2. In the event of an enemy attack on the Second Army Front, the 40th.Division, (less 119th.Infantry Brigade and 1 Company 17th. Worcester Regt.) and attached troops, will man the WEST HAZEBROUCK LINE from 36A/D.25.c. to 27/V.6.central, a distance of about 13,000 yards.
Divisional Headquarters is at RENESCURE 27/T.21.a.1.0.

3. The Divisional Sector is divided into two Brigade Sections as follows:-
SOUTHERN SECTION......120th.Inf.Bde. with H.Qrs.at C.3.c.5.3.
NORTHERN SECTION......121st.   "   "   "   "   "   U.18.d.9.8.

4. The boundaries of Brigade Sections are as follows:-

SOUTHERN SECTION   Southern Boundary. A line drawn from
D.25.c.5.8.to C.25.c.0.8.
Northern Boundary. WALLON CAPPEL along the
Grid line to U.30.b.1.9-U.30.b.8.6-V.25.a.8.8

NORTHERN SECTION   Southern Boundary. Northern Boundary of
Southern Section.
Northern Boundary. A line drawn from
V.12.b.50.95.(exclusive)to V.6.a.5.7.(exclusive)-
V.5.c.5.2-V.4.d.5.7-V.3.a.0.4-V.1.a.0.3-U.6.a.0.1-
U.9.a.5.9.

5. Field Ambulances will be responsible for the collection of all casualties from the areas within the following boundaries:-

135th.Fd.Ambce. S.Boundary.- A line drawn from D.25.c.5.8.to C.25.c.0.8.
N.Boundary.- C.6.d.8.2-C.6.c.0.6-C.5.d.0.3-C.4.d.5.2-C.3.d.2.0.

137th.Fd.Ambce. S.Boundary - The same of N.Boundary of 135th.F.A.
N.Boundary - V.21.b.9.0-V.15.c.5.7-V.14.b.6.0-U.17.a.0.0-U.13.a.0.0.

136th.Fd.Ambce. S.Boundary - The same as N.Boundary of 137th.F.A.
N.Boundary - V.12.b.50.95-V.6.a.5.7-V.5.c.5.2-V.4.d.5.7-V.3.a.0.4-V.1.a.0.3-U.6.a.0.1-U.9.a.5.9.

6. A.D.Ss. will be established at the following points:-

By 135th.Field Ambce............at 36A/C.16.c.8.8.
By 137th.   "   " ....at 27/U.20.b.9.4.
By 136th.   "   " ....at 27/V.1 d.9.5.

7. Car Posts will be established in front of the A.D.Ss. at the discretion of the Os.C. Field Ambulances.

8. 136th. Field Ambulance will establish a M.D.S. at T.18.c.8.7. for the stretcher cases collected by 136th. and 137th. Field Ambulances.
   135th. Field Ambulance will establish a M.D.S. at B.18.c.0.0. for stretcher cases collected in this Ambulance area.
   137th. Field Ambulance will form the Corps Walking Wounded Collecting Station at T.22.a.3.4. for all walking cases in the Divisional Area.

9. "A. & D" Books will be kept, and A.T.S. given at the M.D.Ss. and C.W.W.C.S.
   Attention is drawn to A.D.M.S.40th.Division 115(M) dated 11/6/18, re the use of the letters A.T.S.+ O when ordinary A.T.Serum is given.

10. Each Field Ambulance will set aside accommodation for gassed cases.

11. The Medical Officers i/c Labour Groups will proceed with their attached Ambulance Cars and place themselves at the disposal of Os.C. Field Ambulances as under :-

   M.Os.i/c 33rd. and 64th.Labour Groups to 135th.Fd.Ambce.
   (36A/B.18.c.0.0.)
   M.O. i/c 26th.Labour Group to 137th.Field Ambulance
   (27/T.22.a.3.4.)
   M.Os. 1/c 5th.and 31st.Labour Groups to 136th.Field Ambce.
   (27/T.18.c.8.7.)

12. 300 Stretcher Bearers are being provided from 5th, 31st. and 64th. Labour Groups, and will report as under:-

   100 men from 64th. Labour Group to 135th. Field Ambce.
   100 "   "   5th.   "   "   " 137th.   "   "
   100 "   "   31st.   "   "   " 136th.   "   "
   These men will be rationed by the respective Field Ambulances, by whom they will be supplied with stretchers and S.B. Armlets.

13. A Dump of 150 Stretchers and 250 Blankets is formed at C.W.W.C.S. at 27/T.22.a.3.4.

14. Any man reporting at an A.D.S. suffering from very slight wounds etc., and whom the Medical Officer thinks is fit to return to the line, will be detained at the A.D.S. and handed over to the Military Police who are arranging to visit A.D.Ss. periodically.
   All facilities for re-arming or re-equipping these men are to be accorded to the Police.(156(M) dated 19/6/18).

15. Evacuations from A.D.Ss. to M.D.Ss. and C.W.W.C.S. will be by Divisional Ambulance Cars.
   Evacuations from M.D.Ss. to C.C.S. BLENDECQUES, will be by M.A.C.Cars, and evacuations from C.W.W.C.S. by T.A.T. from EBBLINGHEM, or Lorries to 4 Stationary Hospital, ARQUES.

16. Os.C. Field Ambulances will furnish brief reports 4 hourly on the situation giving numbers evacuated, awaiting evacuation etc., to this Office.

17. Os.C. Field Ambulances will forward any amendments to the schemes already in force to this Office as soon as possible.

18. Attention is directed to Q.M.G.Memo.82 (Q.A.1.) of 18/4/18, forwarded under this Office No.137(M) dated 29/4/18, (Field Ambulances only), regarding the use of Ambulance Cars in forward areas.

19. Acknowledge. (Fd Ambces.,R.M.Os. & Labour Group M.Os.only).

Issued at 9.p.m.

[signature]

A.D.M.S.40th.Division.

Distribution:- Normal plus -

    D.D.M.S.VIIth.Corps.
    A.D.M.S. 9th.Division.
    " 29th. "
    " 31st. "
    " 1st.Aust.Division.
    O.C. 14.M.A.C.
    " 5th.Labour Group.
    " 26th. " "
    " 31st. " "
    " 33rd. " "
    " 64th. " "
    M.O. 5th. " "
    " 26th. " "
    " 31st. " "
    " 33rd. " "
    " 64th. " "
    O.C. 17th. Worcester Regt.(P).
    Labour Commandant VIIth.Corps.
    " " XVth. "
    War Diary.
    File.

SECRET.   COPY No. 16

40TH. DIVISION R.A.M.C. ORDER NO. 80.

Reference Maps,
Sheets 27 & 36A.   29/7/18.

1. On relief of the 119th. Infantry Brigade in the line by the 121st. Infantry Brigade on the night 31st/1st August, 1918, the 119th. Infantry Brigade will come under the orders of 40th. Division, and the 121st. Infantry Brigade will come under the orders of the 1st. Australian Division.

2. By arrangement with A.D.M.S. 1st. Australian Division, all evacuations from the 121st. Infantry Brigade, will be carried out by the 1st. Australian Division.

3. Location of Medical Posts:-

   R.A.P.(Right Bde.)...   E.4.d.3.1.
   A.D.S.   ....   BORRE (Brasserie)
   M.D.S.   ....   V.9.b.1.5.
   D.R.S.   ....   U.5.a.9.3.

4. (a) All wounded of 40th. Division will be shewn in "A.& D" Books of 1st. Australian Division.
   (b) No sick cases of 40th. Division (except as specified in para.5.) will be entered in "A.& D" Books of 1st. Australian Division. Such cases will be sent to Australian D.R.S. at U.5.a.9.3.

5. Cases of sick of the 40th. Division who require immediate evacuation to C.C.S., will be entered in the "A.& D" Books of the Australian Field Ambulance concerned, and a copy of the entry will be sent on A.F.W.3210 to O.C.137th. Field Ambulance for his information, and for transmission to this Office.

6. 135th. Field Ambulance will continue to collect the sick of the Australian Infantry Brigade in the RACQUINGHEM Area daily, and will send them to 137th. Field Ambulance.

7. 137th. Field Ambulance will forward the Australian sick to the Australian D.R.S. at U.5.a.9.3., and the returning cars will bring back sick of 40th. Division to 137th. Field Ambulance.
   Australian sick will not be entered in "A.& D" Books of 40th. Division, except cases sent direct to C.C.S., when a copy of the entry on A.F.W.3210 will be forwarded to the Australian D.R.S.

8. Acknowledge.

   Issued at 4.p.m.

                                                  [signature]
                                                  Colonel,
                                                  A.D.M.S. 40th. Division.

   Distribution:-   D.M.S. Second Army.
                    D.D.M.S. XVth. Corps.
                    A.D.M.S. 1st. Australian Division.
                    "G" 40th. Division.
                    "Q" 40th. Division.
                    H.Qrs. 119th. Infantry Brigade.
                    H.Qrs. 121st.   "   "
                    135th, 136th, & 137th. Field Amboes.
                    M.Os.i/c 23rd.Lancs.F. 23rd.Cheshire Regt.
                         & 8th.R.Irish Regt.
                    War Diary.
                    Office.

CONFIDENTIAL.

MEDICAL SERVICES.

WAR DIARIES.

OF

A.D.M.S. 40TH. DIVISION.

O.C. 135TH. FIELD AMBULANCE.

O.C. 136TH. FIELD AMBULANCE.

O.C. 137TH. FIELD AMBULANCE.

FOR MONTH OF

AUGUST 1918.

VOL. XXVII.

Lt. Col. R.A.M.C.
a/ ADMS 40th Divn.

WAR DIARY
INTELLIGENCE SUMMARY

Army Form C. 2118.

A.D.M.S. 40th Divn.

Place	Date	Hour	Summary of Events and Information	Remarks and references to Appendices
RENFSCOAF. 27/T.20.d.26.	1 8/19	-	A.D.M.S. visited 136 F. Amb. re the establishing plan of an Advanced Army Depository Centre. Instruct submitted to B.G.S. for S.O. to do so as to make a complete & efficient hospital. Capt. McLEOD. to 11 Mobile (BAC) Laboratory visits R. Stns. on the installation of his apparatus & then proceeded to 135. F.A. when to talk matters over with O.C. R. Stns. visits 137 F. Amb. re increase in the patients of the detained then & visited from M.T. Coy. & LOUDENESSE to the Soda water factory recently installed & the Church of 1 Motor Ambulance Conv. the Army Dental & Ophthalmic Centres were also visited regarding cases from the Division.	
"	2 8/19	-	A.D.M.S. visited the tent extension of 135 F. Amber. at 28.7/A.28.4.25. where they are making the Corps Slem Depot. There are about 15 marquees to be put up & tent beds, continue to be built. Heavy rain is delaying the work a little. I. D & S. Capt. is arranging the supply of material required. Then visited R.S. Tons 31. Divn. regarding arrangements for the 121. Inf. Bde. when coming under the orders of Divn. & 4/5-8-18. Arranged that 31. Divn. will carry out the evacuation of sick wounded. Also arranged for 3 medical officers (MOTC) of the attendees to 31. Divn. for instruction.	
"	3 8/19	-	A.D.M.S. inspects outpost of 13th Fr. EAST LANES & after then two F.Amb's to the line and sent them to Base about 48.	Alixim Jell Major F Ams

WAR DIARY
or
INTELLIGENCE SUMMARY.   A.D.M.S. 40 Division
(Erase heading not required.)

Army Form C. 2118.

Place	Date	Hour	Summary of Events and Information	Remarks and references to Appendices
RENESCURE 57/T.20.d.8.6.	4/8/18	—	A.D.M.S. attended the Army Chest Parade Service at TERDEGHEM today, as an of the Representative Officer of the Division. R.O.A.S. visited 136 F.Amb. and saw the two wards fitted up for the Army Retained Dysentery Cases. They are being equipped with 50 beds to form B.R.C.S.	
	5/8/18.	—	40 Div R.A.M.C. Sports were held today and were very successful. After a cool night and a dull morning the prom was on but condition, but in the evening heavy rain came on during the last events, and the Performance by the Divisional Troops had to be cancelled.	
	6/8/18.	—	A.D.M.S. visited Nos. 12 N. STAFFS. and notified about 20 n.p.b. Matron, 2 Officers and 8 O.Ranks were sent to Base. Capt J.S. STEWART. M.C. R.A.M.C. proceeded today as M.O. i/c 10. K.O.S.B. vice Lt. J.M.H. CALDWELL R.A.M.C. who on relief joins 135. Field Ambulance. The Retained Army Dysentery Centre for the two Northern Corps of 2nd Army was opened today at 136 F.Amb. at 4 p.m. G.O.R. for 25 cases in wards at Brutry Aug.	

WAR DIARY or INTELLIGENCE SUMMARY

A.D.M.S. 40th Division

Army Form C. 2118

Place	Date	Hour	Summary of Events and Information	Remarks and references to Appendices
RENESCURE 27/T.20.d.86.	7/8	–	A.D.M.S. visited 132, 135 Field Ambulances and the Cyclist Coy. Depot at 36 M.A. 28 a. D.D.M.S. visited the home FUs in the line & 31 Divn, the C/O MMMS and the 8. R.I. Regt. fld. 121 Fd. Bee attached to 31 Divn.	
	8/8	–	New census allotment times are only three stretcher 2. O.R. Orderly for A.D.M.S. to allot. Stretchers visited 135 F. Amb.	
	9/8/20	–	A.D.M.S. visited 136 + 137 F. Amb. + from the A.O.D. Cante. very full. Shewed (Sen) + advice on Pathology with the A.D.D. Cante.	
	10/8	–	A.D.M.S. visits 15th K.O.Y.L.I. and 11. Camerons' and sent down to Base, 2 O.R. from K.O.Y.L.I and 7 O.R. fm Camerons.	
	11/8	–	A.D.M.S. visited Dn. A.H. Deputy Contr. at 136 F. Amb. to arrange for issue of accommodation, and also visited 137 F. Amb. M.H.R.S. attend at Special Henry Peenet Service at which the King was present; this was followed by a march past of representation of the troops to the 2nd Army	
	12/8		A.D.M.S. visited the Corps Septum Station (1st Ent. sub division 135: F. Amb.) Corp MECOM noted Special Censor. 14 day. F.K.R. At P.H.F.R.B has taken over mot and large temporarily	a.e.g.

Army Form C. 2118

WAR DIARY
or
~~INTELLIGENCE SUMMARY~~
(Erase heading not required.)

A.D.M.S. 40. Division

Instructions regarding War Diaries and Intelligence Summaries are contained in F.S. Regs., Part II. and the Staff Manual respectively. Title Pages will be prepared in manuscript.

Place	Date	Hour	Summary of Events and Information	Remarks and references to Appendices
PERNESCURE. 27/T.2od.P.6.	13/8/18	-	A.D.M.S. visited 135 Field Ambulance, the inquired into the treatment and disposal of cases of pyrexia. A.A. Dysentery Convoi of 136 Fr. another men moved by another 30 hrs. JOHNSON. A.J. BEVERIDGE M.C. proceeded on 14 days leave U.K. today. Lt. MILLS. M.R.C. V.S.R. rejoined 137 Field Ambulance today from temporary duty with XV Corps. Reinforcement Battn. 121 Inf. Bde. rejoined this 40 Division today, in relief in the line with 31 Division by 123 Inf. Bde.	
	14/8/18	-	A.D.M.S. inspected about 30 unfit Q.17s WORCESTERS and sent about 8 to Base. Divisional Clothing store was also visited & clean clothing received from Army Laundry was examined. As many of them showed many eggs of lice, a sample was sent to D.A.D.S. Corps in support of a complaint recently made by this office on the subject.	
	15/8/18	-	A.D.M.S. attended to review a recent photograph taken from aeroplane of the Divl. Rest Stn. accompanied by J.M. Davis (San) 2nd Army re the Clean Clothing Question, and later & REQUESTS shown the clothing, appears to be efficiently treated, although it was noted that the system of marking the seams of garments allowed to dist.	
	16/8/18	-	A.D.M.S. attended Conference of D.D.M.S. XV Corps re General Hosp'l arrangements, disinfestation, instruction of Officers & O.Ranks on Sanitary matters etc. A.D.M.S. then visited 136 & 137 Field Ambces.	

1875 Wt. W593/826 1,000,000 4/15 J.B.C. & A. A.D.S.S./Forms/C.2118.

WAR DIARY or INTELLIGENCE SUMMARY

Army Form C. 2118

A.D.M.S. 40 Div

Place	Date	Hour	Summary of Events and Information	Remarks and references to Appendices
REMESCURE 27/T.20.a.8.6	17/8	-	A.D.M.S. attended the 118 Bde. Sports & Lunch; then visited Old Road Camp & was present at the movies in the Divisional Competition.	
	18/8	-	R.D.M.S. 31 Div. called on A.D.M.S. today, & went to see detachment of 137 F. Ambce, demong. the XV Corps Scabies Centre. Experiments with a simple disinfector consisting of blankets in a framework over a charcoal fire were carried out, and a temp. of 105° F. centigrade was obtained.	
	19/8	-	A.D. Divisional Horse Show was held at REMESCURE, and was very successful. Several Prizes were awarded off to the Field Ambulances.	
	20/8	-	Corps Commander, XV Corps & DDMS Divisional Commander, DDMS inspected 136 Field Ambulance. The G.O.C. Corps & Divisional expressed great satisfaction with the turnout. A.D.M.S. visited 137 F. Ambce, and the C.W.W. C.S. at U.19.a.5.1/27. Taken over today by a new unit. P.137 F Ambce from the 31 Div. The A/DMS inspected inspects of the 12 N Staffs, and Sat Don an Officer & F.P. R.S this Major A.D.M.S. 31 Div arranges for service on Exchange over then Sept. shortly. The Enemy by the Brig. Fleet is returning to get into touch with him.	29

WAR DIARY of ADMS 40th Div

INTELLIGENCE SUMMARY

Army Form C. 2118.

Place	Date	Hour	Summary of Events and Information	Remarks and references to Appendices
RENESCURE	21/8/18		Visited 23 Lanc. Fus. & 23 Cheshires to see men for re-classification. Orders for 40 Div. to take over front held by 31 Div.	
			R.A.M.C. personnel no 83 issued to this effect. D.A.D.M.S. granted leave in turn from 22.8.18. to 29.8.18.	
	22/8/18		The Division relieved the 31st Div. in the right sector of the XV Corps front, with two Bns. in the line & one in reserve. A.D.M.S. Officer moved to WALLON CAPPEL.	
WALLON CAPPEL 30/1/72 27/V.30.c.0.7.	23rd		135 Field Amb. Took over A.D.S. at 36/A D.18.a.5.2. with H.Q.M 27/U24 c.12.0. 136 F.A. remained at 27 T 18.c.8.7.	
			137 F.A. moved to 36/A c.5.a.5.g. taking it over as the M.D.S. A.D.M.S. Officer moved up to D.H. camp at 27/V.30 c.0.7.	
	24		Went round A.D.S. & R.A.P.s of 119 & 120 Bde Sectors.	
	25		Went round R.A.P.s & relief parts of left 13th Sector.	
	26			
	27		Went round Units of 121 Bde in reserve. Minor operation today by 119 & 120 Bdes. Objectives not entirely gained. About 150 casualties.	
	28		Examined some men of Re Tank Reg. to recommend 18 to be sent to Boom en Amfut for homework.	

WAR DIARY or INTELLIGENCE SUMMARY

A.D.M.S. 40. Divn.

Army Form C. 2118

Place	Date	Hour	Summary of Events and Information	Remarks and references to Appendices
WALLON CAPPEL	29/8	—	ADMS visits 138 Field Ambulance. 120 Inf Bde moves & moves operation order was successful — about 25 casualties.	
"	30/8	—	ADMS visits hospitals & barbers and arranged for A.D.S. and M.D.S. to be moved forward. Operation Order No 84 issued to all concerned. DADMS visited the morning front leave 1st Phase. The enemy commenced withdrawing on this divin front from Stray Lhr 7.2.1. Inf Bde in follow up. ADMS visits F. Ambces sit at 38 M/C. S. a. S. 9. Lorry trsn attachment of 136. F. Ambce instructed thus.	Appendix 1.
"	31/8	—	137. F Ambce move thus morning & reported up a main dressing station at LA MOTTE (360/D 20.Central) at 9. a.m.	
		10 a.m.	ADMS telephoned to say that 136 F Ambce was required to leave EBLINGHEM today & to 6 C.C.S. is moving up. Night Order No 85: moved tent covered. Appendix 2. Fm 136 F Ambce to move to site at 38 M/C.S.a. S.9. Leaving Attachment to run the Army Advanced Dressing Centre at EBLINGHEM.	
			ADMS visits the A.D.S, BRITANNIA Fm 300/E.20. Central, and then to the new MDS in process of construction at the Flemans, & the SCHOOL, VIEUX BERQUIN. The Road are passable in an interval of time V. Berquin for some mile or two. ADMS met Col. 131 F Ambce here (VC of proposed Evacuation) & ascertained that a Clear Post was being established at HAUTE MAISON (F. 14. a. 4.4.).	
		6 p.m.	Wounded wounded [?] 1. Off. 5. ORs. A.D.S. A.D.S.S. (M.D.S.) and attended G.O.C.s conference at night. A.J.	

WAR DIARY
or
INTELLIGENCE SUMMARY

Army Form C. 2118

A.D.M.S.
40. Divn.

Place	Date	Hour	Summary of Events and Information	Remarks and references to Appendices
WALLON-CAPPEL 27/v.30.C.o).			Up till the 22nd inst the Brigades of the Division were attached to 31st Divn. On the 22 inst the 40 Divn relieved the 31 Divn on the Right Section of XV Corps front. 135. F. Amb. was put in charge of the forward evacuation arrangements. 137 F Amb took charge of the M.D.S. and 136 F. Amb. returned to man the A.A. Byzantine Centre. Two main questions arose carried out by the 119 and 120. but Bdes with intricate success. On the 30. inst. the enemy commenced activity on this Corps front and the 121. Bdg Bde are following up & have invested DOULIEU hill. Our liaison is being maintained by Bc.135 F. Amb. & Myr BOYEDIDES Msc. 130 F Amb in between R.M.Os. & F. Ambces, so that the runs of M.A.S. & M.D.S. are known to all. Sick wastage this month has been low. The weather on the whole has been good, but during the short three nights has been cold & wet. Every effort is being made to ensure the line parties & portable BLANKET chambers accompanied by XV Corps has been brought into use in several units, but the present movement of trops has stopped the trial.	Austin T. Jack Major RAMC. A.D.M.S

SECRET.   COPY NO.

40TH. DIVISION R.A.M.C. ORDER NO. 82.

Reference Maps.
Sheets 27 & 36A.   10/8/18.

1.   The 121st. Infantry Brigade will be relieved in the line by the 120th. Infantry Brigade on the night 12/13 inst.
On relief, the 121st. Infantry Brigade will come under the orders of the 40th. Division.

2.   By arrangement with the A.D.M.S. 31st. Division, all evacuation from the 120th. Infantry Brigade, will be carried out by the 31st. Division.

3.   Location of Medical Posts.

          R.A.P.(Rt. Bn. of Lt. Sector) E.14.d.5.3.
          Relay Posts............... E.8.c.5.6.
                                  E.19.b.8.3.
          A.D.S..................... D.18.a.5.3.
          (Reserve A.D.S.).......... D.9.d.1.8.
          M.D.S..................... C.3.a.6.9.
          H.Qrs.of Fd.Amb.in Line... U.24.c.2.0.

4.(a)   All wounded of the 40th. Division will be shewn in the "A.& D" Books of the 31st. Division.
  (b)   No sick cases of the 40th. Division(except as specified in para.5) will be entered in "A.& D" Books of 31st. Division.
Sick cases will be sent to the 31st. Division M.D.S. accompanied by their 'Sick Reports' to await collection by 135th. Field Ambulance.

5.   Sick cases of the 40th. Division who require immediate evacuation to C.C.S., will be entered in the "A.& D" Books of the Field Ambulance concerned, and a copy of the entry will be sent on A.F.W.3210 to O.C. 137th. Field Ambulance, who will keep a record of such cases in a special book. The man's unit will be notified by the 31st. Division Field Ambulance.

6.   O.C. 135th. Field Ambulance will arrange to collect daily from the 31st. Division M.D.S. all sick cases of the 40th. Division, and will convey them to 137th. Field Ambulance, who will 'admit' these cases.

7.   O.C.135th. Field Ambulance will arrange for a Car to collect any Dental and Ophthalmic cases at the A.D.Ss. at times to be arranged with Medical Officer i/c of the Battalion.

8.   In the event of severe fighting in this Sector, O.C. 135th. Field Ambulance will be prepared to send Stretcher Bearers to evacuate casualties from this Brigade, on receipt of orders from this Office.

9.   Acknowledge (Field Ambulances only.).

Issued at 1.p.m.

                                               Humphry
                                                Colonel.
                                     A.D.M.S.40th. Division.

Distribution :-
    D.M.S. Second Army.   D.D.M.S.XVth. Corps.
    A.D.M.S.31st. Divn.   "G" 40th. Division.
    "Q" 40th. Division.   120th. Inf. Bde.
    121st. Inf. Bde.   135th. Field Ambce.
    136th. Field Ambce.   137th.   "   "
    M.O.i/c 10th.K.O.S.B.   M.O.i/c 11th.Cameron Hldrs.
        "   15th.K.O.Y.L.I.
           War Diary.
           Office.

SECRET   COPY NO.

40TH. DIVISION R.A.M.C. ORDER NO. 83.

Reference Maps.
Sheets 27 & 36A.   21/8/18.

1.   The 40th. Division will take over the front now held by 31st. Division.

2.   The front to be taken over will be from the Corps Southern boundary to the PLATE BECQUE RAU at F.14.c.3.5.

<u>Divisional Southern Boundary.</u> L.7.d.0.0-K.12.a.0.0-K.11.b.9.6-K.4.a.9.0-K.2.a.0.0-K.1.c.4.3-D.30.c.8.3.

<u>Divisional Northern Boundary.</u> F.21.a.3.5-F.14.c.3.5-F.13.cent.-E.12.c.7.0-E.11.a.0.0-E.4.c.0.0-E.3.a.0.5

3.   Right Infantry Brigade Headquarters D.24.a.9.0.
        Left Infantry Brigade Headquarters   D.11.d.5.8.

4.   135th. Field Ambulance, less 1 Tent Sub-division which will continue in charge of the Corps Skin Depot, will take over the Headquarters of 94th. Field Ambulance at U.24.c.2.0., the A.D.S. at D.18.a.5.2. & all forward posts, and will be responsible for the evacuation of the front area.
        Move to be completed by 10.a.m. 24th.inst.

5.   136th. Field Ambulance will remain in its present site.

6.   137th. Field Ambulance, less a holding party of 1 Officer and 2 other ranks at T.22.a.3.4., also the holding party at Corps Walking Wounded Post at U.19.a.5.0., will take over the M.D.S. at 36A/C.5.a.5.9. from 93rd. Field Ambulance, 31st. Divn.
        Move to be completed by 10.a.m. 24th.inst.

7.   Arrangements to be made direct by Os.C. Field Ambulances concerned.

8.   Completion of moves and map locations to be reported to this Office.

9.   A.D.M.S. Office will close at RENESCURE at 3.p.m. 22nd.inst., and reopen at WALLON CAPPELL at the same hour.

10   Acknowledge.(Field Ambces. only).

        Issued at 10.p.m..
                                                    Colonel.
                                            A.D.M.S. 40th. Division.

Distribution - Normal plus A.D.M.S. 31st. Divn.
                          "   "   " 29th "
                          "   "   " 61st "

SECRET.   COPY NO.

40TH. DIVISION R.A.M.C. ORDER No. 84.

Reference Maps.   30/8/18.
Sheets 27 & 36A.

1.   O.C.137th. Field Ambulance will move forthwith to the Church at LA MOTTE, and open up a Main Dressing Station by 9.a.m.31st.inst.

2.   O.C.136th. Field Ambulance will detail a Senior Officer and 12 other ranks including a clerk and a dispenser and equipment of one Tent Sub-division to take over the site at C.5.a.5.9., and will form a Divisional Rest Station there.

3.   This party will be reinforced by 1 officer and 12 other ranks, detailed by 137th. Field Ambulance.

4.   O.C.135th. Field Ambulance will open forthwith, an Advanced Dressing Station at BRITANNIA FARM E.20.central, and will move his Headquarters to D.18.a.5.3. He will also reconnoitre and prepare an Advanced Dressing Station - location to be reported.

5.   Completion of moves with map references, to be reported to this Office

6.   Acknowledge (Field Ambces. only).

7.   Issued at 6.p.m.

                                        J Humphry
                                        Colonel.
                                        A.D.M.S.40th.Division.

Distribution - Normal plus A.D.M.S.29th.Divn.
                            A.D.M.S.61st.Divn.
                            M.O.i/c 104th M.G.B.

SECRET   COPY NO.
******   ********

                    40TH. DIVISION R.A.M.C. ORDER NO. 85.
                    ****

Reference Maps   31/8/18.
Sheets 27 & 36A.

1.   136th. Field Ambulance, less 2 Officers and 30 other
ranks, will move forthwith to Field Ambulance site at
36A/C.5.a.5.9., and open as a D.R.C.

2.   The party of 2 Officers and 30 other ranks on relief
by a C.C.S. will rejoin their Headquarters

3.   On the arrival of 136th. Field Ambulance at 36A/C.5.a.5.9.
the party of 137th. Field Ambulance left behind at that place
will rejoin their Headquarters.

4.   Acknowledge (Field Ambces only).

5.   Issued at 11.a.m.
                                                    Colonel.
                                            A.D.M.S. 40th. Division.

        Distribution - Normal

CONFIDENTIAL.

MEDICAL SERVICES.

WAR DIARIES

O F

A.D.M.S.   40TH., DIVISION
OFFICER COMMANDING   135TH., FIELD AMBULANCE.
     "   "   137TH.,   "   "

136

F O R

MONTH   OF   SEPTEMBER,

1918.

VOLUMES XXVIII

Humphry
Colonel,
A.D.M.S., 40th., Division.

1/10/18.

WAR DIARY or INTELLIGENCE SUMMARY

A.D.M.S. 40. Divn.

Army Form C. 2118

Place	Date	Hour	Summary of Events and Information	Remarks and references to Appendices
WALLON-CAPPEL 27/U.30.c.0.7	19/8	—	The 121. Inf. Bde. continued today to follow the enemy's retirement and moved through DOULIEU. A.D.M.S. visited 13o F. Amb. this morning, who are forming a divisional A.D.S. at Ln MOTTE and [illegible] in the afternoon the A.D.S. visited 137 F. Amb. who after anxiously for the turn of 137 F. Amb. to 36A/E.21.a.7.4. (CAST Fm), proceeded to N.DS at VIEUX BERQUIN and Fm there proceeded to inspect car post & relay posts up to F.22.a.9.4., where it is hoped to make an A.D.S. if the present mounted can be turned out. Ford car can reach to there point & during dry weather, it is hoped to put by Austin cars to DOULIEU with a day or two. Wounded admitted during 24 hours to 6pm today 14 O.R. H.Kpnel adm. No. 86. Wound. Nomme. 137 F.Amb. to E.21.a.7.4.	
LA MOTTE 36A/D.30. c.9.7.	20/8		A.D.M.S. Office moved to LA MOTTE today at 2 pm. A.D.M.S. proceeded on 14 days leave to U.K. Lt. Col. R.N. HUNT D.S.O. is acting in his absence. The 121. Inf. Bde. continued the advance today & entered CROIX DU BAC this evening. The A.D.S. at 36A/F.22.d.9.4. has now become a Car Post and the A.D.S. moved to 36/A.19.d.6.6. early this morning and led the afternoon was moved again to 36/A.21.b.2.8. Large Australian cars evacuated from A.D.S. to Car post F.22.d.9.4. as the road on this section was bad from their point back to Clu M.53. to Mont [illegible] [illegible] an steel nature and for the large cars to use & [illegible] ambulance to 6 pm - 14 ORs.	

WAR DIARY or INTELLIGENCE SUMMARY

Army Form C. 2118

A.D.M.S. 40. Division

Place	Date	Hour	Summary of Events and Information	Remarks and references to Appendices
LA MOTTE. 36T/D.30.c.9.7.	3/9/18	—	A.D.M.S. visits 137 Field Ambulance who are now running the M.D.S. at 36T/E.21.a.7.4. R.O.M.S. then proceeds to inspect the Car Post and Adv Post at VIEUX BERQUIN, the Car post at CASEY FARM and the new A.D.S. at 36/A.21.c.2.8, which was made a evening & 2nd Sept. R.O.M.S. then proceeds to select a site for 136 F Amb to establish a M.D.S. at an suitable and sheltered site at 36/F.30.d.4.6. which has previously been recommended evacuated by Major CRAWFORD of 136 F Amb. Orders issued for an action of 136 F Amb to move there by 5th inst. staying night of 4/5 inst at E.20 central. Three marquees to be taken at once and accommodation to be erected later. Under the arrangements from BOULIEU back are emptied the M.D.S. of (3) F Ambs will continue to function. Our line was advanced to their TRAM HARNES - E of CROIX-DU-BAC. wounded up to 8 pm today. — D.R. **31**.	
"	4/9/18	—	R.O.M.S. visits 137 F. Ambce (M.D.S.) today and found all ranks well. 19 cases of Sentries there evacuated from the 10. K.O.S.B. yesterday evening. The A.D.M.S. visits 136 F Ambce 16 K.O.S.B. and found that all the cases were put at the M.O.'s ordering them sickness after 15 days in the line in support when such conditions of baths could not be arranged. R.O.M.S. also visits the 17 K.O.Y.L.I. and 11 Cameronians of the Same Brigade. He explains to location of Divisional Posts adopted today. wounded admitted to 8 pm today — L. Off. 9. O.R.s. 1 Section 1/136 F. Ambce moved to 36/F.17.a-MBB. 5pm today and continuing the march 1/6 BOULIEU owns to 119 Inf Bde arrived proceed for VIEUX Berq. relieving the 121 Inf Bde in the line in V Berq.	

Army Form C. 2118

WAR DIARY
or
INTELLIGENCE SUMMARY   A.D.M.S.
(Erase heading not required.)   40. Division

Place	Date	Hour	Summary of Events and Information	Remarks and references to Appendices
La Motte. 36"/D.30. C.9.7.	5-9/18	—	A.D.M.S. visited 137 F. Amb. and the entrenchment of 136 F. Amb. who are making a M.D.S. near DOULIEU. He returned visited the R.D.S." which was now moved this morning from 36/A.21.b.2.8. to 36/A.24.d.2.1. The site of an enemy hospital which had been destroyed by fire during the retirement. Evacuation from here is by Ambulance Car through STEENWERCK R.D.S. 12 Walking Cases thro' No 87 issued on form of 136 M.S.R. & DOULIEU and the during of the M.D.S. there on 6 cases. 137 F. Amb. now open the A.D.S. Am. above the relief of 135 F. Amb. on the lines of (3) F. Ambs. — 14 O.Rs. Wounded admitted to 6 p.m. today, since 6 p.m. yesterday.	Appendices
"	6.9/18		M.D.S. at DOULIEU was opened at noon today by Major CRAWFORD R.C. in section of 136 F. Amb. 137 F. Amb. at this same time teams to the A.D.S. no change in position of R.D.S. today. A.D.M.S. visited 136 F. Amb. today. R.Gen. there on Duct to join the M.D.S. at DOULIEU R.G.T.C Inspected hospits. J.120 Inf Bde & recommended for the Base:— 5. OR. K.R.Rs.; 22 ORs. K.O.S.B.; 14. OR. CAMERONS. Wounded admitted for 24 hours ending 6 p.m. 20th Inst. OR. 14. OR. 1.; Other ranks OR. 5.	
"	7.9/18	—	A small operation was carried out this morning by 92nd Bde on our left to the 119 Bde. Friend the Rivers LYS. The 119 Bde reached the objective but later had to retire to the means line on the 52nd Bde area to up. Casualties 28. OR. OR. Several Reports that a Company of the have been lost for this today.	A.J.

Army Form C. 2118

WAR DIARY
or
INTELLIGENCE SUMMARY

(Erase heading not required.)

A.D.M.S. 40 Div.

Instructions regarding War Diaries and Intelligence Summaries are contained in F.S. Regs., Part II. and the Staff Manual respectively. Title Pages will be prepared in manuscript.

Place	Date	Hour	Summary of Events and Information	Remarks and references to Appendices
LA MOTTE 36A/D.30.c. 9.7.	7/9/18	—	A.D.M.S. visits 137 F.Amb. D.C.S. and M.D.S. The area round the M.D.S. was heavily shelled last night and today — it is proposed to move towards PONT WEMENT. Orders received that 66 Bde. M.G. Coy. came under orders 7.40 am today. Wounded admitted for 24 hours ending 6 p.m. 1.H. 134. O.R.	a.f.
"	8/9/18		M.D.S. moved this afternoon to 36A/F.29.6.5.9., owing to considerable shelling in the vicinity of present site. 137 F.Amb. took over the M.D.S. from 137) F.Amb. move today to the M.D.S. A.D.M.S. visits D.R.S., M.D.S., and H.Q. of 137 F.Amb. Wounded admitted for 24 hours ending 6 p.m. — 1.H. 27. O.R. Capt L.S. PILBEAN Dental Surgeon attached to this Division from 10. Stationary Hospital, proceeds to ENGLAND today on duty.	
"	9/9/18		A.D.M.S. visits 137 F.Amb. (D.R.S.) today, has Dental arrangements made today in Dental Surgeon from 18 Cas. Clearing Sta., D.R.S on Tuesday & Wednesday each week. A.D.M.S. visits detachment of 136 F.Amb at WATEOU CAMP and the detachment of 136 1st Amb. running the Advanced Army Dysentery Centre at ETELINGHEM. Wounded admitted for 24 hours ending 6 p.m. — 1.H. 1. O.R. 2.	a.f.

1875 Wt. W593/826 1,000,000 4/15 J.B.C. & A. A.D.S.S./Forms/C. 2118.

WAR DIARY
INTELLIGENCE SUMMARY

A.D.M.S. 40 Div.

Army Form C. 2118

Place	Date	Hour	Summary of Events and Information	Remarks and references to Appendices
LA MOTTE 36J/D.30.c.9.7.	10/9/18	-	A.D.M.S. inspected further units of "Camerons" and recommended 23 to be sent to Don for reclassification. Shewed their parade to MAJOR POWELL. (3) F. Ranks admitted BRIGHT left-legs & 16 days to V.K. (136 F. Amb.). Wounded admitted during 24 hour entry 6 p.m. - 5. O.Rs.	
"	11/9/18	-	The A.D.M.S. visited the D.Rs, M.D.S and H.Q. (3) F. Ranks and found all correct in spite of the heavy rains every day during the past week. The roads in the forward area are fairly good. MAJOR LINNELL R.A.M.C. (3) F. Amb. returned from Leave today. 39. M.C.Bn. appointed to the 102-M.G.Bn. Wounded admitted during 24 hours entry 6 p.m. today — O.R. 1.	
"	12/9/18	-	Still raining heavily. A small function was carried out this morning by the 13 N. STAFFS. to repel the enemy, S.Y.S. and was apparently successful. Casualties to wits: 22 wounded, 12 F. Ranks admitted (3) F. Ranks and the M.D.S. and the R.B. Ps Lt. Bele. D.Mchns. and Lt (3) F. Ranks. Capt McCLANAHAN M.R.C. E. 39. M. G. Bn. called in advr. J. in the time. Capt McCLANAHAN M.R.C. — 2 Off. 26. O.Rs. Wounded admitted during 26 hours entry 6 p.m. today.	
"	13/9/18	-	Lt P.R. SHANNON R.A.M.C. reported for duty today & posted 6(13). F. Ranks A.D.M.S. visits 135. + 136 F. Amb. rear. Continued loading up & to-day. Heavy showers of rain. Wounded admitted for 24 hours entry, 6 p.m. — 10. O.Rs.	ref.

WAR DIARY or INTELLIGENCE SUMMARY

A.D.M.S. 40 Div.

Army Form C. 2118

Place	Date	Hour	Summary of Events and Information	Remarks and references to Appendices
LA MOTTE au B°/D.30.c.9.7.	14/9/18	—	120 Inf. Bde. relieved the 119. Inf. Bde. in the line last night. ADMS visited the Divisional Baths, 36th/ D.18.c.8.2., & suggested various improvements. Also visited O.C. 56 Sani. Section re accommodation B/121 Inf Bde & 140 U Worker. & the I.W.R. 121 Inf Bde — 23 Lancs. Fus: Heavy rain all day long. Wounded admitted in 24 hours ending 6 p.m. — S.O.R.	
"	15/9/18	—	A.D.M.S. visited 135, 136, 137 F. Amb. and the M.D.S. 13. R. Innis. Fus and 73 E. Lancs and inspected their camps. Ordinated Capt and 2 Col. G.ON.Y. R.A.M.C. visited the Divisional baths to see the system and of letting they men. Shaving &c. Wounded admitting for 24 hours ending 6 p.m. — Off 1. O.R. 5. Telephone message from D.D.M.S. this morning that we complete F. Amb will be temporarily detached from the Division shortly. 136. F. Amb re numeration. R.A.M.S. visited 135. 136. 137. F. Amb. on the arrangement of the staff. Walter made & a warning order. Wounded admitted much improved today. MDS notes: N.Y. Res.N.Y. V.O.M.S.	Appendix
"	16/9/18	—	Wounded admitted for 24 hours ending 6 p.m. — O.R.8. No medical enemy shoots mean day.	
"	17/9/18	—	ADMS visited 121. Bde in Harebreck to enquire into sanitary condition and suggested various alteration. The interviewing the M.O.'s of 23rd Cheshires and R.I.R.. Major Cooke called at noon. 136 F Amb at 10 am 1916 Appendix Ralph ned no PD revealed O.C. 136 F Amb called on ADMS. Capt. Humphry C.M.S. ADMS returned from leave today. Recommend chats by mothers.	

WAR DIARY or INTELLIGENCE SUMMARY

Army Form C. 2118.

A.D.M.S.
40 Division

Place	Date	Hour	Summary of Events and Information	Remarks and references to Appendices
LA MOTTE 36a/D.30.c.4.7	18/9/18	—	A.D.M.S. visits 135, 136, 137, F. Ambces and the "A.D.S." 137 F. Ambce took over the M.D.S. from 138 F. Ambce at 11. am. Coy 138 F. Ambce to "parked at 36a/L.5.a.6.0. (La BRIELLE Fm) awaiting orders to move to another formation. (La BRIELLE Fm) Commenced shelling. was upheld round the M.D.S. yesterday. All personnel from A.A. Defence Units reported 12654. Wounded admitted during 24 hours to 6 pm — 19 O.Rs.	
	19/9/18	—	2nd Army wire desires to 126 F. Ambce about 3 am to proceed by [?] Road to PROVEN (27/E.6.d.4.3) + to come under U. control arranged by the Divisional Ambulance Convoy in by Lorries of 2th and transport and 7 F. Ambce, [?] temporary transport by 827 F.Ambce, lorries of 12) Mtg 81L taking Sec S2., RAMC. under 1/27 F. Ambce, packed 7 RDS, and F.F.H.P.s. Rode to the lines 30 to the Base personnel, voted 7 Bale in the lines. Wounded admitted for 24 hours ending 6pm. — 20 Div. D.R. 1. Bttn. O.R. 21.	
	20/9/18	—	A.D.M.S. wires the LO from M.T. Coy to hasten along the completion of the relief of the Divisional Ambulance Cars. A.D.M.S. visits A.D.S.s to Get further information. Bthes + Adm'd visits the M.D.S. and 2th 13 BRIELLE Fm (L.5.a.6.0) moving visits the 66 Div Battalion Plans + Coms on this Div. front. Rides, wishes w/ref of 23rd CHESHIRES— this arrangt. recommended 9.L. Ram. Wounded admitted for 24 hrs. ending 6 pm — 40 Div. Off.1 O.R. 3. 81 Div. D.R. 1.	B.J.

WAR DIARY
~~INTELLIGENCE SUMMARY~~ A.D.M.S. 40. Div

(Erase heading not required.)

Army Form C. 2118.

Place	Date	Hour	Summary of Events and Information	Remarks and references to Appendices
LAMOTTE 36 T/D 30.c.9.7	21/9/18	"	A.D.M.S. visits the A.D.S. to-day. A.D.M.S. visits D.D.M.S. IVth Corps and 136 F. Amb. when on complaints attached to IVth Corps A.D. are 4 left after Gunners in the area. They have only 3 large cars working & 1 unserviceable. at present as a result of the so called exchange. Nor have they any standard cars. A car & then driver. 1 Wounded admitted during 24 hrs ending 6 p.m. — 1. O.R. 5. O.R.	
"	22/9/18	"	Ambulance post instructions issued to F.Amb.s. A.D.M.S. visited 135,137) F.Ambulances and then proceeded to Cork & new A.D.S." prior to taking over some frontage from the 3/ Division on our left. It was decided to carry on at the present N.D.S's 38/ A.24.d.2.1. Wounded admitted during 24 hours ending 6 p.m. — 40 Div. O.R. 3. 51. Div. O.R. 4. A.D.M.S. inspects the Bath at A.22.c.4.5./28. When an Auxt-truck jut treatment room is being established. Rome order No. 88. issued.	Wharves
"	23/9/18	-	A.D.M.S. inspects units 1/13 East Lancs and 12 N. Staffs. this morning and arrangements 3 Off and 22 O.R.s to be sent to Base. 119. Lep. Rest m.o. to take on the time to be seen. Cancelled Rome order 89. Cancelled 137). F. Amb. they moved the N.D.S. Am F.29.a.6.9. & L.S.a. 6.D. A.D.S's might possibly be taken later at A.27).C.2.2. but it is rather out of the way for us. N.D.S's visited M.D.S. & /35.F.A. Wounded admitted for 24 hours ending 6 p.m. — 40 Div. 8. O.R. Cdn. Forces. 2. O.R.	ap

WAR DIARY
or
INTELLIGENCE SUMMARY. A.D.M.S.
40 Divn.

Army Form C. 2118.

Place	Date	Hour	Summary of Events and Information	Remarks and references to Appendices
LA MOTTE 36A/D30.c.g.7.	24/9/18	—	A.D.M.S. visited Divn. Baths & Anti trench foot treatment rm at 36/A.22.a.5.4. and arranged various improvements. Motored then held a medical Board on Capt McKeown 10. K.O.Y.L.I. who proceeded to inspect the water sterilizing lorry in STEENWERCK and the M.D.S. and M.D.S. Capt B. ROBERTSON returned from Special leave to U.K. Wounded admitted for 24 hours ending 6 p.m. 40 Bn. O.R. 4. 31 Divn. O.R. 2.	Appendix
"	25/9/18	—	A.D.M.S. visited 135. M137 F Ambces and inspected the M.D.S. R.Stas. inspected about 40 units of 120. Inf Bde and recommended a number for transfer to the Base for reclassification. R.Place Offr No 90 visited. Wounded admitted for 24 hours ending 6pm — nil.	
"	26/9/18	—	Orders received from Lt Col K.H.HUNT DSO to proceed to Command 42 C.C.S. This Offr has proceeded on leave to U.K. A.D.M.S. accompanied motored gave instructions for M.D.S. & A.D.S. the Court played advance. R.O.M.S. visited (35) Field Ambulance. Wounded admitted during 24 hours ending 8 p.m — M.R. 4.	appx.
"	27/9/18	—	Man ofturkin this morning, not successful. about 50 casualties. D.A.D.M.S. proceeded to U.K. on 14 days leave.	18

WAR DIARY
INTELLIGENCE SUMMARY. A.D.M.S. 40 D.I.

Army Form C. 2118.

Place	Date	Hour	Summary of Events and Information	Remarks and references to Appendices
LA MOTTE 36A/A30 c.9.7	28/9/18	—	Visited A.R.S.	A
"	29/9/18	—	Nil	
"	30 "	—	A.D.S. moved to B.9.c.8.2. Our front line is advancing slowly. Objective is to held the main L/S from JESUS FARM B2&D5.0 to C.16 central, with two Bns in line & one in support.	A

SECRET.

COPY NO.

40TH. DIVISION R.A.M.C. ORDER NO.86.

1/9/18.

Reference Map.
Sheet 36A.

1. 137th. Field Ambulance will move the Main Dressing Station from LA MOTTE to selected site at CAST FARM E.21.a.7.4. Move to be completed by 9.a.m. on Tuesday 3rd inst

2. Issued at 10.p.m.

3. Acknowledge (Field Ambces. only.)

Humphrey
Colonel.
A.D.M.S.40th.Division.

Distribution - Normal plus 14.M.A.C. A.D.M.S.29th.Divn.
A.D.M.S.61st.Divn.

SECRET.   COPY NO.

40TH. DIVISION R.A.M.C. ORDER NO. 87.

Reference Maps.
Sheets 36 & 36A.   5th. Sept. 1918.

1. The Main Dressing Station will be opened at 12 noon on 6th.inst., at 36A/F.30.c.4.6., by a Section of 136th. Field Ambulance. All Sick and Wounded from the Field Ambulance in the Line, will be sent to the Main Dressing Station.
   Cases for Divisional Rest Station will be sent from the Main Dressing Station in Divisional Ambulance Cars.

2. At 12 noon 6th.inst., 137th. Field Ambulance at 36A/E.21.a.9.4. will cease to function as a Main Dressing Station, and will become the Divisional Rest Station.

3. O.C.136th. Field Ambulance will close down the present Divisional Rest Station and move his Headquarters to the Main Dressing Station at 36A/F.30.c.4.6. as soon as possible.
   He will leave an Officer and sufficient personnel and equipment, with a large Ambulance Car, at 36A/C.5.a.5.9. to deal with the evacuations from the Brigade in Reserve.
   These cases will be sent to Divisional Rest Station or Casualty Clearing Station as considered necessary.

4. The detachment of 136th. Field Ambulance at the Advanced Army Dysentery Centre at EBBLINGHEM, will be left intact. They will draw rations locally.
   States and Returns will be rendered as heretofore.- copies for this Office to be sent by D.R.L.S.

5. Sick at present in 136th. Field Ambulance will be disposed of as follows :-

   (a) ~~To Duty~~. Those likely to be fit for duty in four days, will be transferred to Divisional Rest Station, at 36A/E 21.a.9.4.
   (b) Those not likely to be well in four days to C.C.S.

6. Until 136th. Field Ambulance Headquarters moves to the Main Dressing Station, separate 'A.& D' Books will be kept at each place, and separate Daily States will be rendered direct to this Office by the Main Dressing Station and by Headquarters 136th. Field Ambulance.

7. 136th. Field Ambulance will move their present tentage to the Main Dressing Station, less two marquees to be sent to the Divisional Rest Station.

8. D.D.M.S.XVth.Corps is arranging for M.A.C.Cars to evacuate cases from the Main Dressing Station and Divisional Rest Station to Casualty Clearing Station.

9. O.C.137th. Field Ambulance will take over from O.C.135th. Field Ambulance the Advanced Dressing Station and all Bearer Posts, and will be responsible for the evacuation of all casualties from the Divisional Front.
   Details to be arranged by Os.C. concerned.
   Headquarters will be at 36/A.21.b.2.8.
   Relief to be completed by 12 noon 8th.inst.

- 2 -

10.   O.C.135th.Field Ambulance will take over the Divisional Rest Station from 137th.Field Ambulance by 6.p.m.8th.inst.
     Headquarters 135th.Field Ambulance will move to the Divisional Rest Station and all personnel relieved in the forward area will rejoin their Headquarters at the Divisional Rest Station.

11.   If O.C.137th.Field Ambulance should require additional Ambulance Cars, wagons, Bearers etc., application will be made to this Office.

12.   Completion of moves and reliefs to be reported to this Office.

    Issued at 10.p.m.

    Acknowledge (Field Ambulances only.)

                  Lieut-Colonel,R.A.M.C.
                    A/A.D.M.S.40th.Division.

Distribution - Normal plus A.D.M.S. 31st.Division.
                          A.D.M.S. 61st.Division.
                          O.C.14 Motor Ambce.Convoy.
                          O i/c Adv.Dressing Station.
                          M.O.104th.M.G.B.
                          M.O.28th.A.F.A.Brigade.
                          M.O.31st.Divl.Amm.Col.

SECRET.

COPY. NO.

40TH. DIVISION R.A.M.C. ORDER NO. 88.

Reference Maps.
Sheets 36 & 36A.

17th. Sept. 1918.

1. 137th. Field Ambulance will take over the Main Dressing Station at F.29.b.6.9. from 136th. Field Ambulance by 11.a.m. 18th. inst.

2. 136th. Field Ambulance will remain at LA BRIELLE FARM (L.5.a.6.0.), parked. They will be ready to move at 2 hours notice from the Divisional Area, probably on the afternoon of 18th. inst.

3. D.D.M.S. XV Corps is arranging to send the personnel and equipment from the Advanced Army Dysentery Centre to rejoin the Unit on morning of 18th. inst.

4. 136th. Field Ambulance will take only Mobilization Equipment and Stores authorized by G.R.O's.
Surplus stores will be handed over to 137th. Field Ambulance.

5. Rations for two days will be carried on the transport.

6. Detailed instructions for the move will be sent later.

7. Acknowledge. (Field Ambulances only).

Issued at 7.30.p.m.

Alastair C. Jebb, Major

Lieut-Colonel, R.A.M.C.
A/A.D.M.S. 40th. Division.

Distribution - Normal.

SECRET.   COPY NO.

40TH. DIVISION R.A.M.C. ORDER NO. 89.
==*=*=*=*=*=*=*=*=*=*=*=*=*=*=*=*=*

Reference Maps.   22-9-18.
    Shotts
27, 36 & 36A.

1. The 119th. Infantry Brigade will take over from the Right Battalion 94th. Infantry Brigade, 31st. Division on the night 23/24th.

2. The Northern Divisional Boundary will run from C.1. central - B.5.c.3.5 - along road to D.10.a.85.90 - B.8.b.1.4 - A.10.a.6.4 - A.16.a.6.6. thence along present boundary.

3. The 39th. Bn. M.G. Corps will relieve guns of the 31st. Bn. M.G. Corps in this area with one Company.

4. 119th. Infantry Brigade Headquarters will be established at B.7.c.1.1.

5. R.A.P for Left Battalion in the line is situated at B.10.a.4.5.
R.A.P. for Right Battalion in the line is at B.21.a.5.4.

6. The A.D.S. situated at A.24.d.2.1. will collect casualties from both Brigades.

7. O.C. 137th. Field Ambulance will arrange for Bearer Posts and Car Posts to be established.

8. The M.D.S. will close at F.29.b.6.9. at 6.p.m. 23rd.inst., and will open at LA BRIELLE FARM (L.5.a.6.0.) at the same hour.

9. The D.R.S. will remain at E.21.a.9.4.

10. A.D.M.S. Office will close at LA MOTTE at 3.p.m. 24th.inst., and reopen at A.21.b.2.8. at the same hour.

11. Acknowledge. (Field Ambulances only.).

12. Issued at 10.p.m.

                                           Humphry
                                          Colonel.
                                A.D.M.S. 40th. Division.

Distribution - plus A.D.M.S. 31st. Division.
                    A.D.M.S. 61st. Division.
                    O.C. 14.M.A.C.

SECRET.   COPY NO. 31

40TH. DIVISION R.A.M.C. ORDER NO.90.

Reference Map.
Sheet 36.   25-9-1918.

1.   The 119th. Infantry Brigade will take over from the
      92nd. Infantry Brigade, 31st. Division, on the night 26/27th.
      inst., the front line system from C.1.d.2.9. to the present
      Divisional Northern Boundary.

2.   The Northern Divisional Boundary will run from C.1.d.2.9 -
      B.5.c.3.5 - along road to B.10.a.85.90 - B.8.b.1.4 - A.10.a.6.4.
      - A.16.a.6.6. thence along present boundary.

3.   One Company 39th. Bn. M.G. Corps is relieving a Company of
      the 31st. Bn. M.G. Corps in this area on night 25/26th. inst.

4.   119th. Infantry Brigade Headquarters will be established
      at B.8.a.4.2.

5.   The Advanced Dressing Station situated at A.24.d.2.1.
      will collect casualties from both Brigades.

6   Officer Commanding 137th. Field Ambulance will arrange for
      the evacuation of the new front, and will forward to this
      Office, locations of new Regimental Aid Posts, Bearer and
      Car Posts.

7.   Acknowledge. (Field Ambulances only).

      Issued at 10.30.p.m.

                                            [signature]
                                            Colonel.
                                            A.D.M.S. 40th. Division.

Distribution Normal plus A.D.M.S. 31st. Division.

16/3323

AMS 20th DD

COMMITTEE FOR THE
MEDICAL HISTORY OF THE WAR
4 DEC 1918
Date

Oct 17/16

WAR DIARY
or
INTELLIGENCE SUMMARY. 1/1 A.S./N.S.
40 S.W.

Army Form C. 2118.

Place	Date	Hour	Summary of Events and Information	Remarks and references to Appendices
LA MOTTE	1/10/18		Orders issued for move of M.D.S. & D.R.S. copy attached	
36/a 30.c.9.7.				
36/A 21.6.2.7.	2/10/18		A.D.M.S. Office moved to 36/A 21.6.2.7. Visited A.D.S. and two R.A.P.S of right Bde who were pushing out patrols across the river LYS. The enemy is rapidly withdrawing. Town of ARMETIERES placed out of bounds. 119 Bde advancing to N North & then moving South of ARMENTIERES. D/ri =LILLE roadway, 120 Bde advance South of ARMENTIERES D/ri up with 119 Bde. Pontoon bridge over LYS are being placed.	
"	3/10/18		Visited A.D.S. & walked thro' ERQUINGHAM & noted the ERQUINGHAM infirmarie for traffic at present, there. Found thro' ERQUINGHAM impossible for traffic at present, 119 Fd Bde in old front line E of ARMENTIERES. 120 Fd Bde in emergency out & N.W in reserve.	
"	4/10/18		Visited A.D.S. for its right Bde at H4.C.5.4. established then this morning & this ERQUINGHAM is passable this morning, & a pontoon for traffic in being put down across the LYS at H4&H.5.	
"	5/10/18		Visited A.D.S. of right Bde left 13 hrs sent on orders to amoving temples & leaving wing of advancing front line	
"	6/10/18		Evacuation is now entirely thro' ARMENTIERES, ERQUINGHAM to STEENWERCK & quite satisfactory.	

Army Form C. 2118.

WAR DIARY
or
INTELLIGENCE SUMMARY. 2/2 2/M.S. 20 S.W

(Erase heading not required.)

Place	Date	Hour	Summary of Events and Information	Remarks and references to Appendices
36/A2162.1.	7/10/18		136 & 142 Bdes. arrived from II Corps and took over the M.D.S. from 137 F. Amb. who moved to B.28.6.7.0. & are now working the front line only.	
	8/10/18		Nil.	
	9/10/18		Selected the Civil Hospital ARMENTIERES as a Main Evacuating Station in case of the next advance.	
	10/10/18		Nil. About 60 gas cases passed thro' M.D.S. today	
	11/10/18		Nil.	
	12/10/18		Orders issued for 135 F.A. to take over evacuation of front line from 137 F.A. & 137 F.A. to open a D.R.S. & take over patients remaining in present D.R.S.	
	13/10/18		Major Tebbs & A.D.M.S. returned from leave.	
	14/20/18		Went round M.D.S. & A.D.S. & R.A.P.s owing to an attack on the North enemy expected to retire on our front.	

(A7092). Wt. W12539/M1293. 75,000. 1/17. D. D. & L., Ltd. Forms/C.2118/14.

Army Form C. 2118.

WAR DIARY
or
INTELLIGENCE SUMMARY. A.D.M.S. 40 DIV.

(Erase heading not required.)

Place	Date	Hour	Summary of Events and Information	Remarks and references to Appendices
36/A.2.16.7.	15/10/18		Patrols pushed out today & advanced about 1000 yds to our front. Major Todd. 8/A.D.M.S. went to C.C.S. with Influenza.	
"	16/10/18		Enemy retiring very rapidly. 135 F.A. following and advanced H.Q. and established an A.D.S. at HOUPLINES. 136 F.A. established an M.D.S. at 1st Civil Hospital ARMENTIERES.	
"	17/10/18		Orders issued late last night for 136 F.A. to move to ARMENTIERES. 135 F.A. to HOUPLINES. Winter front area to form an evacuation station taking 135 F.A. pushing up thru A.D.S. to J.12.b.4. Amaquin. Established in 137 F.A. to C.C.S. & ARMENTIERES. for wounded from 135 F.A. to move to PERENCHIES and 137 F.A. Order issued for 135 F.A. to move to WAMBRECHIES on 18th inst.	
ARMENTIERES R.10/18			D.H.Q. arrived here today. Visited PERENCHIES & WAMBRECHIES. 137 F.A. at WAMBRECHIES took over large building used by the enemy as a hospital.	
"	19/10/18		Division strength of 4 lower today. One Bde M.L.A. PREVOTE area Bde in WAMBRECHIES and 1 Bde in MARCR near K.11. J. Ambulances among the same, except 1 Sect of 135 F.A. in bush, Hosp. CROIX 36/J.7.	
MOUVAUX 36/7.C.17.7.	20/10/18		D.H.Q. moved to MOUVAUX 721.C.7.7.	

Army Form C. 2118.

WAR DIARY
or
INTELLIGENCE SUMMARY.

A D M S
40 DIV

(Erase heading not required.)

Instructions regarding War Diaries and Intelligence Summaries are contained in F. S. Regs., Part II. and the Staff Manual respectively. Title pages will be prepared in manuscript.

Place	Date	Hour	Summary of Events and Information	Remarks and references to Appendices
MOUVAUX 36/T.c.7.7.	21/10/18		NIL	
"	22/10/18		135 F.A. arrived up 16/1 am then advanced further at CROIX	
"	23/10/18		119 Fd Amb. moving on to BONDUES. 136 F.A. Rein 1 Section/2 moves to WAMBRECHIES. The section of 136 F.A. to remain at ARMENTIERES & clear off its patients remaining to 1st D.A.D.S. Hdrs.	
"	24/10/18		Ordered the section of 136 F.A. to clear down transfer remaining patients to 137 F.A. at WAMBRECHIES & again this Hdrs Qrs. 31 Div in the line. Issued Op. Order	
"	25/10/18		Orders for the Div to relieve 31 Div in the line. Issued Op. Order No 21	
"	26/10/18		No 99 Fd Amb. Arrangements in the present quarters 135 F.A. being taken Owing to the lack of accommodation to the cond top in ROUBAIX, to Hopital en Second, RUE de SAGASSE	
LANNOY 37/G.15.cent.	27/10/18		D. H. Q. moved to LANNOY 37/G.15 central. Visited the A.D.S. at 37/H.2.6.2.7. of the M.D.S 37/B4940rth/t moved by 136 F.A.	
"	28/10/18		135 F.A. moved to T.20.c.2.6. RUE DE SAGASSE ROUBAIX, an onsurance and Hospital. Influenza is becoming about 12 cases daily	

WAR DIARY
—OR—
INTELLIGENCE SUMMARY.
(Erase heading not required.)

Army Form C. 2118.

Place	Date	Hour	Summary of Events and Information	Remarks and references to Appendices
L'ANNOY 3//G.15 Central	29/10/18		No of cases of Influenza increasing. 135 F.A. will have accommodation for 250 cases.	
"	30/10/18		Owing to Influenza recurrence church services for the present be suspended. A.D.R.O. was warned the following day to the subject.	
"	31/10/18		A.D. Sir. ordn. no 228 issued today. In consequence of this have arranged that 137 F.A. shall evacuate all their cases & men up to the 2nd Nov to CHATEAU LEONDERIE. 37/G.14. C.7.2. Major Scott. A.D.M.S returned from Hosp yesterday.	

Montgomery
Lt Col A.D.M.S
40 Div

'SECRET.   COPY NO.

40TH. DIVISION R.A.M.C. ORDER NO.91.

Reference Map.   1/10/18.
Sheet 36 & 36A.

1.   137th. Field Ambulance will move to A.17.d.5.6., and open up the Main Dressing Station at that place on Oct. 2nd. Move to be completed by 1600 hours.

2.   135th. Field Ambulance will move to L.5.a.6.0., the site of the present Main Dressing Station, and open as the Divisional Rest Station at 900 hours 3rd. Oct.
     A sufficient personnel will be left to wind up the present Divisional Rest Station at E.21.a.9.4.

3.   Acknowledge (Field Ambulances only).

Issued at 10.00.

                                                    Colonel.
                                          A.D.M.S. 40th. Division.

Distribution - Normal plus 66th. Divl. Artillery.

SECRET.

COPY NO.

40TH. DIVISION R.A.M.C. ORDER No. 92.

Reference Map.
Sheets 36 & 36A.

5/10/18.

1. 135th. Field Ambulance less one Section at LA MOTTE, will remain at L.5.a.6.0., and continue to run the Divisional Rest Station.

2. 136th. Field Ambulance on arrival from II Corps Area will take over the Main Dressing Station from 137th. Field Ambulance.

3. 137th. Field Ambulance on handing over the Main Dressing Station to 136th. Field Ambulance, will move to LA HAYS FARM B.28.d.7.8., and be responsible for the evacuation of the front line.

4. Acknowledge (Field Ambulances only).

Issued at 13.00.

Colonel.
A.D.M.S. 40th. Division.

Distribution - Normal plus   A.D.M.S. 31st. Division.
                             A.D.M.S. 59th. Division.

SECRET.

COPY NO.

40TH. DIVISION R.A.M.C. ORDER NO. 93.

Reference Map.
Sheets 36 & 36A.

12/10/18.

1. 135th. Field Ambulance, less sufficient personnel to run the Divisional Rest Station at DOULIEU, will move on 14th. October to C.9.c.8.1., and take over all forward posts from 137th. Field Ambulance, and be responsible for the evacuation of the front line.

2. 137th. Field Ambulance on 14th. October, will open a Divisional Rest Station at their present site at LA HAYS FARM, B.28.b.7.0., and on 15th. October will send sufficient personel to relieve the personnel of 135th. Field Ambulance at DOULIEU The latter will then join their Headquarters.

3. 136th. Field Ambulance will continue to run the Main Dressing Station at STEENWERCK, but will send an advanced party to prepare the CIVIL HOSPITAL, ARMENTIERES, for future use.

4. Acknowledge.(Field Ambulances only).

Issued at 18.00.

Colonel.
A.D.M.S. 40th. Division.

Distribution - Normal plus A.D.M.S. 31st. Division.
                           A.D.M.S. 59th. Division.

SECRET.

COPY NO.

40TH. DIVISION R.A.M.C. ORDER NO. 94.

Reference Map.
Sheet 36

16/10/18.

1. 136th. Field Ambulance will move to Civil Hospital, ARMENTIERES, on 17th. instant.

2. 135th. Field Ambulance will move their Headquarters to the Factory at C.27.b.6.7. on 17th. instant.

3. Acknowledge. (Field Ambulances only).

Issued at 22.00

Humphrey
Colonel.
A.D.M.S. 40th. Division.

Distribution - Normal plus A.D.M.S. 31st. Division.
                                        A.D.M.S. 59th. Division.

SECRET.   COPY NO. 36

40TH. DIVISION R.A.M.C. ORDER NO. 95.

Reference Map   17/10/18.
    Sheet 36

1.   135th. Field Ambulance will move on 18th. October to
PERENCHIES, J.14.b.2.9., and establish a Dressing Station.

2.   137th. Field Ambulance will move on 18th. October to
WAMBRECHIES, E.26.d.cent. and open a Dressing Station on the
19th. October, and be responsible for the evacuation of the
front line, in advance of that place.

3.   Evacuation of Patients will still be to 136th. Field
Ambulance, Civil Hospital ARMENTIERES.

4.   Acknowledge. (Field Ambulances only).

        Issued at 18.00.

                                            J Humphrey
                                            Colonel.
                                    A.D.M.S. 40th. Division.

Distribution - Normal plus:-
        A.D.M.S. 31st. Division.
        A.D.M.S. 59th. Division

135/6/7

SECRET.

COPY NO.

40TH. DIVISION R.A.M.C. ORDER NO. 96.

1. 155th. Field Ambulance will remain at WAMBRECHIES, but be responsible for the evacuation of all Sick and Wounded from the Advanced Guard Brigade.

2. 137th. Field Ambulance will open an ~~advanced~~ Main Dressing Station, and Divisional Rest Station at WAMBRECHIES, and will collect Sick from Brigade in Support.

3. 136th. Field Ambulance will remain at ARMENTIERES and will collect Sick from Brigade in Reserve.

4. Acknowledge.

D.H.Qrs.
18/10/18.

Colonel.
A.D.M.S. 40th. Division.

SECRET.

COPY NO. 32

40TH. DIVISION R.A.M.C. ORDER NO. 95.

22/10/18.

Reference Map.
 Sheet 36.

1. 135th. Field Ambulance will move to CROIX, L.3.d.6.4. on morning of 23rd. October, 1918.

2. Acknowledge. (Field Ambulances only).

Issued at 10.00.

J Humphrey
Colonel.
A.D.M.S. 40th. Division.

SECRET.

COPY NO.

40TH. DIVISION R.A.M.C. ORDER NO. 98.

Reference Map.
Sheet 56.

23/10/18.

1. 136th. Field Ambulance less 1 Section, will move to WAMBRECHIES on the 24th. October, 1918.

2. Issued at 17.00.

   Acknowledge. (136th. Field Ambulance only).

   J Humphry
   Colonel.
   A.D.M.S. 40th. Division.

SECRET.   COPY NO.

40TH. DIVISION R.A.M.C. ORDER NO.99

Reference Map.   25/10/18.
Sheets 36 & 37

1. The 40th. Division will relieve the 31st. Division in the line on 26th. and night 26/27th October.

2. 136th. Field Ambulance will move to 37/G.19.b.4.4. on the 27th. October, and take over the Main Dressing Station from 94th. Field Ambulance, 31st. Division. Move to be completed by 12.00.

3. 136th. Field Ambulance will detail 2 Officers and 34 Other Ranks with Advanced Dressing Station equipment and 3 Motor Ambulances and take over Advanced Dressing Station at 37/H.2.b.2.7. on the morning of the 26th. October.

4. 137th. Field Ambulance and 135th. Field Ambulance, will remain in their present locations.

5. A.D.M.S. Office will close at 36/F.21.d.5.7. and open at LANNOY at 10.00. 27th. October.

6. Acknowledge. (Field Ambulances only).

Issued at 13.00.

                                                                    Colonel.
                                    A.D.M.S. 40th. Division.

Distribution Normal plus:- A.D.M.S. 14th. Division.
                              A.D.M.S. 31st. Division.
                              A.D.M.S. 59th. Division.

SECRET.
*****

COPY NO.
****

40TH. DIVISION R.A.M.C. ORDER NO.100.

Reference Map.
  Sheet 36.

26/10/18

1.   135th. Field Ambulance will move to the HOSPITAL DE SECOURS, RUE DE LA SAGASSE at F.30.c.2.6. on the 28th October, 1918, and form the Divisional Rest Station.

2.   Issued at 18.00.

3.   Acknowledge. (Field Ambulances only)

J Humphrey
Colonel.
A.D.M.S. 40th. Division.

Distribution - Normal.

16/3403

Army Form C.

WAR DIARY
or
INTELLIGENCE SUMMARY A.D.M.S. 40 Div.
(Erase heading not required.)

Place	Date	Hour	Summary of Events and Information	Remarks and references to Appendices
LANNOY. 37/G.15.c.4.d.	1/11/18		Enemy reported still active on this Divisional front along the river. 119 Inf Bde moved today to the LEERS-NORD area. 137 F Amb at WAMBRECHIES closed down today. A.D.M.S. visited the proposed Divisional Battn in LANNOY today and the 136 F Amb at 37/G.14.c.2.0. D.A.D.M.S. visited the A.D.S. at LEERS-NORD and the R.A.P.s & left & right Battns in the line and Battn in support at ESTAIMBOURG. (37/H.5.d.9.4.) O.R.DAS. also visited R.A.P (135. F Amb.) at RUBAIX. Major W.R.P. MIDNIGHT 135. F Amb. admitted 67 PP with Influenza. 136 F Amb. to attend 2 Officers of 135. F Amb. to temporary duty.	
	2/11/18		A.D.M.S. & O.R.Das. visited 135. F Amb. (D.R.S.) One infl'enza Midwen M.Ssrgts D.M.Ds visited 38 Admission during day. 26 Sick M.Ssrgts. D.M.Ds visited M.D.S. & Coll. Bn. R.A.P. 137. F Amb. moved today from WAMBRECHIES to Chau LIPONDERIE (37/G.14.d.7.1.) 30 Gas casualties in 23 Lane Fus evacuated to ESTAIMBOURG.	
	3/11/18		A.D.M.S & D.A.D.M.S. visited 136. F Amb. (M.D.S.) A.D.M.S visited 11. C.C.S. he Officer Patients from these Region. DAS to Capt called and left today. DADMS visited MO. I.N.C. & 17 WORCESTERS in LANNOY.	
	4/11/18		A.D.M.S. visited 134 F Ambulance (M.D.S.) D.A.D.M.S visits 17 Bde P.F.A. ab 37/I.3.14.	

WAR DIARY
or
INTELLIGENCE SUMMARY

(Erase heading not required.)

Army Form C. 21

A.D.M.S. 40. Div.

Place	Date	Hour	Summary of Events and Information	Remarks and references to Appendices
LANNOY. 37/G.15/Cent.	5/11/18	—	A.D.M.S. visits A.D.S. and visits French N.C.O. ROUBAIX re examination of all known prostitutes in the Divisional Area. G. 40 men sent instructions what to do in the event of the enemy retiring from the river. A.D.M.S. held conference with O.C. 136 & 137 F. Ambces.	
	6/11/18	—	A.D.M.S. & D.A.D.M.S. visits 135. F.Amb.ce. A.D.M.S. visits the Divisional Baths LANNOY. About 30-20 civilian pro cases/attn were examined in LEERS last night by gas-shelling.	
	7/11/18	—	D.A.D.M.S. visits the 121.I.Bde. in LANNOY, D.A.C. & S.T.M.By. re billets, Sanitation & institution of 'blue room'. A.D.M.S & D.A.D.M.S. visits M.D.S. and Right Bn. R.A.P. in view of a further early advance of the division.	
	8/11/18	—	A.D.M.S. held conference with O.C. 135, 136, 137. F. Ambces re prospects moves in the event of an enemy retirement. O.C. an attack to cross the river SCHELDT, is at an early date in district of Pecq can operate. A.D.M.S. visits W.C.E.S. in district of Pecq can operate. O.C. 137 F.Ambce reconnoitres the area round PECQ (8.37)/H 6+7) in site for F.Amb. H.Q. & work the line across the river, and for the few Shelter & heavy [?] casualties awaiting the attack to cross the river. A.D.S.	

WAR DIARY
INTELLIGENCE SUMMARY

A.D.M.S. 40 DIVISION

Army Form C. 2118.

Place	Date	Hour	Summary of Events and Information	Remarks and references to Appendices
LANNOY. 37/G.15 central	9/11/18.	—	The Enemy has withdrawn in this front to the 119 Inf. Bde are following up & reached CLIPET. (Road mile) 137 F. Amb. which had moved up to PECQ this morning 126. 1st Amb. moved up the M.D.S. to the Chateau at H.6.a./37 this morning. Stretcher Bearers proceeded to join the R.M.O. the batts in line and found them at J.3.a. and D.28.c R.A. respectively. He arranged with 13.F. Amb to establish car post near NOLEMPRIX D.26.d. an Amb Care Post was sent a parade. Amb ambulances could not get across the river or the night but by the bridge in the area of the Division were put across to station could not get forward HERINNES. An amb at PECQ was established by 2100 hours.	
	10/11/18.	—	Advance continued this morning toward VERMMES when the XI Corps were tapped at 1151 Bde on withdrawn to VERTE & GRAND RENET 137.F.Amb area up CHENIN VERTE & GRAND RENET 137.F.Amb U.S. & Franco to PECQ & to look after the troops area as 31 Div. Cavs. St ANDRÉ to the river Arras. A/ADMS write 11. C.C.S Enquire re Divisional Medical Officers who are palace the	
	11/11/18	—	W.F.O. U.S. Cease fire at 11.00 hours & all troops (part of stopped. A/ADMS Visited village (part of occupied British retreat) in Enemy LANNOY when Divisional Headquarters of Advance	

FREDRICH BRITISH Retreat Quarters

WAR DIARY
or
INTELLIGENCE SUMMARY.

A.D.M.S. 40. Division.

Army Form C. 2118.

Place	Date	Hour	Summary of Events and Information	Remarks and references to Appendices
LAPUGNY 57/G.15.central	12/11/18	—	119 Inf Bde withdrawn to HERIMIES WARCOING area. 120 Inf Bde withdrawn to TOUFFLERS BUCQUOI area. Troops & aux per. remain in present site & collect sick from respective Brigade Rptrs & Stations. visits 132 & 121 F. Amb'gs & T.F.C.Q. Rptrs attended Conference at 3rd Army H.Q.rs. at T pm. re M.I.(c). 130 F. Amb'ce.	
	13/11/18	—	ADMS visited 3 F.R.S. today. DADMS went round the billets &c of 232 Labor Functn'y.	
	14/11/18	—	G.O.C. XXII Corps held Conference of all C.R.G. Division & their Staffs in the Education Theatre. ADMS attended.	
	15/11/18	—	ADMS held a Conference of O.C. F. Rptrs and their Sub Education Officers re Study & classes in the future. Sch Education Officer attended. ADMS & DADMS visited the Hospice CROIX into Sheet 13) F. Ambs. ADMS & DADMS went into the New M.T. Cy ce Ambulance Line in 16 but came in contact with. N. C.C.S. & see Divisional A.D. who are patients there.	
	16/11/18 17/11/18	— —	ADMS visited 136 F. Ambce. D.ADMS visited 135 137 F. Ambc'ce. ADMS & DADMS attended the 2nd Army Thanksgiving Church Parade at [TOURNAI]	

WAR DIARY
or
INTELLIGENCE SUMMARY.
(Erase heading not required.)

Army Form C. 2118.

A.D.M.S. 40 Division

Place	Date	Hour	Summary of Events and Information	Remarks and references to Appendices
LANNOY 37/G.15.central	18/10	-	2nd & 3rd Army delivered a lecture of all the L. of C. Div. F. Mintres at ROUBAIX and expressed his satisfaction with their work. R.O.M.S. & Matrons attended.	
"	19/10	-	Rotrns. & sundry notes D.M.S. 5th Army. Hrs 2nd & 3rd Army. Transfer of their Divisions.	
"	20/10	-	D.A.D.M.S. went round the Divisn. with the 8 F.Regt. R.O.M.S. & Matron attended a lecture on the "Work of the British Navy" given at ROUBAIX.	
"	21/10	-	R.A.Regs. inspected a few empty of the 11 Divisions of the Divisn. Round visits to C.C.S. in district. Arrangements for the Divisn. Stretcher visits. 23 Glos'shires & 121. T.M.B.Ty.	
"	22/10	-	Rotrns. attendances visits. D.D.M.S. on forming a Cyclist Skin Centre at Chateau 36/F.15.d.9.1. and then proceeded to the CCS with the details of 135. F. Ambce. who were also involved of the transfers.	Attach 1
"	23/10	-	R.D.M.S. Stretcher visits 136 F. Ambce. BAIUL. adm. No. 102. Round Camouse D.136 & Site at 36/F.14.d.a. 24 init.	
"	24/10	-	A.D.M.S. attended conference with D.D.M.S. 15 Cops. re introduction of anti-phus inoculation in this Divisn. 136 F. Mintre moved to-day to 36/F.14.d.	

Army Form C. 2118.

WAR DIARY
or
INTELLIGENCE SUMMARY. A.D.M.S. 59 Div

(Erase heading not required.)

Place	Date	Hour	Summary of Events and Information	Remarks and references to Appendices
ROUBAIX 36/L.S.7.a 4 Rue des Arts	25/11/18	-	A.D.M.S. Office moved from LANNOY to ROUBAIX from STATIONS visited the Battn. of 1/20 Inf. Bde. at MECHIN & TOUFFLERS.	
"	26/11/18	-	A.D.M.S. visited A.D.M.S. Corps re introducing of Anti influenza vaccine prophylaxis in 119 Inf Bde. STATIONS visited to K.O.S.B.s at TOUFFLERS and 33. M.G. Bn. at LEERS.	
"	27/11/18	-	A.D.M.S. visited 135 F Amb. STATIONS visited 12 N. STAFFS. 13. EAST LANCS. Field Amb Bde.	
"	28/11/18	-	A.D.M.S. visited 137 F Amb. re inoculation with Anti influenza vaccine STATIONS visited 12 R. Innis Fus.	
"	29/11/18	-	A.D.M.S. visited 135. F Amb STATIONS visited 181. Bde RFA and 178. Bde RFA and A.D.R.C. in MARVRECHIES area.	
"	30/11/18	-	A.D.M.S. & STATIONS visited 136 F Amb where a new functioning as a Corps Skin Centre, and called on A.D.M.S. X Corps.	ay

Army Form C. 2118.

WAR DIARY
or
INTELLIGENCE SUMMARY. A.D.M.S. 40 Div.
(Erase heading not required.)

Place	Date	Hour	Summary of Events and Information	Remarks and references to Appendices
ROUBAIX 4 Rue des Arts.	30/11/18		Throughout the whole of this month there has been an epidemic of Influenza in the Division, and came during the highest at Rousies for one day. The epidemic has been diminishing for the past 10 days. The rate of Influenza cases notified has been 1113 in the 119. Inf Bde. Commenced on 29' inst. Convoyment in the troops being billeted in 2 new large villages there has been an increase in Venereal Cases. 4th Canad Army this month. Blue Cross' are established in all units, can be obtained. The Educational Programme of the Active Service Army Schools is being pushed on with classes have been running in all units for several weeks.	Alunto T. Jeff Major

SECRET   COPY NO.

40th DIVISION R.A.M.C. ORDER NO. 102.

Ref. Sheet 36.

23/11/18.

1.   136th Field Ambulance will transfer all patients to 137th Field Ambulance or C.C.S., forthwith, and will move on the 24th inst. to the late site of No. 2 Canadian C.C.S. at 36/F.14.d., and will open a Corps Skin Centre as soon as possible. O.C., 136th Field Ambulance will report to this Office date on which the Centre will be open to receive patients.

2.   O.C., 137th Field Ambulance will continue to collect the sick of the 119th Infantry Brigade, CROIX.

3.   O.C., 136th Field Ambulance will collect the sick from the Divisional Artillery in WAMBRECHIES area, and will convey them to the D.R.S., by whom they will be "Admitted". To commence on 25th inst.

4.   O.C., 135th Field Ambulance will collect the sick of the 121st Infantry Brigade in LANNOY, and of 120th Infantry Brigade in NECHIN and TOUFFLERS areas, and 39th Bn. M.G.C. LEERS; from 25th inst. inclusive.

5.   The Dental Surgeon will be accommodated at 135th Field Ambulance, ROUBAIX, (Rue de Sagasse) from the 24th inst. inclusive. O.C., 136th Field Ambulance will arrange for the necessary transfer.

6.   Acknowledge.

Issued at 1200 hours.

Colonel,
A.D.M.S., 40th Division.

Distribution - Normal plus 14th and 59th Divisions.

A. D. M. L. 40th Div.

WAR DIARY
or
INTELLIGENCE SUMMARY.

Army Form C. 2118.

A.D.M.S. 40. Division

Place	Date	Hour	Summary of Events and Information	Remarks and references to Appendices
ROUBAIX	1/7/16	-	Arrangements made with 9th Army Mechanical Jenling Centre OES	
4.Ouds.ARIS	2/7/16	-	Officers to attend "dental" students for instruction	
"	"	-	ADMS ROUBAIX moved 1730 to Roubaix.	
"	3/2/16	-	Major Instructions telephoned from OSMS XV Corps to attend two M.O. to report for temporary duty to NAMUR, ROUBAIX for work with a French Ambulance in connection with returning P. of W. and refugees.	
"	4/7/16	-	ADMS visited 136. 1730 F.Amb ctc. 1730 F.Amb. The French Ambulance returned today as there is not sufficient work for them. Arrangements made for 1 m.o. to visit daily at 9.30 am the alluding post for Refugees at Pond d'AVELGEM.	
ROUBAIX				
March 5				
"	5/7/16	.		
"	6/7/16	.	ADMS visited 135 + 136 F Ambces.	
"	7/7/16	.	Major Capt. L HAMPTON MANK, MO 23rd CHESHIRES to England for duty	
"	8/7/16	.	MC Capt J HAMAD RAMC, 131 RAMC invalided to England " " Scott	
				Christopher Major RAMC

WAR DIARY
or
INTELLIGENCE SUMMARY. N.O.M.S. 40 Divn
(Erase heading not required.)

Army Form C. 2118.

Place	Date	Hour	Summary of Events and Information	Remarks and references to Appendices
ROUBAIX	9/12/18	-	NOMS meets Gen. 118 I 20/21. Enf. Bde. NOMS visits French authorities re inspection of refugees. This services of British M.O. are not required at present. They will be working for their own).	
4 Rue de Paris	10/12/18	-	NOMS & NOMS visits the Artillery HQ Bleur and NCO in WAMBRECHIES area.	
"	11/12/18	-	Nil.	
"	12/12/18	-	Cap L HUMPHREY CAMC NOMS proceeds on 10 days Special leave to U.K. Lt Col. LR HODLESTON RAMC 126 F Amb is acting for him. NOMS visits D. A & Q in WAMBRECHIES re medical arrangements consequent on expression of Capt NORTON RAMC & right to W.O. & no relief being available. GNOMS visits 126 F Amb. NOMS interviews D.M.O.	
"	13/12/18		121 Inf Bde re working of new arrangements of F.L. M.O. Infy Bde. & finds all satisfactory Medical Arrangements No 23 issued	Appendix 1.

WAR DIARY
or
INTELLIGENCE SUMMARY

Army Form C 2118.

A.D.M.S. 40 Div.

Place	Date	Hour	Summary of Events and Information	Remarks and references to Appendices
ROUBAIX 4 Mon Battn	14/12/18		ADMS attended G.O.C. conference at H.Q. Inf. Bde. H.Q. re General welfare of the personnel. RAMC Officers attended the first meeting of the Corps Medical Society held at 136 F. Amb. Where short addresses were given by Col: FRANKAU RAMC, Consulting Surgeon 5th Army, and Major J.B. LINNELL RAMC 137 F. Amb.	
"	15/12/18		ADMS visits units of 120 Inf. Bde. regarding Baths, accommodation etc.	
"	16/12/18		120 Inf. Bde. H.Q. re improvement of accommodation. ADMS with O.C. 120 Inf. Bde. inspected new quarters being prepared for LANNOY F.A. Cameron. RAMC also visits 231 M.G. Bn. Officers Mess in Ey. 136 Fd. Ambulance	
"	17/12/18	-	ADMS visited 136 F. Amb. RAMC held a conference re Further Arrangements re General Medical Attention & instructions on visit to LILLE &	
"	18/12/18	-	ADMS visits Baths at CROIX and 137 F. Amb.	
"	19/12/18		ADMS attended G.O.C. conference on general welfare of the troops & visits 136 Field Amb, ADMS visits 15 KOYLI and the Baths at LANNOY. A.J.	

Army Form C. 2118.

WAR DIARY
or
INTELLIGENCE SUMMARY.
(Erase heading not required.)

A.D.M.S. 40 Div.

Instructions regarding War Diaries and Intelligence Summaries are contained in F.S. Regs., Part II. and the Staff Manual respectively. Title pages will be prepared in manuscript.

Place	Date	Hour	Summary of Events and Information	Remarks and references to Appendices
ROUBAIX L. Sac des ARTS	20/3/19		G.O.C. 40 Division inspected the D.R.S. (133rd F.Amber.) Accy. Sh. D.M.S. attended. ADMS inspected Medl. C.O.C. 119, 120, 121 Inf. Bdes. Re Medical arrangements, and also called on O.C. 39. M.G. Btn. at LEERS.	
"	21/3/19		ADMS called on MOs of N Campaign 165, 120, 121 He etc. appointment of MOs i/c OMs to 120 Inf Bde Medical Officer M.C.	
"	22/3/19			
"	23/3/19		ADMS visited 135 F Amber. ADMS visited D.M.T Coy re emotion Ambulance Car	
"	24/3/19		ADMS visited 135 and 136 Field Ambulance	
"	25/3/19		knew say amusements in all events	
"	26/3/19		Capt F.M. S.Rwa R.Mlee became MO. to 120 Inf. Bde. Sh. Sten. MO's opm field Ambulance.	
"	27/3/19		ADMS visited 136 F Amber.	
"	28/3/19		2nd Meeting of Xi Corps Medical Society held at 136 F Amber. & well attended.	A.D.S.

Army Form C. 2118.

WAR DIARY
or
INTELLIGENCE SUMMARY. A.D.M.S.   40 Division
(Erase heading not required.)

Place	Date	Hour	Summary of Events and Information	Remarks and references to Appendices
ROUBAIX	29/1/19	—	Mis Entreneumed for the Anti-Influenza Inoculation & Lt. Col. Sir Humphrey Rolleston	
4 Rue Brûleurs	30/1/19	—	Instructions received from Corps that Field Ambers amount to be reduced below 2/3rd strength by demobilization of personnel	
"	31/1/19	—	ADMS midst 135 & 136 Field Ambulances. ADMS midst AD'ms S & O.C. Ambers	
			During the month the Division has received its second billeting area & has never attacking all units are now comfortably installed. The Batt. MOs were called to the F. Ambers on Brigade MO appointed in lieu & this arrangement is working well. The influenza epidemic, or rather outbreak, in Corps 3 & 9 cases only & no serious complication have been noted in three last month. The XV Corps Medical Society has held two successful meetings this month at the Corps Schain Centre. (136 F. Amber)	

Alastair F. Speith
Major V. Mane
A.D.M.S.

A.D.M.S. 40th Div.

Box 2418

16

WAR DIARY
or
INTELLIGENCE SUMMARY.
(Erase heading not required.)

A.D.M.S. 40th Division

Army Form C. 2118.

No. 32

Place	Date	Hour	Summary of Events and Information	Remarks and references to Appendices
Roubaix	1/1/19		A.D.M.S. & A.D.M.S. visited 5. Army Dental Centre also 39 St. B'n at Lille	
L'C de Arts			A dentist appointment for the Division	
			The A.D.M.S. then to Tcr. gave a very successful demonstration to Anatomy Staffs of British C.C.S. & stationary hospitals	
			in Tourcoing area.	
"	2/1/19		A.D.M.S. visited 135 Field Ambulance & visited the	
			Divisional Baths. Rec LONGUE HAIE & RUBAIX	
"	3/1/19		A.D.M.S. visited 120-121 Inf. Bde & med the 121 Inf Bde	
		4/1/19	D.D.M.S. visited Baths at Croix. 137 Field Ambulance	
		5/1/19	Nil.	
"	6/1/19		A.D.M.S. & A.D.M.S. visited G.O.C. 119, 120, 121. Inf. Bdes & one of the	
			were satisfied with Med arrangements to the rest the 121 Inf	
			Bde & 127 F. Amb. were also visited.	
	7/1/19		A.D.M.S. visited 136" Field Amb.	
	8/1/19		A.D.M.S. & A.D.M.S. called on the C.R.A.40 Div. & Mother 181, 120	
			Bdes R.F.A.	

Monte Campo Ronde

WAR DIARY
or
INTELLIGENCE SUMMARY.
(Erase heading not required.)

Army Form C. 2118.

A.D.M.S. 40 Div.

Place	Date	Hour	Summary of Events and Information	Remarks and references to Appendices
ROUBAIX 4 km. des Mairie	9/1/19	—	Nil	
	10/1/19	—	A.D.M.S. inspected 136 F. Amb.	
	11/1/19	—	A.D.M.S. & D.A.D.M.S. attended XV Corps medical Societies meeting	
			A.D.D.M.S. inspected billets for 121 Inf. Bde. area	
	12/1/19	—	Nil	
	13/1/19	—	Col. L. HUMPHRY C in C R.A.M.C. reported from leave troop. W. Col. V.K.	
			HUDLESTON R.A.M.C. reported 136 F. Amb. Winter	
	14/1/19	—	Nil. Most of the day spent in making out the Consolidated	
			reports on Officers D.N.S. 5th Army called in A.D.M.S. & they discussed names & photos of D.D.M.S.	
	15/1/19	—	A.D.M.S. & D.A.D.M.S. visited 135 - 136 - 137 Field Ambulances.	Appendix I
			Instructions issued to Bearers to prepare const to all personnel	
			with a view to establishing the East Index system for	
			unit & officer personnel.	
	16/1/19	22/1/19	Nothing of importance. On jury to cut for 3 S.N.E. D'lys today, so handed	
			over to Lt Col. T. Huddleston R.A.M.C.	
			Humphrey	
			Lt. Col A.D.M.S.	
			40 Div	

Army Form C 2118.

WAR DIARY
or
INTELLIGENCE SUMMARY. A.D.M.S. 40 Division
(Erase heading not required.)

Instructions regarding War Diaries and Intelligence Summaries are contained in F. S. Regs., Part II. and the Staff Manual respectively. Title pages will be prepared in manuscript.

Place	Date	Hour	Summary of Events and Information	Remarks and references to Appendices
ROUBAIX L. de Mts ARTS	24/4/19	-	ADMS called on D.A.C. H.Q. 120/21 Inf. Bde. & C.R.E. re funeral medical arrangements & inspected the Divisional bath WAMBRECHIES.	
	25/4/19	-	D.M.S. 5th Army ADMS & OC L R.A.M.C. Staff attended a successful meeting of Corps Medical Society. Papers were read by Maj. HODGES D.S.O. 29 St. Hosp. and Maj. Marshall of 10. C.C.S.	
	26/4/19	-	Nil.	
	27/4/19	-	ADMS XL Corps called on ADMS & Dorothy etc.	
	28/4/19	-	ADMS XL Corps called on ADMS re funeral medical arrangements.	
			ADMS & ADMS XL visited Divisional Baths at CROIX, LANNOY and ROUBAIX and the 136 F. Amb.	
	29/4/19	-	ADMS visited no 14. 119 Inf. Bde.	
	30/4/19	-	Casualty Physician St. Genevy re-ach ADMS Hy, 1 with him, inspected the NRS.	
			ADMS visited no 4. no 120, 121 Inf. Bde at LANNOY & TOUFFLERS and new system.	
			Further machines need re demobilyation	A.J.F. Alexander

WAR DIARY
or
INTELLIGENCE SUMMARY. A.D.M.S. 40 Division
(Erase heading not required.)

Army Form C. 2118.

Place	Date	Hour	Summary of Events and Information	Remarks and references to Appendices
ROUBAIX 4. Rue des Arts	31/1/19	—	Ont. The Division has been in the same area all the month. Demobilization has been proceeding rapidly at present about 250 a day from the Division. Since the 24 inst. all attached & Ministry of Munitions personnel have been sent to A.D.M.S. home until 5 Feb when we get 4 O.R. daily. Sickness in the Division is very low, so the Field Ambulances can carry on the work with diluted personnel.	Aubrey T. Guest Major RAMC A.D.M.S. 31/1/19.

Appendix I

Officer Commanding,
    135 Field Ambulance,
    136 Field Ambulance,
    137 Field Ambulance.
----

1. Kindly complete forthwith on F.H.Cards, specimen copy of which is attached, a card for each W.O., N.C.O., and man on the strength of your Unit, including attached men of other units shown as such in your War Establishment, (excluding attached Venereal Convalescents and men of other Corps lent for special employment).

R.A.M.C. personnel attached from other R.A.M.C. Units will be included, but their unit must be shown on the front of the card.

These Cards to be sent by the quickest possible means to Demobilization Officer, A.D.M.S. 40th. Division.

2. The personnel forming your Cadre Establishment must be stated as such on the front of the Card.

3. You should choose your Cadre Establishment at once from the following classes if possible :-
    A. Volunteers (your senior N.C.O's. and men on whom you rely will be usually in this category).
    B. Regular soldiers with less than 2 years colour service to complete.
    C. Men belonging to industrial groups not likely to be for early demobilization.
    D. Men, irrespective of their group, you consider essential for the requirements of your unit.

All casualties affecting the personnel of your Unit must be notified immediately by letter to Demobilization Officer, A.D.M.S. 40th. Division.

Should a member of your Cadre Establishment be necessarily demobilized, he must be replaced by you, and the Demobilization Officer notified of the change.

If you are closed as a Medical Unit members of your Cadre Establishment may be borrowed by the Demobilization Officer for reinforcing other Units. If you require reinforcements or information, wire, or better still, see your Demobilization Officer who will be available at A.D.M.S., 40th, Division Office after 10.00 hours daily.

                                      Humphry
D.H.Qrs.,
15/1/19.   Colonel,
                            A.D.M.S., 40th, Division.

A.D.M.S.,
40th DIVISION.
No. 176/116(17)
Date 15.1.19

Date of entry and medical unit admitting must be recorded immediately on admission. Brief clinical notes to be added later and signed by M.O.

No. of C.C.S. Date of entry	No. of Hospital Date of entry
1 Date of Enlistment.	1
2 Terms of Enlistment.	2
3 Date of joining B.E.F.	3
4 Length of Service with E.F.	4
5 Married or Single.	5
6 Dispersal Centre.	6
7 Present Employment in unit.	7
8 If qualified for other Employment.	8
9 Whether willing to remain until disbandment.	9

This F.M. Card must not be destroyed, and it must be transmitted with the patient if he is evacuated to U.K. Temperature charts or additional clinical notes may be sent with it, either in the same or in another envelope attached to the patient.

Specimen Card   Army Form W 3118.

FIELD MEDICAL CARD.

No. 9999   Rank private
Name Brown A.
Unit 8 CCS RAMC

Battle Casualty — Accidentally Wounded — "Sick"
(Strike out description which does not apply)

No. of F.A. On Cadre Establishment
Date of admission or not.
F.A. diagnosis
Group Number
Code Number.

Additional F.A. Notes to be written on back of card.

C.C.S. diagnosis (if altered from above)

A Slipman or not.

Base Hospital diagnosis (alterations or additional)

A.T. Serum } 1st
Dose and date
                2nd

FIELD AMBULANCE NOTES.

Morphia }
Dose and time

Date of wound or }
onset of illness

Religion

Officer Commanding,
   135th. Field Ambulance.
   136th.   "   "
   137th.   "   "

Further to this office No.176/116(m) dated 15/1/19.

1. It has been decided that the Demobilization Index Cards for Field Ambulance personnel should be retained by the Field Ambulances concerned.

2. Officers Commanding Field Ambulances will notify the A.D.M.S. office daily by 11.00 hours, on the attached pro-forma, all alterations in O.R.Personnel, e,g:- leave, priority, receipt of Guarantee letters and A.F.Z56 and 232, men whose age has been verified over 41. Alterations to Cadre personnel, departure on demobilization &c.

3. An allotment will be made to each Field Ambulance from this office, and in all probability this allotment may be utilized for any dispersal station.

4. If difficulty is experienced in filling the allotment, then a full report must be rendered at once to this office.

5. The allotment will be made 5 clear days before the men are due to reach the Concentration Camps. On the same day as allotment is received, units will notify the A.D.M.S. office the Number, Rank, Name, and Dispersal Area of each man in this allotment.

6. This will come into operation on the 31st inst, inclusive.

J. R. HUDLESTON.

Lieut.-Colonel,R.A.M.C.,
A/A.D.M.S.,40th. Division.

D.H.Qrs.,
30/1/19.

A.D.M.S. 40th Division

WAR DIARY
INTELLIGENCE SUMMARY

Army Form C. 2118.

14/3

A.D.M.S. 40 Div.

Vol 33

Place	Date	Hour	Summary of Events and Information	Remarks and references to Appendices
ROUVROY La Corne du Bois	1/1/19	-	ADMS attended Conference at Army HQ re equipment of Field Ambulances in this Sector area.	
	2/1/19	-	Nil	
	3/1/19	-	ADMS visited 119 Inf. Bde. HQ, 120, 121 Inf Bde HQ and MO's 121 Inf Btn. and OC 1) Worcester Regt. re general medical arrangements.	
	4/1/19	-	ADMS visited the tactical H.Q. LANNOY. There is to be an advanced medical post at CROIX now closed down as we are also the tactical at CROIX. Orders issued of Lieut. Col. J.K. RH BDS RAMC to report to Military Hospital, UPPER EDMONTON for duty. NAMC visited A.D.M.S. VI Corps.	
	5/1/19	-	OC 40 Div met the Medical Officers of the Field Ambulances today, discussed the general attitude of be adopted between Officers & men. Also asked if the enemy kept in any way the demobilisation if any should case.	Austin J Jobb Major RAMC ADMS 40 Div
	6/1/19		Nil	

Army Form C. 2118.

WAR DIARY
or
INTELLIGENCE SUMMARY: A.D.M.S. 40. Division

(Erase heading not required.)

Instructions regarding War Diaries and Intelligence Summaries are contained in F. S. Regs., Part II. and the Staff Manual respectively. Title pages will be prepared in manuscript.

Place	Date	Hour	Summary of Events and Information	Remarks and references to Appendices
ROUBAIX 4th Aus Hosp.	7/1/19		Nil.	
	8/1/19		ADMS attended Conference at DDMS XV Corps about Revised Syllabus of Field Ambulance. ADMS & DADMS attended XV Corps Evening meeting.	
	9/1/19		Lieut Col V.R. Huddleston RAMC ADMS proceeded on 14 days special leave to England leaving Off to Lieut Col A.Thok the Curragh as to the same.	
	10/1/19		ADMS & ADMS visited H.Q.s RIF RGA & M.O.S 7. 178 & 781 Bgs RFA. Also the bath at WAMBRECHIES.	
	11/1/19		ADMS visited G.O.C. 40th Div discussed the supplies of clothing & men leaving the army who are in need of them. He also visited G.O.C. 119 Bde.	
	12/1/19		Nil.	
	13/1/19		Major M Beverley RFC Rear a warrener of duties DADMS XV Corps. Major M Prestly RAMC warrener of duties DADMS 40 Div. Capt. Street RAMC reported.	

Army Form C. 2118.

WAR DIARY
or
INTELLIGENCE SUMMARY. ADM.L 40th Division
(Erase heading not required.)

Instructions regarding War Diaries and Intelligence Summaries are contained in F.S. Regs., Part II. and the Staff Manual respectively. Title pages will be prepared in manuscript.

Place	Date	Hour	Summary of Events and Information	Remarks and references to Appendices
PONTRUET	1917			
3 months 1919	13/4/19		to England prior to Demobilization	
	14/4/19		ADD'sn visited 120 Bde + 121 Bde Hd Bn. Med Inspection rooms. Major W.R. McKnight R.A.M.C. relinquished his comm. & returned to England prior to demobilization.	
	15/4/19		General routine	
	16/4/19		General routine	
	17/4/19		General routine	
	18/4/19		General routine	
	19/4/19		General routine	
	20/4/19		General routine	
	21/4/19		ADMS visited CRA & inspected the fort. Col W.H.Ch. Schallass A/DDMS handed over to Col. Humphrey who returned from A/DDMS IV Corps.	
	22/4/19		Returned from IV Corps today. Humphrey Lt Col AMS 40 Div	

Army Form C. 2118.

WAR DIARY
or
INTELLIGENCE SUMMARY. *of A.D.M.S. 40 D IV.*
(Erase heading not required.)

Instructions regarding War Diaries and Intelligence Summaries are contained in F. S. Regs., Part II. and the Staff Manual respectively. Title pages will be prepared in manuscript.

Place	Date	Hour	Summary of Events and Information	Remarks and references to Appendices
AUBIGNY	Feb 23	-	Nil	
	24		Nil	
	25th		Orders issued to 135 T.A. to close and hand over the building to the Civilian Authorities. 137 F.A. at Croix to act as S.R.S.; Major Judd proceeded to England & in strength of the Strength of A.D.M.S. H.Q.	
	26th		} Nil	
	27th		}	
	28			

Murphy
Lt Col A.D.M.S. 40 D IV

17 JUL 1919

Army Form C. 2118.

WAR DIARY
INTELLIGENCE SUMMARY.
(Erase heading not required.)

ADMS 40th Div

MARCH

WC3

Place	Date	Hour	Summary of Events and Information	Remarks and references to Appendices
Roubaix	1/3/19			
Noy Rue des	2/3/19			
Arts	3/3/19			
	4/3/19			
	5/3/19		Lieut G.H Martin MORC demobilised.	
	6/3/19			
	7/3/19			
	8/3/19			
	9/3/19			
	10/3/19			
	11/3/19			
	12/3/19			
	13/3/19		Lieut Col L Humphry ADMS despatched to UK for duty and struck off the strength	Lumpy Colonel (Bet)
			Lieut Col W.McK.H. McCullagh RAMC assumed duties of A/ADMS.	of Col Brise
	14/3/19		Capt J. Grant Norin demobilised	

WAR DIARY
INTELLIGENCE SUMMARY.
(Erase heading not required.)

Army Form C. 2118.

ADMS
40th Dis
MARCH

Place	Date	Hour	Summary of Events and Information	Remarks and references to Appendices
	13/3/19		Capt J RYAN RAMC and Lieut A.B. MILLS MORC proceeded to the 2nd Army	Invisence
	14/3/19		Capt Carl Pessler RAMC demobilised	Invisence
	15/3/19		Nil	Invisence
	17/3/19		Nil	Invisence
	18/3/19		Capt J CRAWFORD RAMC relinquished rank of A/MAJOR and proceeded to 2nd Army for duty	Invisence
			Capt W.H. STONER MORC demobilised	
	19/3/19		Lieut E.F. BREAKEY RAMC and Capt J.B. WOODROW RAMC proceeded to 2nd Army for duty	Invisence
	20/3/19		Nil	Invisence
	21/3/19		Nil	Invisence
	22/3/19		Nil	Invisence
	23/3/19		Capt GOUGH McR RAMC demobilised on leave	Invisence
	24/3/19		Nil	Invisence
	25/3/19		Orders received for Capt McCLANAGHAN MORC to proceed to US Army on 26th	Invisence
			ADMS office closed at 12 noon and opened as SMO's Office at 137 F.A. CROIX	Invisence
	26/3/19		Capt McCallaghan proceeded to U.S. Army for demobilisation	Invisence
	31/3/19		Lt Col HARDING RAMC proceeded to DMS II Army for duty on the Rhine	Invisence
			Capt RAMC	

www.ingramcontent.com/pod-product-compliance
Lightning Source LLC
Chambersburg PA
CBHW080922230426
43668CB00014B/2177